CHARLESTON HORSE POWER

CHARLESTON HORSE POWER

Equine Culture in the Palmetto City

——

Christina Rae Butler

THE UNIVERSITY OF
SOUTH CAROLINA PRESS

© 2023 University of South Carolina

Published by the University of South Carolina Press
Columbia, South Carolina 29208

uscpress.com

Manufactured in the United States of America

32 31 30 29 28 27 26 25 24 23
10 9 8 7 6 5 4 3 2 1

Library of Congress Cataloging-in-Publication Data
can be found at http://catalog.loc.gov/.

ISBN: 978-1-64336-402-5 (paperback)
ISBN: 978-1-64336-403-2 (ebook)

FRONTISPIECE: Saddle horses rest in front of McLeish's
Vulcan Ironworks factory on Cumberland Street in 1865.
Library of Congress.

For Tommy Doyle

CONTENTS

✦ ILLUSTRATIONS ✦

❧ ACKNOWLEDGMENTS ❧

I am so fortunate to have the opportunity to meld two lifelong passions, horses and history, into one book, and I owe a debt of gratitude to family, friends, archivists, and fellow horsemen for their knowledge and support that made its completion possible. The librarians and archivists of the South Carolina Room and Charleston Archive at the Charleston County Public Library, especially Amanda Holling, Dot Glover, and Sarah Murphy; Jennifer McCormick with The Charleston Museum; Karen Emmons, Grahame Long, Valerie Perry, and Sarah Ferguson with the Historic Charleston Foundation; Meg Moughan and Rebecca Schultz with the Charleston City Records Management Division; and the staff at the South Carolina Historical Society, especially Virginia Ellison and Molly Silliman, were all helpful in providing insight and access to their institution's wonderful collections. Fellow historians W. Scott Poole, Beth Phillips, Charles Lesser, and Wade Razzi have been immensely supportive friends. University of South Carolina Press Acquisitions Editor Ehren Foley provided expert editorial advice and content guidance over the past three years.

My parents, Dave and Rita Oberstar, deserve credit for fostering my love of horses from the youngest age, driving me through Cleveland blizzards to the barn and sacrificing countless weekends for horse shows. They have always supported me in every way, and I am eternally grateful. Terri and Jerry Moody, both no longer with us, encouraged equine interests for so many young people in northeastern Ohio through the Caps N Chaps 4-H club. Over time, that interest turned into a profession, and I owe much of my equine management knowledge and driving skills to Tommy Doyle of Palmetto Carriage Works, a mentor, boss, and friend for almost two decades. Tommy, his father Tom Doyle, and Tony Youmans, director of the Old Exchange and Provost Dungeon, graciously provided interviews about the carriage tour industry over the past fifty years and about city equine management. Gratitude is also due to the horses and mules who patiently let me learn with them and who showed me that human–horse bonds are among the deepest we can experience, especially Jerry the quarter horse, Mitchell the mule, Mello, and DeBlasio.

The book would not have been possible without endless support and historical insight from my husband, Nicholas Michael Butler. He shared useful context through his Charleston Time Machine podcasts, brainstormed about content and organization, and offered helpful source ideas for the colonial era. Thanks to Nic for tolerating the endless mule photos, horse smells, and equine stories past and present.

ACKNOWLEDGMENTS

⚘ INTRODUCTION ⚘

"More than half a century a volunteer fireman in this town, Mr. Levy recalls the days of the fire horses and hand-drawn hose reels rattling bravely over cobblestone Charleston streets during visits with relatives in the neighborhood of Cannon Street engine house. 'I said then that if I ever grew to be a man, I would be a fireman.'"[1] Such was the impact, the thrill of watching horses gallop through the city as they raced to the scene of a fire to protect life and property—and it was a site every resident of Charleston, South Carolina, would have experienced before the 1930s. In the twenty-first century, it is easy to forget that less than one hundred years ago, metropolises were equine cities, with horses and mules working and sometimes living side by side with humans in a variety of jobs and city departments.

In Charleston, as elsewhere, equines (members of the horse family including donkeys and mules) pervaded every aspect of urban life and contributed to the building and maintenance of the city, providing the power to make it operate through public and private transportation, food and fuel deliveries, and myriad other work that equines did more efficiently than humans. An American Society for the Prevention of Cruelty to Animals (ASPCA) essay from 1925 captures both the contributions of equines and the value of our relationships with working horses:

> Everything that contributes to the existence, comfort, and pleasure of human beings is inseparably linked with the service of the horse, which has been man's unpaid partner through the centuries . . . he cannot be paid for his services in money so the only way we can show our partnership is by giving him the very best treatment in our power . . . 'tis love that makes the world go round' was not written merely for humans- it applies equally well to the animal world, and when a horse knows that his master loves him his daily task becomes a pleasure, and with a light heart and perfect confidence he gives the best that is in him to this human comrade.[2]

Charleston Horse Power chronicles the history of working equines and the humans who worked with them in Charleston from 1680 to the present and seeks to immerse the reader in the equine city of the past. Equines powered single commuter and public transportation, they provided the literal horsepower to operate machinery to dig ditches and street beds; they carted goods for shipping, one of many facets of an international maritime trade network, through the port–they even operated cranes and hoists to load the ships; they pulled fire engines and conveyed the city's police force on their beats; and they hauled building materials to construction sites and fuel and commodities to residences. Equines also provided entertainment and companionship. We do not know what horses thought of their human cohorts, but it is possible to infer a mutual respect, codependence, and comradery from the stories left by the people who worked with them. Residents—rich and poor alike—would have seen, heard, and smelled the ubiquitous equines daily.

Charleston's equine culture offers a new lens through which to view the city's social history. Carriage is a general term for an equine-drawn vehicle, but there are many varieties tailored for specific purposes, and vehicle selection gives insight into the socioeconomic backgrounds of Charleston consumers. A large, heavy carriage might give an heir of grandeur, or be considered too bulky and slow, depending on the owner's tastes. Some Charleston carriages were painted with coats of arms in true English fashion, driven by coachmen kitted in full livery, emulating the European elite.[3] By contrast, drays and carts were often homemade, and their condition and simplicity reflected the relative poverty of their drivers.

Thousands of Charlestonians made their livings in the equine sector in a variety of jobs ranging from unskilled to sought-after, high paying positions. Vestiges of the horse-dominated world of the past persist in popular phrases such as horsepower or chomping at the bit, but many equine occupations have left the contemporary American lexicon and warrant a description here. Hostlers, also known as ostlers, were often employed by inns, hotels, or larger delivery companies to care for horses in residence. Hostlers, grooms, stablemen, or barn hands worked and often lived at a stable to provide for horses' daily needs. Duties included feeding, grooming, bathing, harnessing, and general care, as well as cleaning and maintaining tack and harness, and cleaning stalls. Hostlers and grooms needed fewer skills than did others working in more specialized equine-related positions.[4]

Carriage drivers went by many names, indicating a specific type of driving or client. Draymen or carters hauled goods; hackmen operated taxi carriages for hire; coachmen, whips, or coachees were chauffeurs who drove private carriages; and stage men drove stagecoaches on long-distance routes. Teamsters drove two or four horses, which required advanced driving ability because the animals had to pull in tandem to convey the cart evenly and there was twice as much activity to mind. Teamsters and hackmen had a reputation for boisterous behavior, seeking to be their own men even if they were employees who did not own their carriage and animals. James Garland wrote disparagingly in 1899 that, "coachmen and grooms do not form a class from which angels are exclusively chosen, and drunkenness, brutality, moral obliquity, profanity, laziness, sullenness, and bad manners were frequent traits."[5] The job took physical strength and courage in times of stress. Like most equine jobs, males dominated the teamster field; of the 368,000 teamsters in the United States in 1870, only 264 were women.[6]

Livery stables offered boarding for privately owned horses and also supplied stable-owned horses and coaches for hire. Dray masters and livery stable managers operated these full-care boarding facilities and managed delivery and hiring schedules for various drivers in their employ. Equine support occupations included harness makers, saddlers, carriage makers, and fodder dealers. Farriers trimmed hooves, addressed minor podiatric issues, fitted new shoes, and nailed them onto horse hooves. Before the rise of professional veterinarians, farriers also treated ailments. Riders, jockeys, trainers, and breeders made their living preparing equines for races or city work, while knackers were involved at the end of a horse's life, to collect their remains for burial or rendering into various consumer products.[7]

Charleston Horse Power enhances our knowledge of the southern urban experience, a region largely absent from previous books on urban equines, by discussing southerners' heavy reliance on mules, a unique phenomenon in the American South, and by examining racialized occupational tendencies and hiring practices. Enslaved workers were employed in a multitude of equine occupations that were integral for the operations of southern cities. From the early colonial period, Charleston had a majority-enslaved population, and even though native-born and immigrant white men worked in equine occupations, they were outnumbered by Black Charlestonians, enslaved and free. Enslaved men held esteemed positions as liveried coachmen, driving the finest carriages pulled by teams of well-matched horses for the local gentry. At the other end of the spectrum, the city scavenger department had a crew of three "Negros" with mule and push carts who collected street sweepings.[8] Employers actively sought Black coachmen and draymen for hire both before and after the Civil War.

Joel Tarr and Clay McShane's seminal book, *The Horse in the City,* analyzes horses' work, urban equine regulation, stabling and feed, "his use in leisure activities . . . and his decline and persistence as an important factor of the urban economy" in northern cities, topics I investigate in Charleston and to which I add architectural analysis and the legacy of horses in the city today.[9] Though smaller than New York or Philadelphia, Charleston was one of the largest and wealthiest cities in the South. Analyzing its equine history and infrastructure adds the southeastern experience to our understanding of transportation, technology, and the role of horses in American cities.

Charleston government and residents' responses to their equine neighbors illuminates their priorities and attitudes towards technological change. The local government sought to balance efficiency versus livability in regulating transportation, and to balance cost versus efficacy in its paving choices. Dirt roads may have been the cheapest, but horses struggled with pulling heavy loads on substandard paving, and wealthy residents complained about the dust, so better materials such as Belgian block and plank roads were introduced over time.[10] The breeds preferred, the types of work they did, vehicle materials and styles, paving types and circulation networks, and even the number of equines pulling carriages also evolved over time as the city grew and new technologies arrived. Eighteenth century equines, for example, were much smaller than later draft breeds like the Percherons bred in the Midwest and shipped by rail to the city, or draft mules who were carefully bred to create larger, stronger animals.

Equines existed alongside modern technology, working side by side with steam rail as part of an intricate shipping network from plantation to city to ship and, later, sharing the streets with cars. There was and remains a struggle over how finite space should be used in the growing city. Residents who did not have yard space, for example, fed their horses and cows "on the Pavements of the Streets (especially after Dark) to the great Annoyance of the Inhabitants" trying to pass by.[11] Pressures mounted with Victorian ideas about cleanliness, culminating in zoning changes to push noisome animal activities out of the city center. Automobiles arrived on Charleston's streets in the summer of 1900 and brought the most profound and lasting change of any technological innovation in the city's history, although horses and mules worked in the city

well into the twentieth century for economic reasons.[12] Some residents clamored for modernity, while others expressed nostalgia for the slow pace of the past. This is still true today in Charleston, where some welcome carriage tours in their neighborhoods and others complain of traffic congestion and the smell of manure.

Charleston Horse Power also analyzes the tangibly evident equine city of today through the surviving architectural environment. To prevent the wholesale architectural loss other cities experienced, Charleston created a historic district in 1931, setting regulations for restoring or reusing historic buildings and outbuildings, ultimately contributing to Charleston's burgeoning tourism industry as visitors flocked to the city to step into the past.[13] With the largest contiguous historic district in the nation and a bustling heritage tourism industry, the past remains ever-present on Charleston's landscape, and, if one knows where to look, there is ample physical evidence of the former equine-dominated city through adaptively used stables and carriage houses. As the last delivery horses and private carriages left the city's streets following World War II, a new working horse industry emerged in 1949 with the carriage tour trade. There are up to thirty-six carriages on city streets during daytime operating hours. This allows the city to retain its urban equine legacy in the twenty-first century as carriages continue to roll through the quiet residential streets, providing visitors with what has become a rare experience in the urban United States—equine interaction and transportation that is punctuated by hoofbeat. Few cities have had such an unbroken continuity with their equine heritage.

Sources and Organization

The book is organized thematically, with subheadings for ease of reading. Each chapter could be a book unto itself, but I hope to create a starting point for future research by providing an overview of city equines and their jobs over three and a half centuries. Chapter 1 describes early working breeds in Charleston, the rise of mules, and the later prevalence of larger European draft breeds. It also discusses equine composition, draft power principles, and the fundamentals of harnessing. Chapter 2 analyzes how horses influenced town planning and paving choices, and the ways that local government regulated horse-based transportation. Equines' fundamental needs, including forage, farriery, and veterinary care/welfare are discussed in Chapter 3.

The following four chapters explore the types of jobs equines did in Charleston, and the people who worked with them. Chapter 4 discusses horse racing, private carriage use, coachmakers, and coachmen. Commercial transportation, including multi-person vehicles with fixed fares such as omnibuses and streetcars, private rented options such as hack taxis, and livery businesses where clients could rent a horse and carriage, is covered in chapter 5. Chapter 6 examines the arduous work of transporting goods to and from wharves, the delivery industry, and the "machine horses" who powered equipment. The city's fire and police departments, and public

works equine fleets are explored in chapter 7.

Chapter 8 gives a tour of the buildings in which equines lived and worked throughout the city. The impact of automobiles, which slowly but surely eroded Charlestonians' reliance on equines is addressed in chapter 9. By counterpoint, I provide examples of repurposed equine buildings that leave solid evidence of the horses who lived here. A final chapter explores the ongoing legacy of working horses in Charleston through carriages and heritage tourism in the city today, drawing correlations between regulations of the horse drawn city, past and present.

The book utilizes manuscript collections and public records to peer into the equine past. The *Sanborn Fire Insurance Maps* provide statistics on the numbers of stables, carriage houses, and support shops at the turn of the twentieth century; how many were extant by 1955; and how they were repurposed. They also provide data for the building materials, forms, and sizes of stable that were most prevalent, and where equine buildings were the most highly concentrated in the city. Select extant buildings are analyzed as examples of successful adaptive reuse. The Charleston city council proceedings, fire department records, ordinances, and city *Yearbooks* document the regulations governing equines, creation of streets and infrastructure, and licensing practices that give insight into the number of carriages and drays in the city. These public records also allow us to meet city fleet equines, while historic newspapers, *City Directories,* censuses, and other vital records illuminate the lives of the humans who worked with them.

Manuscript records from the South Carolina Historical Society including the business records for Lockwood's Sale and Feed Stables, E. W. Lloyd carriage warehouse, and that of C. D. Franke and Co. describe carriage manufacturing and feed supply. The Horlbeck Brothers Construction records include invoices for hiring drays and carts and for building stables and kitchen houses. The Charleston City Railway company records covering the years 1862–1895, and Enterprise Rail Company records, covering the years 1871–1872, chronicle operations of the city's equine-drawn streetcars. The Historic Charleston Foundation and the Charleston Museum's collections provided photographic evidence and manuscripts from private businesses.

Working Equine
Traits and Breeds

Equines come in a variety of sizes and have been bred over the centuries to cultivate desired aesthetic characteristics and performance traits necessary for specific jobs. They have contributed to, shaped, and enhanced human activities over several millenniums of coevolution.[1] Although their drivers, owners, and handlers formed bonds with them, equines were often viewed as tools for profit rather than sentient beings. Clay McShane likened the attitude in comparing the shooting of a lame horse to junking a car engine or rendering a carcass to recycling scrap iron.[2] It is important to remember, however, that animal husbandry results in a mutually beneficial relationship in which the animal receives care—and possibly companionship and love, although these terms were rarely used for human–animal relationships before the late nineteenth century, and the human receives the animal's labor.

Working equines have nearly constant contact during the workday with their humans through physical touch, voice commands, and harnessing and care routines. Horseman Lynn R. Miller aptly said that "driving the horse is, in its finest sense, the true reward of understanding, trust, and communication between the animals and the teamster."[3] Palmetto Carriage Works owner Tom Doyle echoes Miller that, "it's a trust relationship and you're asking the animal to do something it might not know how to do. If he's treated right and trained well, he'll do what he's supposed to."[4]

Training ranged from fear-based approaches based on assumptions that horses only respond to force, creating often-unstable relationships devoid of affection and respect, to positive reinforcement and patient acclimation of a horse to new experiences and tasks. Trainers and drivers must know the personality of each equine to place them in appropriate jobs for their dispositions.[5] Horsemen teach animals to accept harness and loads on their back or a carriage behind them, and to steer via reigns and voice commands. By the mid-nineteenth century, training manuals advised avoiding the whip, and instead quickening the gait "by the use of some kind word, to which all horses should be accustomed."[6] Another suggested gentle acclimation to "objects of fear," allowing the horse to "stand and look at the object, and drive him as close as convenient, allowing him to smell of it, and see that no harm is intended him; at the same time talk encouragingly to him, and in this manner, he will soon be fearless and confident. Should you whip him for becoming frightened at such things, he will be apt to associate the punishment with the object of fear and be more frightened the next time he sees it."[7] Stable managers and delivery company owners recognized the close relationships that developed between drivers and individual horses.[8] Anne Greene notes that, "managers used horse behavior to rationalize operations. They encouraged bonds between horses and drivers by assigning horses to the same drivers. They permitted drivers to name the horses and encouraged them to groom them, an activity that copied horse grooming behaviors and encouraged horse–human bonding."[9]

The term "horsepower," quantified by James Watt in the late eighteenth century, is a unit of measure for how much power something can produce. An average-sized horse can create an output equal to six or seven men. In a four-hour shift, the average human exerts 4,420 foot-pounds per minute; horses, 24,780; mules, 16,530; and oxen, 22,044. An owner then budgeted for the "fuel consumption" cost of a draft animal versus the power they could produce, balanced with the animal's individual personality and trainability. Galloping, the fastest gait, is an inefficient use of energy, as horses can pull longer and farther when travelling at a trotting or walking pace.[10] Oxen, members of the bovine family, can pull heavy loads but are slower than equines and can comfortably work five to six hours a day compared to six to ten for horses and mules, making the latter two the more popular choices for city work. Horses have extra red blood cells in their spleen that release during strenuous exercise, and they have more glycogen in their muscles than oxen, which gives them more endurance and speed.[11] Oxen and water buffalo were used on Lowcountry plantations, but there is less evidence of them in the city.[12]

Equines' draft power comes from their strong shoulders and chests for carriage work or plowing, and they have sturdy spines and backs that make them ideal for riding. As a horse pushes against his collar, the action is converted to a pull on the traces, or straps, that connect to the carriage or plow to move it forward.[13] As William Youatt explained in *The Horse, with a Treatise on Draught* in 1833, "a horse by the formation of his body, can relieve his weight partly from his forelegs; and extending his hind legs, can throw the center of gravity a considerable distance in front of his feet. He is in fact, by his mechanical construction, a beast of draft."[14]

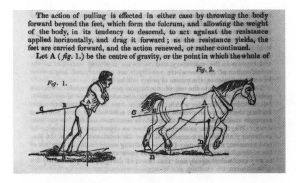

The action of pulling is effected in either case by throwing the body forward beyond the feet, which form the fulcrum, and allowing the weight of the body, in its tendency to descend, to act against the resistance applied horizontally, and drag it forward ; as the resistance yields, the feet are carried forward, and the action renewed, or rather continued.

Let A (*fig.* 1.) be the centre of gravity, or the point in which the whole of

Fig. 1.   Fig. 2.

Figures from *The Horse: With the Treatise on Draught* show a human and a horse using their weight to pull an object forward, demonstrating draft principles. Letter C on figure 2 represents the trace that affixes to the carriage.

There are different types of harness and tack geared towards specific breeds, animal size, or desired work, but the purpose is always to attach an animal comfortably to a vehicle or machine to allow them to efficiently power it, while providing a way to guide both him and the vehicle.

Large draft breeds wear a collar that fits loosely around their neck and rests on their shoulders above the breast. A metal or wooden set of hames, curved arms that fit into a groove in the collar, are lifted and buckled into place. From these, a set of traces run the length of the equine and are attached to the carriage. The traces are connected to a singletree or whiffletree, a hinged bar that pivots, on the front of the carriage, which acts as an evener because a horse pulls with different shoulders as he walks. Wooden or metal shafts run parallel to the equine and are connected to the carriage alongside the traces to help steer the vehicle. The hames are also attached by back straps to

a hip drop assembly or "spider" and breeching, so called because the straps look like spider legs when viewed from the driver's vantage point. The spider rests on the rump of the horse. Breeching harnesses feature a brake strap that is attached to the shafts of the carriage to facilitate stopping. These are well suited to heavy carting and city traffic. Plow harnesses, by comparison, do not usually have brake straps.[15]

Single animal harness often includes a saddle with both an inner and outer girth, through which the shafts pass. For lighter vehicles, the collar and hames might be replaced by a simple breast strap that passes over the horse's neck and across his chest, and from which the traces continue to the carriage. Driving lines or reigns pass from the driver to the equine's bit and bridle. Driving bridles typically have leather protrusions called blinkers or blinders to block the horse's peripheral vision to prevent him from being startled.

Team harness includes several additional components that allow two or more equines to steer and pull together. A pole strap is affixed below the collar of each team member, which connects to a pivoting yoke in front of the animals and a pole that runs between the two equines, in place of shafts found on a single hitch. The pole strap acts as the breaking and reversing system.[16] The traces are attached to double trees on the carriage frame. Team driving requires a double set of lines attached to the bits, crisscrossed, then reduced to a pair of reigns to allow the driver to steer both animals at once. Drivers and hostlers must be intimately familiar with their harness

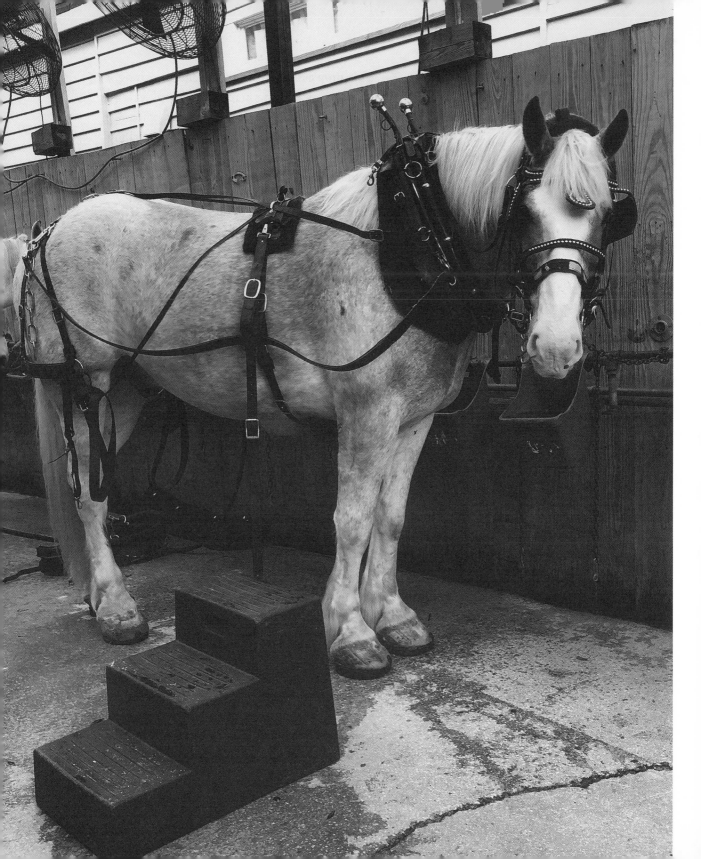

Chester, a 2,000-pound roan Belgian draft horse, wears a traditional harness with collar and hames, a saddle and belly band/girth, and spider and breeching straps. His bridle features blinders. The trace running along his side hooks to a carriage to allow him to pull a vehicle. Belgians historically pulled delivery wagons and fire trucks in Charleston. Photo by Author.

and carriage, for an ill-fitting piece of tack can cause injury and an improperly hitched vehicle can cause dangerous accidents. Equestrian authors advised gentle steering; "jerking on the reins . . . is unworthy even of a peddler or city huckster. A driver should be in communion with his horse. Human nature is fallible, and horses are very uncertain. Carelessness in the driver, however, is responsible for ninety and nine of every hundred driving accidents that happen."[17]

American verbal commands for driving equines, which are reinforced by steering with the driving lines, are: gee/turn right, haw/turn left, woah (stop), hike or back (reverse), and giddy up/get up/step up (time to go). Equines are receptive to the voices of the humans they know. City work manuals instructed drivers to, "watch for objects likely to alarm your horse. Sing, talk, or whistle to them to keep them calm."[18] Equines are intelligent herd animals that understand social order, "which explains willingness to adapt with remarkable success as a work companion to man both in field and city."[19] As flight animals in a sometimes-chaotic urban environment, "horses had to rely on their drivers for direction and reassurance. A skilled driver could steer through traffic, avoid accidents, and

limit unwelcome horse behaviors by using his voice as well as reins and brakes in the cacophonous streets."[20] Preservationist and former Charleston tour guide Valerie Perry recounted Fritz, a newly arrived carriage horse in 1986, who did not respond to common verbal commands. Knowing he was bred in Pennsylvania by the Amish, she switched to German commands and his ears perked up and he was immediately responsive. Another guide noted, "only a handful of people could get Fritz to do anything, he trusted the lady drivers."[21] Equines are also acutely aware of visual stimuli, hence the blinders on driving bridles. The author has driven horses and mules that recognize traffic light patterns and will pull on a green light before being prompted. All equines know the halfway point in the city's various carriage routes and will speed up for the last trip of the day, like humans anxious to relax at the end of the workday.

Equine breeds are as diverse as the aesthetic characteristics their owners desire and the work they are intended for. Richard Mason offered advice on selecting the right equine for the job in his popular 1848 *Pocket Farrier*: "when a horse is purchased for the saddle alone, he must be clear of all defects, strike the fancy, entirely please the eye, [with] happy symmetry and due proportion of form . . . A horse that has been frightened from the harness, never again is safe for that employment; so retentive are their memories that they do not forget an alarm of that kind during their whole lives. It very often happens that horses are kept together as a match on account of their colour and similarity of their marks, when no respect is paid to their difference in form, spirit and movement, which often differ as widely as the mettled racer from the dull cart horse."[22]

Height, fat mass, bone structure, confirmation, the shape or structure of a horse, and muscling all impact strength and ability. Long, thin muscle structure is suited for speed, and thick muscle with a stocky build is ideal for heavy work. Heavy horses include Clydesdales bred originally in Scotland, Percherons from the north of France, Suffolks and Shires from England, and Ardennes, Brabants, and Belgians from Belgium. Cleveland Bays and thoroughbreds from England; Standardbreds, Appaloosas, Quarter horses, and Morgans, of American origin; Arabians from the Middle East; and Holsteiners and Gelderlanders from Germany, are categorized as light horses which are ideal for riding, trotting races, or for pulling small carriages.[23] The breeds found in urban Charleston are described in more detail below.

Equine populations grew with urban expansion, even after the rise of the automobile. Large cities averaged one equine per twenty people; at peak, Philadelphia had 51,000 equines and Chicago had 74,000, most of which were bred and trained in the countryside and then brought to the city.[24] Charleston had approximately one equine for every thirty residents around 1880, while a later—likely inflated—estimate claimed there were once 5,000 equines in the city, or approximately 1 for 10 people.[25] Cities boasted more breed variety than the countryside, given the diverse nature of work equines did in the urban setting. Purebred drafts were more numerous in town because they were a status symbol; envision perfectly matched, well-muscled teams pulling glossy painted carts emblazoned with company logos. Urban draft horses worked year-round rather than only during planting season, which justified the increased cost of grain consumption for their size. Geldings, castrated male horses, were most common in cities because they had the fewest behavioral problems, followed by mares.[26] Stallions, which could be unpredictable and dangerous especially around estrous mares, were the least commonly used in town.[27] Few inventories specified gender, although some nineteenth-century advertisements did, such as one advertisement of a horse for sale that described a "fine large mare, suitable for beer or ice wagon" that worked for the Champion Cotton Press.[28] Besides size and gender, handlers also consider breed susceptibility to disease, predilection for certain kinds of work, and an animal's character and innate ability to adapt to an urban environment. Matching pairs is a true art that balances size and strength, aesthetics of matching coats and markings, and personalities, because horses, like people, form bonds and cannot always be forced to work with a partner they do not like.[29]

Imports and Domestic Horses in Early Charleston

Breeds varied by era, price, availability, desired physical attributes, and even by region. The English settlers who arrived in 1670 did not bring horses with them, and early South Carolina colonists' choices were limited to horses they could purchase from established northern colonies and those they could trade from the indigenous population. Thomas Colleton recommended purchasing horses and cattle from New York and New Jersey instead of Virginia because those animals were cheaper and Carolina commodities worth more in trade. Governor Joseph West conferred in a March 1671 letter that, "horses [in New York] are very cheap and of a good Breed," and would be useful for plowing and transporting timber.[30]

To encourage South Carolinians to breed horses locally, the General Assembly set an importation tax on equines after 1701. By March 1705/6, the Commons House proposed setting a fair day, set aside for holding livestock sales, "now that horses are become [sic] plentifull and Oxen fit for the Plow."[31] John Lawson remarked in 1707 that Charlestown had, "a well-disciplin'd militia; their Horse [troop] are most[ly] gentlemen, and well mounted, and the best in America."[32] Equines became an integral part of life and a valuable commodity in early Carolina and the first issues of the *South Carolina Gazette* in 1732 contain numerous advertisements for strayed and stolen horses, and individual mounts for sale.[33]

Carolina's capital was a marketplace for imported horses, while backwoods settlers rode small Chickasaw and Chocktaw horses descended from equines left behind in previous Spanish explorations.[34] English naturalist Mark Catesby, who was in Charleston from 1722 to

1725, wrote that South Carolina horses were "of the Spanish breed, occasioned by some hundreds of them being drove as plunder from the Spanish Settlements. They are small, yet hardy, and will endure long journeys, and are not subject to so many maladies as are incident in horses in England. As stallions have been introduced from England, the breed must necessarily be improved, Carolina being in a climate that breeds the finest horses in the world."[35] John Irving described these "Chickasaw horses" as, "well-formed, active and easily kept, but small. The mares seldom exceeded thirteen hands and a half; but being remarkable for their muscular development and great endurance, when crossed with the imported thoroughbreds, produced animals of great beauty, strength and fleetness." Settlers used "Indian breed" horses for both riding and draft work.[36] A pair of "black marsh ponies" were offered for sale in town in 1853, but the breed seems to have been used mostly on plantations. The registered rare breed Carolina Marsh Tacky descends from these early Spanish/Native American horses. Tackies rose to fame when Captain Francis Marion rode one in his backwoods campaigns in the swamps of South Carolina during the American Revolution. Tackies have a strong constitution and a tolerance for marsh grass resulting from having lived in the swamps and marshes along the coast. [37]

Elite residents imported horses from England or brought them from other colonies in pursuit of specific bloodlines and athletic attributes.[38] Early advertisements mentioned "blooded horses" including thoroughbreds from England, and Arabians brought from the Middle East to England centuries earlier. These breeds are generally nervous, energetic, and fast, making them suited to racing or speedy coach travel. Young white men with disposable income clamored for the fastest horses for their sport, and owners proudly listed their prize-winning stallions available for stud service each season at their plantations. Benjamin Barra offered for sale an Arabian horse named Crawford who was bred by the Duke of Cumberland in 1767.[39] Abdalah, an Arabian horse, arrived in Port Royal, South Carolina by way of Gibraltar and Cade, a five-year-old English horse born to "Old Cade, a son of Lord Godolphin's Arabian and Mrs. Hutton's famous Wormwood" had been imported by Thomas Creswell and was available for breeding at the Stono plantation in 1762.[40] Barrock Billy, a chestnut thoroughbred and another of Cade's progeny, offered cover (a historic term for stud service for a fee) at Capt. Samuel Elliott's plantation under the supervision of the groom Richard Williams. Several horses imported from England on board the *Nancy* could be viewed at Mr. Pike's Stable on Tradd Street prior to their sale, which was to take place at Nightingale's farm on Charleston Neck.[41]

Equine advertisements in the *South Carolina Gazette* rarely specified breed but typically listed color; height measured in in hands; and markings or other distinguishing features, the latter being helpful in identifying lost horses. A unique ad in 1743 offered a "good draught horse and likewise a valuable Rhode Island natural pacer," which may have been a Narragansett pacer, a

A stud service advertisement for Pharaoh, at Drayton Hall for breeding season. *South Carolina Gazette,* 30 March–6 April 1765

now extinct colonial-era breed.[42] Early sale ads for "draft," "draught," or "dray horses" indicated the type of work rather than a specific breed or size. Sellers used the terms "draft horse" and "carriage horse" for equines trained to pull, and often listed "saddle and draft horses," indicating versatility of work.[43] "A pair of elegant and handsome blacks, sixteen hands tall, well broke either to the carriage or chair and also excellent riding horses"[44] and "a very likely horse, remarkably easy and gentle under saddle, and has been much used in both single and double draft", demonstrate this adaptability.[45] Size mattered, even if breeds skewed smaller than their modern counterparts bred over the last two centuries for increased height. The Troop of the Horse Guards for example, which was organized under the colonial militia acts, required their mounts to be no less than fourteen hands tall.[46]

"Family horses" stood patiently and were calm enough for children to drive. For example, a seller offered "a good draught horse, used to the chair, free from all vicious tricks, and so remarkably gentle a child can manage him. He would answer very well to draw children to and from school. Wherever he is left to stand, there he will stay patiently."[47] "Match horses" came as a pair and were similar in size and appearance. Auction houses sold horses and carriages as package deals, as well as parcels of horses brought to Charleston from the countryside and from Virginia and North Carolina.[48] In 1824, "a good draft horse with dray and harness and license for nine months" offered the purchaser a complete business package, and in 1839 a seller offered a horse and omnibus with a license to operate through October.[49] Someone even offered a docile "large work horse, blind, suitable for a cart or dray" in 1852.[50]

In the antebellum era, ads indicated age, size, whether a horse pulled as a team or single, and if it was acclimated to urban work. For example, auctioneers Verree and Blair listed "a strong, able draft horse, used some time in the city, and well calculated for a cart or dray" in 1806, and another seller listed "a good draft, accustomed to draw a chair or carriage in this city, young, perfectly gentle, and free from tricks" in 1812.[51] Draft horses in the early nineteenth century ranged from 15 to 17 hands, and the most prevalent color was bay, followed by black. Sellers noted valuable bloodlines, like a horse "raised at Columbia, got by one of Col. Hampton's stud horses, an uncommonly fast trotter,

first rate draft horse, and good saddle horse" for sale in 1843.[52] Gantt and Mortimer Auctioneers offered, "a very large and well-formed sorrel, 6 years, 17 hands high, a fine mover and works well in anything; for a four-wheel carriage, used for one horse, he would be very valuable. A large, fine black horse, 6 years, 16 hands high, a very fine draft horse either in single or double harness, a fine mover, and handsome. An unexpectedly fine mare, 6 years old, of immense power, perfectly gentle in all kinds of harness, near 16 hands high. The above stock is raised in this state. In addition to draft, they are all good under saddle."[53]

Rarely do we know why an animal was sold. Equines might find themselves at auction because they did not suit the needs of the owner, or the owner was in debt and/or trying to profit from the sale, was retiring from business, or had died, after which their horses were sold through probate. A few advertisements mentioned reasons for the sale: "an uncommonly handsome and well-formed gelded draft horse" was "only being sold because his match was dead," a "fine large draft horse suited to a family or physician, sold because his owner has no further use for him, and a bay draft who was being sold "on account of risk of former owner, not having proved sound."[54]

Riding horses on the Charleston market included a Galloway, an extinct breed of Scottish pacing horse, "being very gentle under saddle and a very easy gate, would suit well for a lady's riding horse."[55] Antebellum era sportsmen looking for speed could purchase stud service at Mills House Stables from Young Membrino Chief, bred out of Kentucky, already able to "trot in three minutes to harness" at age four.[56] "Cleveland Bay's" stud advertisement offers a detailed account of pacing breed characteristics and performance preferences of the mid nineteenth century:

> A brown bay, 15 ½ hands high and 6 years old, docile in disposition, and works kindly in harness and naturally a very fast trotter. He was got by the imported horse Cleveland Bay out of a full bred Morgan mare, who was got by the celebrated horse Flying Dragon . . . A stallion of this stock was imported some years ago by Mr. Robert Patterson, of Maryland, and G. Tolet, Esq., and eminent breeder and farmer in Staffordshire, England, said in a letter to him—"the breed of the Cleveland Bays of which your colt is of the pure blood, was the native sort of the improved English horse before introduction of the Arabians and Barbs . . . by crossing mares with race horses, the Yorkshire breeders have supplied, for many years, the metropolis with high priced coach horses. *The cross with the blood horse is admirable, as it combines strength and power with fleetness.*" The original Morgan horse was raised by Justin Morgan in Vermont, the year 1795. They are celebrated in this country for their great speed and endurance on the road. Cleveland Bay was exhibited in Charleston, at the S. Carolina Institute, and received a silver cup.[57]

As local planters established their own bloodlines, importing horses from abroad or other states became less common.

Mules

Born from female horses sired with donkeys, mules are a hybrid that have worked as draft animals since 3000 BCE in Egypt. They were uncommon in England, which might account for their limited numbers in early English colonies in North America.[58] They were viewed in the northeast with suspicion "as immoral and untrustworthy," in part because of notions of race purity against hybrids.[59] Mules' heartiness and heat tolerance made them popular in the South, where four-fifths of the US population resided by the early twentieth century. They were the unglamorous equine of the working class and sharecroppers, while overseers and planters rode expensive horses. Glenn Hinson notes that, "the lives of African American workers and mules are intimately linked in every period of southern history," both during slavery and post-emancipation with the dashed hopes of "forty acres and a mule."[60]

John Gilmer Speed described mules as "the ideal farm animal. They would find it hard to get along without him on the plantations in the South. A horse must be attended, or it will get ill and die. The mule seems if not to thrive in neglect, at least not seriously to deteriorate. On many southern plantations mules know neither currying comb nor brushing during all their long lives. And they live to a great age."[61] William Faulkner described mules unflatteringly in his 1927 novel, *Flags in the Dust:*

> father and mother he does not resemble, sons and daughters he will never have; vindicative and patient (it is a well-known fact that he will labor ten years willingly and patiently for you, for the privilege of kicking you once), solitary but without pride, self-sufficient but without vanity. Outcast and pariah, he has neither friend, wife, mistress nor sweetheart . . . He can be moved neither by reason, flattery, nor promise of reward; he performs his humble monotonous duties without complaint.[62]

Despite their reputation as vicious, stubborn, and slow, proponents claimed that a mule took better care of himself with an incompetent driver, would not undertake risky work even if beaten, and would refuse to work if underfed—we might call it self-preservation rather than stubbornness.[63] My observation in driving mules and horses for seventeen years in the city is that they are generally slower and harder to steer, but are calmer, more calculating about their footing, and less likely to be alarmed in new situations, making them well suited for urban work. They are quite affectionate to humans they trust.[64] Charleston mules did the odious work of pulling the city's trash carts and overloaded drays for the lumber yards. Sale stables advertised "plantation" or "rice mules" accustomed to rural work and "timber and turpentine

mules" trained to work in the city for lumber yards and affiliated businesses.[65]

Donkeys arrived in the Americas during Spanish exploration but were less common than mules in cities because they were so small; the 1910 census recorded only 2 asses to 1,184 mules in Charleston County.[66] Draft mules, whose dam was a draft mare and whose sire was a large donkey, were an almost exclusively American phenomenon. George Washington is called the "father of the American mule" for his role in breeding in the early republic, extolling "the great strength of mules, on their longevity, their hardiness, and cheap support which gives them a preference over horses that is scarcely to be imagined."[67] Washington created the "American Mammoth Jackstock" by breeding Andalusian and Maltese horses with donkeys he had received from the King of Spain and from the Marquis de Lafayette. He sent his jackass Royal Gift on a breeding tour throughout the South, including to his cousin William Washington's Sandy Hill plantation thirty miles from Charleston, in the 1790s to cover draft mares to produce large mules, while King of Malta mated with smaller breeds to yield riding or chair mules.[68]

Mules were already working in the Lowcountry, however, before Washington promoted them. They are referenced in Charlestown by 1732, when an enslaved man named Aaron, "who used to go about the town with a cart & mule," ran away.[69] John Waring had a jackass "very good for getting mules" on his plantation in 1766.[70] The British stole several from William

Williamson's plantation during the Revolutionary War.[71] John Hatfield on East Bay Street advertised a "very fine mule broke to drawing," or trained for draft, in 1783.[72] As early as 1771, South Carolinians were importing jackasses for breeding tours, such as "the famous Ass Rosano, just arrived from Spain," descended from lines owned by Pope Innocent and Queen Isabella, whose predecessors had been imported from the Middle East.[73] Gell and Garnet's livery stable imported a fourteen-hand tall Spanish jackass, "of the largest breed, as large as any on the continent, and presumed to be the largest in South Carolina,"[74] while an unspecified breeder boasted "a real Egyptian Stone Jackass" for cover.[75]

Mules came to Charleston from the northern states and beyond in the early nineteenth century. For example, thirteen "large mules, from 13 to 14 hands high, from two to three years old, sired by the great Jack, *Royal Standard,* on Plainfield, Connecticut" were for sale at a King Street livery stable in 1798, and John Gell offered forty large mules for sale brought "from Spanish Main."[76] In 1803, Benjamin Merrell sold fifty "mules of an uncommon large size, bred from Mexican Mares, and well adapted for this climate and for immediate use," which he estimated would reach fifteen hands when fully grown.[77]

A team of large mules parked on Church Street with a delivery wagon during the 1920s. They are distinguishable by their long ears and flat faces. Library of Congress.

Some mules were acclimated to the state and trained for draft work, while others were sold immediately on arrival without an acclimation period, such as forty mules from Buenos Aires who arrived on the brig *Warrior* in 1819, 110 "prime mules for sale on board the ship *Neutrality,* at Smith's Wharf," and a pack of Mexican mules sold "reasonable for cash or negroes."[78]

Mules cannot procreate so jackasses were continually shipped to the Lowcountry for breeding stock into the antebellum era, but native-born mules also came directly to Charleston from Kentucky by the 1830s.[79] Sale stables at the turn of the twentieth century sold rail carloads of equines from out of state. Harper Brothers sold nearly 1000 horses and mules in 1907 alone. Al and Lon Harper operated the Charleston branch of the business, while Herman and Frank Harper were in Havana, Cuba, and St. Louis, Missouri, respectively, operating branch businesses and procuring animals. Henry and Nesbitt Harper ran the Atlanta facility.[80] J. E. O'Hearn and Brothers sold fifty mules at a time ranging from 1,100 to 1,400 pounds, ideal for "merchants, transfer companies, and draymen."[81] South Carolina's mule population peaked at 210,000 animals in the 1920s, mostly imported from Texas and Missouri.[82] Mules worked in the city until the last livery stables closed and the ice companies switched to vehicle fleets in the 1950s. They made their local resurgence in 1972 when the Palmetto Carriage company opened. Speaking to the long-standing predilection for horses, Palmetto is the only local company to use mules alongside other draft breeds. The company's founder preferred mules and purchased them from suppliers who broker for the Amish. Tom Doyle cites their stoicism and intelligence; "they're not really good at hiding a behavior. What you see is what you get. They're very smart, Beaufort [a Percheron mule] was so smart. He'd swish his tail all day and the minute you'd walk behind him he'd freeze so he wouldn't swat you. And he was playful, he'd chase you around the pasture at feeding time."[83] Mules are ideal for the southern heat and humidity, thrive on coastal hay, and are strong, durable, and smart, seconds Tommy Doyle Jr.[84]

"Modern" Draft Horses

Horse populations proliferated across the nation in the nineteenth century, with a twelve percent increase in urban populations between 1840 and 1850, and a fifty-one percent increase from 1850 to 1860. In the late nineteenth century, urban equine populations increased by over 350 percent and horse populations grew even faster than that of the humans.[85] Charleston sellers began to list breeds in their ads, like a "northern draught horse of Morgan stock" or R. Arnold's "fresh arrival of Northern horses and a pair of Morgan mares and some first rate single horses for buggy or family use" in 1859.[86] Buyers still sought "fine ponies" for their private carriages, but delivery companies and city departments required horses of large size and of great strength. Americans selectively bred European draft horse breeds for increased size and by the 1880s, the size of carriage horses ranged from 900–1100 pounds and

fifteen hands, to 1800–2000 pounds and seventeen hands tall or more.[87] Charleston sellers used the terms "draft horse" and "harness horse" versus "buggy horse" and "saddle horse" to differentiate size. Dealers advertised "well-broken horses and mules that weigh from 900 to 1,500 pounds; a fancy pair of dapple grays that weigh 3,000 pounds; barouche, carriage, buggy, and saddle horses, horse not afraid of cars, and rice, field, timber and plantation mules," showing the variety of equine available in 1900.[88]

"Breeds of Draft Horses" in the *USDA Farmer's Bulletin* of 1914 shows that by that time, "draft" denoted specific breeds and characteristics:

> the draft type is charactered by massiveness, and the particular field for this type is the hauling of heavy loads at a comparatively slow rate, usually at the walk. Their power and not speed is desired, and in order to possess this power the horse should be generally blocky or compact, low set or short legged, and be sufficiently heavy to enable him to throw the necessary weight into the collar to move the heavy load and at the same time maintain a secure footing . . . should not weigh less than 1600 pounds and between 16 and 17 hands . . . in temperament the draft horse is generally lymphatic but should not be too sluggish. While the nature of his work requires him to be steady and easily managed, it is nevertheless essential that it should be performed willingly and with some snap and vigor.[89]

American draft breeds originated in the colder climes of Europe and were first bred to carry knights in heavy armor into battle. They typically have leg feathers, stocky builds, and calm dispositions, and they have been bred over the centuries for carriage work and plowing. Percherons were widely imported to the United States after the stallion Louis Napoleon, who was bred with 400 mares in a single year, arrived in 1851. French breeders exported 1500 stallions to the US each year leading to 1880.[90] Percherons average 1,600 to 2,000 pounds, stand at least seventeen hands high, and are black, white, or grey. They were first mentioned in the Charleston papers for sale in the 1880s. The popular breed is known as "one of the best movers and surpassed in style of action only by the Clydesdale."[91]

Belgians were the second most popular draft breed in the nineteenth century. Similar in size to Percherons, they are generally 17 to 18 hands tall and weigh between 1600 and 2200 pounds. They are slower and shorter lived, traits counterbalanced by being "better feeders," (less picky and less wasteful with their grain), docile and easily handled, and with a less finicky constitution.[92] They are usually chestnut or sorrel in color. Shires fell out of favor because grooming their luxurious coats was tedious and their feathers left their legs prone to infection and mites; Clydesdales replaced them for their tall height and strong necks.[93]

The most common breeds of draft horse in Charleston's carriage industry today are Belgians, Percherons, and draft mules, such as Belgian or Percheron hybrids, which all faced endangerment in the post–World War II era when breeding and equine use on farms curtailed drastically in favor of mechanization.[94] Most draft horses and mules working in southern cities today, such as Charleston, Savannah, Beaufort, and New Orleans, are bred and trained by the Amish in Ohio and Pennsylvania, where they work for five to ten years in agriculture prior to their employ in the carriage industry. Some work in the Tennessee logging industry before working as carriage horses in Charleston. Draft crosses, born of a draft mare mated with a lighter breed stallion commonly used for small carriages, riding, or racing, such as quarter horses, Morgans, or thoroughbreds, are also common for smaller carriages. Cross breeds represent the "best of both worlds," as they are slightly smaller and better able to tolerate Charleston's heat, sure footed, strong, and good natured.[95] Spotted Drafts, like draft mules, are uniquely popular in the United States. This newer breed owes their pinto markings to cross breeding with paint horses and draft breeds, most commonly Percherons. Spotted drafts were formally registered as a breed in 1995 but had been in use since the mid-twentieth century.[96] Generally speaking, people walking around the city today see the same breeds as those seen on Charleston's streets more than a century ago.

The Equine Streetscape

English settlers founded Carolina as a proprietary colony in 1670. Charlestown, the colonial capitol, was established at its present peninsular location in 1680, on the high ground next to the Cooper River near the current intersection of Broad Street, the principal east-west street of the city, and East Bay Street, running north-south. Charleston is a subtropical, low-lying coastal city prone to flooding, tropical storms, and long, hot summers. While the heat can be oppressive for humans and equines alike, the city's flat topography caused horses less strain than in hillier towns as they pulled carriages through the few muddy and sandy roads in the early settlement. The town gradually expanded in every direction as residents filled lowlands and created new subdivisions. Local planters established rice and cotton as profitable cash crops, cultivated on nearby plantations by planters using, and,

in so doing, exploiting enslaved labor in the tidal swamps and pine forests near Charleston. Pedestrians and goods coming to town by carriage journeyed down the peninsula through the Charleston "Neck," a general term for the low-lying suburbs and farms outside town limits. The Neck's location moved northward as the city's population and buildable land grew.[1]

Charleston's earliest streets were laid out on an original town plan called the Grand Model. The planned streets were commodiously designed for two-way carriage traffic, while the supplemental streets were narrower but still ample for carts to reach the workshops and stables that lined them.[2] Property owners carved out even smaller alleys and passageways down the sides of their long lots to allow access to various rear buildings utilized by carpenters, bakers, and other businesses. For example, 55 East Bay Street

The 1844 *Plan of the City and Neck of Charleston* depicts the earliest section of the city along the Cooper River wharves and the suburban development to the north, west, and south. The Washington Racecourse lies on the Neck along the Ashley River marshes. Rumsey Map Collection.

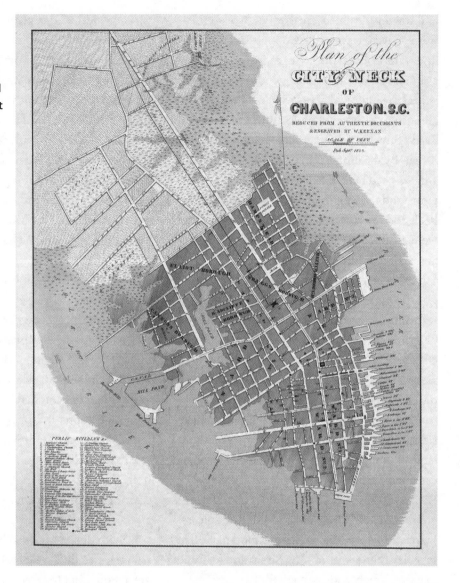

was bordered by a lane just seven feet wide for reaching store houses, carriage houses, and slate-roofed brick stables behind the main building.

Broad, King, and Meeting Streets were wide and well paved for carriages to circulate through the commercial districts. King Street, known as the Broad Path in the colonial era, was forty foot wide and led into the city from the lowlands and plantations further up the peninsula. The three-mile stretch of road outside the town featured taverns, pastures, and livery stables for merchants, planters, and other land travelers.[3] Drays and wagons rumbled, creaked, and rolled their way eastward toward the Cooper River wharves. The waterfront teemed with industrial activity as horses and mules hauled goods to and from ships. The oldest wharves were concentrated alongside the original walled town, between Tradd Street and Market Street along East Bay Street. By the nineteenth century, the original wharves had been filled, extended, and paved to withstand the weight of drays laden with cotton bales and loads of coal. The early railroad depots were grouped between Meeting and King Street above the city limits between Ann and John Streets, where drays gathered to load goods for transporting to the wharves. Single equines and teams pulled omnibuses and streetcars on predetermined routes that led through the commercial corridors, as well as traveling eastward and westward to bring Charlestonians to residential districts.

Bordered by the Ashley River, the western side of the peninsula featured extensive lowlands. Lumber and rice mill owners constructed causeways across the millponds and Ashley River marshes so delivery equines could bring goods eastward for loading on ships or railcars. Harleston, a suburban neighborhood platted in 1770, lay to the west of King Street and featured planned streets wide enough for two carriage lanes. Similar suburbs could be found on the east side of the peninsula, and as the city's population grew, residential development expanded correspondingly to the north and west across the peninsula. Horses took residents to their suburban estates and simpler houses via roads of

varying width and pavement quality, depending on borough demographics.

Colonial era parish-level entities including the Commissioners of Streets and the Commissioners of Fortifications used equines to haul, fill, and move materials for creating the town's defensive walls and roadbeds. Charleston's incorporation in 1783 led to a more nuanced local government and better regulation of the nascent city's activities. The Incorporation Act gave the new city council the power to pass laws respecting everything from the harbor and wharves to streets, to "carriages, wagons, carts, drays" or anything "that shall appear to them requisite and necessary for the security, welfare, and convenience of the said city, or for preserving peace, order and good government within the same."[4] The act created standing committees, established an intendant, also known as the mayor, and augmented colonial laws including speed limit regulations and carriage licensing practices.

Charleston's Commissioners of Streets oversaw road, drain, bridge, and causeway construction. The city council outlawed citizens from creating "narrow and confined streets, lanes, and alleys" after 1799, because ill-planned thoroughfares with densely packed buildings created a fire risk, trapped filth, propagated disease, and "do greatly obstruct the free passage or persons and carriages." All new roads would be approved by the Commissioners of Streets with horse drawn vehicles in mind.[5]

Just as vehicle size and traction performance dictate pavement and road planning for cars today, so did the needs of horses and their vehicles

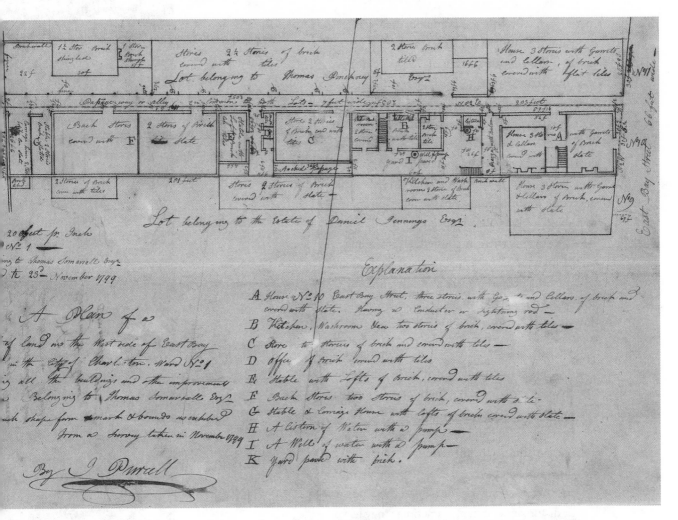

A 1799 Joseph Purcell plat shows Thomas Somersall's densely developed East Bay Street lot. The back buildings on the narrow lot, including a brick stable (letter E) and a stable and carriage house (letter G) were accessed by a small "passageway or alley." McCrady plat 1222. Charleston County Register of Deeds.

in the past. Developing pavements that were hard and smooth for wheels to easily turn but which had an elastic surface that allowed horses to gain traction presented a challenge. Sand or dirt roads were cheap but were dusty, fraught with ruts, and difficult for horses and drivers to maneuver. Decried as exorbitant, early cartage costs in the city reflected bad road conditions that made delivery laborious.[6] Cartwheels sunk deep into unsurfaced roads as equines struggled to pull their loads. Residents complained of "loaded wagons with narrow wheels, traveling on the high roads, by which the said roads are cut up and destroyed, to the great detriment and dangers of all passengers."[7] Timothy Ford described the city's inferior roads in 1785.

> The intermediate space is in its natural state mostly sandy and therefore disagreeable when crossing the streets. But this is atoned for by the inoffensive quietness with which carriages pass along; for being accustoming to having my ears strained by the rattling of carriages I was struck most agreeable by seeing them pass here without leaving behind them noise or disturbance- though sometimes they leave dust.[8]

Frequent flooding caused erosion, sink holes, and muddy street conditions. Residents complained that carriages got stuck in deep ruts and overturned at low spots like the intersection of Rutledge and Broad Streets, the site of the Colonial Lake today.[9] Owners sought remuneration from the city when their horses were injured by poorly paved streets and potholes. Black stable

Street scene in 1920, looking north on Bedons Alley to Elliott Street. A horse and wagon fitted with an umbrella to shelter the driver passes down the sandy, unpaved street near the Cooper River wharves. Library of Congress.

owner Jason Brown requested compensation for damages to his carriage and horses from falling into a pothole on a summer night.[10] H. S. Moore and William Randolph received money for vet bills for their horse who was injured "on account of the defective condition of the street," while George Von Kolnitz got $200 for injuries to a horse who fell into a hole on Smith Street. P. P. Moorer received $200 for a mule who died from falling into a hole on Moultrie Street.[11]

The city's growing equine population meant an ever-greater volume of manure and urine that accumulated in streets, gutters, rear yards, and abandoned lots as the city scavengers struggled to keep up. Early sanitary reform and public health theory rested on empirical evidence that residents who lived in filthy or low-lying areas of the city were more likely to fall prey to various urban diseases, from yellow fever to typhoid to cholera.[12] Street debris and manure created noxious smells that "poisoned the air" and contributed to flooding when refuse washed into the storm drains. The Commissioners of Streets contemplated buying "Franklin stink traps," which were essentially grates fitted to drains or manholes to prevent dung from clogging storm sewers and drains.[13] A City Council report in the 1850s remarked that "if we reflect on the numerous sources of impurity and filth that exist in the old city—grave yards, privy vaults, dung pits, and gas pipes and ill constructed drains, both public and private—we need not wonder at the bad quality of the water in the wells."[14] Victorian era proponents of modernity and sanitation complained about urban horses, pointing to

smells and flies, manure, coachmen and hostlers' lacking moral character, and accidents as reasons to reduce their numbers. A revolted Charlestonian described wayward horses and cows in 1872 as "objectionable promenaders" blocking Rutledge Street for the "numerous church going folks . . . much to the disgust of residents in the vicinity, when they had gone the evidence of their presence was to be seen in many places," by way of manure deposits.[15] However offensive to the bourgeoisie, horses were a necessity, so the city worked to install easy to clean paving and tasked the mule-drawn scavengers carts with removing and depositing ever-increasing refuse in the lowlands on the periphery of the city, near small farms and working class cottages.

The streets department installed and maintained a combination of road surfaces including sand, dirt, shell, macadam, Belgian blocks, plank roads, and asphalt. They followed General Quincy Gillmore's advice from his *Practical Treatise on Roads,* published in 1876, to guide their paving choices: "the essential requisites of a good street pavement are that it shall be smooth and hard in order to promote easy draft, that it shall give a firm and secure foothold for animals, and not become slippery from use, that it shall be as free from mud and dust as possible, and that it shall be easily cleansed, and shall not absorb and retain surface liquids."[16] The city health department commended the city council for approving funds in 1880 for stone paving, as "it is believed from a sanitary point of view, it will add materially to the welfare of the community. The readiness, quickness, and thoroughness with

A mule pulls a two-wheeled delivery cart along a Belgian block-paved stretch of Meeting Street near Queen Street. Mills House Hotel is visible in the background and street-car tracks run through the pavement, ca. 1912. Historic Charleston Foundation.

which it may be cleansed and all filth removed is a material issue in the value."[17]

Plank roads consisted of railroad ties set in the roadbed, backfilled with sand, and covered with thick wooden planks. Engineers and drivers debated about plank road efficacy, and critics claimed the planks were slippery and less elastic, which caused equine joints to stiffen, and that horses could pull twice as much as on a macadam road.[18] Granite blocks became popular after the 1850s and provided good footing, but were so expensive in Charleston, where there is no native stone, that they were reserved for the

business and commercial districts along Market, Meeting, Broad, and Calhoun Streets, and where horses carried out "heavy hauling" along East Bay.[19]

Shell roads eroded quickly but utilized abundant Lowcountry materials and provided both a hard and forgiving surface and good traction. The shell paved stretch of upper Meeting

Pedestrians and riders in private coaches pulled by teams of horses enjoy the well-paved carriage drive and promenade at East Battery. *Leslie's Illustrated*, 1880. Library of Congress.

Street was popular for illegal racing for its good footing. Three buggies in a heated race startled another horse in 1854, who "dashed off at full speed," causing series injury to the passengers. Eugene Brown, a Black livery stableman, was driving along the shell road near Line Street in 1891 when his horse "became unmanageable." Brown collided with George Steffens and they were both thrown from their buggies. It came to light the next day that Brown, "with a party of other owners on horses, was racing on the shell road just before the unfortunate accident."[20] Gala Race Week organizers suggested that the shell road, which was used mostly by farm wagons coming into the city, be devoted to pleasure turnouts during the afternoons of the races, and traffic vehicles relegated to King Street.[21]

Paving advances, better coach design and suspensions, desire to flee city congestion, and increased interest in leisure driving spurred national suburban growth patterns in the nineteenth century. In conjunction with these trends, the Charleston city council began constructing East Bay Street Extension, later renamed East

Battery, to connect the high, original part of the town with the southern end of the peninsula, in 1785. The project was completed in 1818 and included a seawall with a promenade for pedestrians, residential building lots, and a wide carriage drive. The city commenced work on adjacent White Point Garden in 1836. The large park included a drive along its northern edge which connected to "a promenade similar to that of the Battery in New York." The park was expanded in 1852 and the adjacent East Battery promenade widened to facilitate more carriages.[22] "The Battery has recently undergone great improvement," remarked an English visitor. "The greater number of the visitors come in carriages, and while some alight to enjoy the walk, others prefer the slow drive around the road called the South Bay . . . the carriages are all open, so that it strikingly reminded me of The Course at Calcutta."[23]

Three miles northward on the Neck, eight stockholders purchased Magnolia Umbra Plantation on the marshes of the Cooper River in 1849 to create Magnolia Cemetery, modeled after the popular Mount Auburn Cemetery in Boston and Greenwood Cemetery in New York. The *Charleston Courier* reported, "the grounds are already enclosed; the main avenues, embracing an extensive ride, are guarded and constructed . . . we feel great interest in the success of this enterprise, believing it will advance the best interests of the community."[24] *Appleton's Illustrated Handbook of American Travel,* published in 1861, noted, "the environs of the city afford a variety of pleasant drives. The Battery is of great resort on pleasant afternoons; thronged with carriages

and pedestrians. But take a coach and drive to the Magnolia Cemetery—a beautiful 'city of the dead' . . . you will find this a lovely retreat, well laid out, mingled woods and waters."[25] Harriot Pinckney Rutledge Holbrook enjoyed riding by coach to Magnolia to escape from the clatter of urban life.[26]

Charleston hosted the South Carolina Inter-State and West Indian Exposition on part of the nearby Washington Racecourse from December 1901 to June 1902. Organizers hoped the World's Fair-type Exposition would stimulate rail and shipping commerce and boost the local economy out of its post-Civil War slump. The city hired New York architect Bradford Lee Gilbert to oversee the architecture and landscaping, which followed City Beautiful planning principles of improved vehicular circulation, orderly planning, and recreational amenities in place of congestion.[27] After the Exposition, the city converted the fairgrounds into Hampton Park, with strolling paths and a carriage drive along the periphery of the old racecourse track. A cross-park drive was created to, "allow for those in vehicles to view the beauty of the place without leaving their carriages."[28]

The city undertook several paving campaigns after the 1880s for carriages, utilizing vitrified brick, granite, and asphalt, which all allowed for faster travel because they were smooth, while also providing suitable traction for wheels and hooves.[29] Hard paving had the undesired effect of making the bustling intersection of Meeting and Broad Streets "one of the noisiest places in the city, much to the disgust of the city fathers . . .

at the last session [Council's] voices could scarcely be heard over the din."[30] One can imagine the clamor of draymen yelling, traces jingling, hooves clattering on the pavement, and police horses tearing out of the stable at the Guard House across the street from City Hall. The Charleston city council discussed abating vehicular noise by spreading sawdust in the road, which would have made it harder for horses to pull through the area, or installing Nicholson wood block pavement that was known for being so quiet pedestrians could not hear carriages coming.[31] The Committee on Streets settled on vulcanite cement, "suitable for streets or sidewalk paving, in use in Philadelphia and other northern cities for some time past. It can be laid over cobblestones or bricks or any other surface, and in one hour becomes hard as granite, equally durable, and possesses the same noiseless qualification of the Nicholson pavement," while also lasting longer.[32] The streets department repaved Rutledge Street northward from Spring Street into the burgeoning suburbs with cement gravel, to "give a splendid drive for carriages, and the wheelmen . . . it is away from the street cars, and for the bicycle riders is a nice spin."[33] The police department requested asphalt macadam in 1900 in front of their stables, as present dirt paving made it "impossible for the horses to haul the [patrol] wagons through it at a speed necessary to fill a call."[34]

Road conditions varied depending on the tax revenue of a neighborhood, and hack drivers and coachmen had to choose between the most direct and fastest route versus the better paved, quieter, and more comfortable journey. Many opted to take "undesirable back streets" from the passenger stations to hotels, "possessed of the idea apparently that they should make the quickest time, no matter how sorry the streets look" and regardless of the wear to their vehicles from the rough roads. Badly paved roads were also hard on the horses and mules who were jostled as their vehicles rattled over potholes. Their late-night passage probably also created a noisy distraction for adjacent residents as the carriage traces clanked and wheels creaked over bad pavement. The drivers retorted that all the roads in the city were bad, and some only slightly worse than others.[35]

Paving conditions improved with rising city revenue and new products at the turn of the twentieth century. Charleston had five and a half miles of asphalt and wood block roads by 1914 when the streets department assessed their efficacy for horses:

Very little complaint, if any, has been made by teamsters and horse-owners concerning slippery roadways. This fact is quite reassuring, for when this class of paving was adopted three years ago, in preference to vitrified brick . . . there were some misgivings that the asphalt and wood block, although admittedly superior for motor traffic, might prove slippery for horse-drawn traffic. Notwithstanding the change which has taken place whereby automobiles and auto-trucks are in a measure supplanting horse-drawn vehicles, the latter must still be considered . . . our roadways, however, present no problems arising from steep grades, and our new pavements up to this time seem to meet the requirements of all classes of our local traffic.[36]

Speed Limits and Road Regulations

A Grand Jury complaint in 1747 about the "evel [sic] practice of Negroes and other persons riding [sic] horses at full speed through the streets of Charles Town to the endangering several persons lives" indicates that traffic pace was problematic even on the poorly paved roads of the colonial era.[37] Miles per hour were difficult to quantify, so horses' natural gaits, usually identifiable by different hoofbeat patterns, dictated safe and acceptable speed. Hauling animals usually walked, while carriage horses commonly moved at a fast walk or trot. Horses walk an average four to five miles an hour; trot in a range of five to ten miles an hour; canter at ten or more miles an hour; and gallop at around twenty miles per hour.[38] The Commissioners of Streets passed the first traffic law in 1750 to regulate speed and road use, making it illegal to ride or drive "in the said town faster than a moderate trot or pace under pain of forfeiting the sum of five pounds current money for every such offence."[39]

Carriages are far less dangerous than automobiles, but potentially fatal accidents did occur due to driver error, equine behavior, inclement weather, and pedestrians unwittingly entering vehicle rights of way. A horse and rider passing on a muddy or sandy street could be quiet enough for a careless pedestrian to walk into traffic and be struck. Unexpected debris or unfamiliar noises startled horses and led to accidents, such as two incidents in 1846 when a "colored boy driving a dray was instantly killed near the Exchange, his horse running off and he jumped off," and when a "boy of A. Jones driving a cart" had his leg amputated after his horse took fright and he fell from the vehicle.[40] An "Observer" complained that lumber floated up the Ashley River and piled indiscriminately near Rutledge Street was "almost an invariable means of alarming horses, and making them run off."[41] Horses were also injured in traffic accidents and in the dangerous industrial atmosphere along the wharves, such as one who was "instantly killed by cotton, with which the dray was loaded, falling on him."[42]

Speeding draymen pressured by clients and employers threatened public safety as they rushed to make up lost time or to increase their wages by adding another delivery or two, creating incentives to abuse equines and drive perilously.[43] Speeding fines were so common in municipal court that diplomat William Henry Trescott penned this verse in 1855: "to check the wicked and sustain the weak/ to guide the erring with a saintly pace/ to make the Irish hack-men very meek/ and stop the 'runner' in his reckless race."[44] Congestion clogged East Bay and Broad Streets which thronged with drays coming and going from the Cooper River waterfront. There was so much traffic, the fire chief complained, with "some of the drays moving down the street four abreast," that the fire engines could not expeditiously reach a cotton bale fire at the Commercial Cotton Press. The law stated that fire engines had the right of way, "but draymen seem to be a law unto themselves."[45]

Laws required that horses and mules be "properly bridled or haltered and led by some person properly capable of managing them" and forbade handlers from letting equines run at large or driving them through the city. Wayward or unsupervised equines damaged fences, trees, other plantings, and buildings while left tied, prompting fines for tying animals to lamp posts and trees in the city, or for allowing equines to rub the bark off of city trees.[46] The streets department experimented with wooden tree boxes, iron cages, and wire netting to prevent delivery horses from chomping on street trees while unattended.[47] An 1856 ordinance made it unlawful for "any cart, carriage, dray, wagon, or other carriage, laden with cotton, lumber or other merchandise or commodity to be driven through King Street, south of Calhoun Street, except to deliver on said streets," probably to prevent pavement damage and inconvenience to shopping pedestrians. Later versions of the ordinance also included Meeting Street north of Line Street.[48] It also became illegal to leave a carriage or cart in the street for more than four hours at a time, like parking meter limits today.[49]

The training of horses in the city raised safety concerns because unseasoned equines were more likely to bolt when startled. Two horses pulling a brake wagon, equipped with a braking mechanism to prevent a runaway

situation while horses are in an acclimation period, were frightened by a kite and injured two people in the ensuing run in May 1830. "Horse Drover," writing for the *Charleston Mercury*, asked "whether the driving of refractory horses through the streets be not a nuisance; and it is done almost every day . . . the brake wagon is of a peculiar construction—the body hangs high, to be out of the way of the heels of unbroken horses. If they were not designed for wild horses, this construction would not be necessary." Drivers could obtain licenses for brake wagons, even though there was a law prohibiting training horses in the city, creating ambiguity.[50] The city council amended the law to clarify that "two wheel chaises, chairs or sulkeys used by the keepers of livery stables, or other persons, for exercising or exhibiting horses for sale in the city," were liable to taxation, but that "the tax imposed shall not be construed in any manner to permit the breaking of horses within the city limits of Charleston, contrary to city ordinances prohibiting such practices."[51]

The city updated its traffic laws in response to new safety concerns and types of paving that encouraged speeding. An 1868 ordinance quantified speed in miles per hour, stating that no one shall "ride, drive, or lead any horse, mare, gelding, or other animal faster than six miles per hour in any street, lane, alley, market place, public landing or common in said city below Line Street," and no faster than seven miles an hour to the north.[52] An 1897 ordinance required cart, dray, omnibus and carriage drivers, and riders on horseback to veer to the righthand side of the road so faster travelers could pass on the left, similar to modern highway traffic flow.[53] Riders were expected to follow the same speed limits as carriages. Black rider Walter Hamilton was arrested in 1905 for "letting his horse hit the grit" while on his way to the rail depots to receive a drove of horses for the livestock sale yards, when he collided with a bicyclist and was arrested.[54]

Cars necessitated new traffic laws to allow equines and automobiles to share the streets. The 1901 "Ordinance to regulate the use of the streets by mobiles, automobiles, and locomobiles" set a ten mile an hour speed limit and capped speeds at intersections to four miles per hour.[55] Equines continued traveling at their natural pace, and like today, congestion ensued, and frustration flared as two forms of transportation vied for road space. A 1915 law required motorists to stop their vehicles for "any person or persons driving or riding a restive horse, or horses, or driving a domestic animal, or animals . . . as long as may be necessary to allow said horse or horses, or domestic animal or animals, to pass." Modernity took priority by 1924 and "all slow-moving vehicles and all horse drawn vehicles shall at all times proceed along the streets in the city of Charleston as near to the right-hand sidewalks of the streets as possible," to let cars pass.[56] Because speeding vehicles can startle horses, an ordinance required carriage drivers to have "fast hold of the reigns . . . that the driver can, in case of necessity, instantly take hold of such reins."[57]

Country farmers and poor residents used horses and mules to come to the city into the 1940s, taking county roads like King Street extension or Meeting Street to pick up supplies and to bring their goods to town to sell. The two-lane roads had shoulders and were wide enough for cars to safely pass wagons and carriages, but accidents still occurred. A Black man named James Nelson was driving home to Goose Creek from Charleston when he and his mule and coal wagon were struck about 8:15 pm by a car near Heriot Street on upper King Street in August 1937. The area was sparsely populated and at that time was bordered by small farms. Edward C. Jones, a 23-year-old Navy shipyard pipe fitter testified that he was driving his '35 Chevrolet with his wife, baby, and mother traveling northward at 30 miles an hour when a car coming the other direction with very bright lights blinded him, so he did not see Nelson's wagon until it was too late to veer around him. The mule was injured, and Nelson's leg and a rib were fractured, in addition to wagon damage. Thomas P. Stoney's law firm defended Nelson, who was driving in a completely lawful and safe manner, "the mule was entirely on the right-hand shoulder and had two wheels on said shoulder," and he had rear lanterns operating. The Court of Common Pleas found in favor of Nelson, who received $3,000 in damages.[58] Since the late 1940s and still today, there are equines on Charleston's streets pulling tour carriages, and they adhere to customized traffic rules that allow cars and carriages to coexist. The regulations governing their routes and operation are discussed in the final chapter.

Urban Equine Lifestyles

Equines have precise dietary and care needs that allow them to thrive and work efficiently. The ASPCA reminded equestrians of the importance of bathing and grooming, providing adequate stabling, keeping harnesses clean and well fitted, and admonished that, "the man who underfeeds his horse or saves on bedding, blankets, shoeing, or employs incompetent help to save money, practices false economy which invariably results in weak, lame, sore, and enfeebled animals. Plenty of light, fresh air, good food, pure water, and proper housing are as necessary to the horse as they are to the human being."[1] Working horses burn roughly 7900 calories per 500 pounds of body mass daily, compared to an idle horse that burns only 4356 calories.[2] For a working horse, the necessary caloric intake amounts to five to ten pounds of grain, commonly oats, corn, wheat, and barley, per day depending on horse size, in addition to forage, usually grass or hay.[3] Retired or idle horses can subsist entirely on hay or grazing, hence the term, "put out to pasture." Urban horses often worked harder than their rural counterparts but were usually better fed, had a more varied diet, and a longer life expectancy. Fire, carriage, and riding horses often worked into their twenties.[4]

A Lowcountry horse's diet in the eighteenth century consisted of rice straw or husks, which are low in nutritional value; Indian corn, oats, corn blades, or leaves stripped from the stalk; and pasture grazing.[5] Grains were often cracked to aid digestion, which were referred to as the "shorts," or leftover partial grains from the milling process used to make cereals and flour for human consumption. By the mid-eighteenth century, providing proper stabling and forage replaced earlier practices of leaving equines to fend for themselves grazing in fields with limited shelter.[6] In the nineteenth century, wholesalers offered Virginia oats and locally-produced wheat shorts by the bushel, and West Point Mill advertised ground rice as horse feed, which was a nutritious milling byproduct; rice bran remains a popular feed supplement for equines.[7] By the late nineteenth century beet pulp, a byproduct of beet sugar production first used as a fiber source for dairy cows, became common. Dry pulp stores well, making it an ideal city fodder.[8]

Charleston's sandy soil yields coastal variety hay which is less nutritious and harder to digest than Timothy or alfalfa grass, but the region's long growing season meant forage was easier to source consistently than in northern cities.[9] Suppliers shipped hay on flat boats from Ashley River plantations to town for merchants to sell year-round.[10] A unnamed planter had ten thousand pounds of good and inferior grade crabgrass hay for sale four miles from town in 1770.[11] During the American Revolution, the British established forage yards on the city waterfronts for the convenient arrival and sale of corn blades, hay, straw, and grains.[12] The Commissioners of the Markets regulated fodder prices by weight, and inspected feed arriving at the Market Wharf, where it was stored in sheds to keep it dry. As the city's equine population grew, the commissioners opened a second weigh station at the northern end of the city, established an additional forage market on South Bay in 1803, and leased an overflow forage facility near Gadsden's Wharf in 1811.[13]

Grain merchant Otis Mills furnished corn, hay, and oats for the city's equines in the antebellum era on an annual contract basis. Merchants, such as Henry Bulwinkle, located at the intersection of 94 East Bay and 17–19 Elizabeth Street, and William H. Jones, situated at the corner of 76 East Bay Street and 70 Chalmers Street, sold corn, bran, oats, hay, grist, and assorted meal in the late nineteenth century.[14] Warehouses filled with hay and grain occupied whole blocks of real estate in the market and near the wharves along Cordes, North Atlantic Wharf, and Prioleau Streets.[15] Albert Bischoff & Co.'s three-story feed mill had a coal fueled steam grinding engine, an electric grain lift, one-story brick hay house, and a large ell-shaped wooden stable in the rear yard where the delivery horses lived.[16] Sahlman Hay and Grain and Molony and Carter Feed also had horse-drawn delivery wagons.[17] H. T. Foster owned a warehouse on the North Atlantic wharf into the 1920s that had hay, meal, grain, grist, and cow feed for sale.[18]

Charleston equines grazed on underdeveloped lands near the Ashley River or on the Neck, usually by trespass or for a pasturage fee. Despite instructions from the Lords Proprietors to set aside 200 acres as a common for planting and provisions when the town was created, and

OVERLEAF: A horse takes a break to eat while his driver loads his cart with produce at North Adger's wharf alongside the Cooper River. His bridle is off for ease of eating and drinking, and he wears a traditional draft harness. Courtesy of Charleston Museum.

ongoing plans to establish common or pasture, Charlestown did not have a public greenspace set aside for grazing.[19] Tavern, stable, and pasture proprietors rented parcels on the edge of town, such as Mary Eycott, who leased a 130-acre "convenient pasture" in 1750, later part of Harleston neighborhood, and the Lynches, who offered Rhettsbury (now known as the Ansonborough neighborhood) for rent as pasture lands.[20] Landowners installed fencing to confine livestock as the town developed and pasturage moved up the Neck. Abraham Bestatt leased access to a "well fenced pasture" two and a half miles outside the town on a daily, weekly, monthly, or quarterly basis; and Peter and Mary Jeyes also stabled and pastured horses on the Neck.[21] Equines continued roaming free on the edges of town at least until 1875 when New Street residents, "complained of the large number of cows and mules which are allowed to graze in that vicinity, rendering the street at times well-nigh impassible."[22]

Draft horses produce around 35 pounds of manure a day, which translates to a staggering seven tons per year. As cities grew, disposing thousands of cartloads of dung that equines produced, and keeping manure from piling in the streets, was a challenge. Charlestonians found a creative use for horse excrement, slaughterhouse and rice mill offal, and other waste products by using them as fill material placed in lowlands, capping with sand or clay, and then developing the "made land."[23] Feed came into the city and manure went to the countryside as fertilizer in a cyclical and mutually beneficial relationship. The police department, for example, recorded annual income from selling their stable manure, as did the streets department into the late 1920s. A 75-acre Lowcountry farm in the 1880s could utilize up to 4,000 pounds of manure per annum.[24]

Working horses need plenty of fresh water, given Charleston's heat, but there is little early evidence of how and where they drank, or whether public troughs were available. The local creeks are tidally influenced, and much of the ground water is brackish and not potable. Drivers likely kept buckets with them to water their horses at livery stables or public wells during the day. In the nineteenth century, the city provided water troughs and fountains for equines near busy intersections and in parks. The artesian spring-fed trough at Wentworth and Meeting Street was "a favorite rendezvous of dray horses and equine travelers generally. This water is eagerly drunk by horses, and in preference to any other that can be procured, so much so that there is frequently a delay and obstruction from the number of horses awaiting to approach the trough."[25] The city installed brownstone and granite troughs for horses on their way to the railway depots and wharves, supplied by the new waterworks system. Additional troughs were located on Pinckney Street, at Wragg Mall on Meeting Street, and on Alexander Street.[26]

The SPCA built a fountain near Calhoun Street "for daily use by the horses and mules and a large number of farmers who use the Meeting Street Road for hauling their goods to the city," and another at Vendue Range for the equines carting to the Clyde Shipping Line docks and for East Bay merchants.[27] Firemen tapped hydrants to fill the fountains and horse troughs. As late as 1939, the city was still maintaining troughs at Ann and King Street, the Meeting and Mount Pleasant Street intersection on the Neck, Chapel and East Bay Streets located near several rail depots, and at Spring Street and Rutledge Avenue.[28] Tourism carriage operators filled their buckets from the fountain at Meeting Street and White Point Garden until the 1980s, when they relocated departures to the market nearer their barns.[29] Today they water their equines in the market area where tours begin and end.

Charleston retains a few troughs and several carriage mounting blocks, horse ties, and boot scrapers scattered throughout the city. Boot scrapers were installed near front doors for visitors to remove manure and street filth before entering the house. Early examples were hand forged with scrolled side arms and a flat blade between while later models were cast, reflecting modern fabrication practices.[30] There are at least 105 carriage steps and mounting blocks remaining in the city, located South of Broad Street (an elite residential area) and in front of large double houses in the former suburban neighborhoods of Harleston, Ansonborough, Wraggborough, and Elliottborough. They range in style from single slabs of brownstone or granite, to carved marble steps. Stone carver Robert Given imported free stone (soft limestone or sandstone) in 1797, "from Virginia, fit for window sills and arches, steps for doors and carriages, &c," indicating that the some blocks and steps were locally carved.[31] There were likely more horse blocks and stepping stones prior to 1907, when

the streets department complained that they reduced sidewalk widths by as much as two feet, "forming an obstruction to the use of the sidewalk and a menace to pedestrians," and asked for authorization to remove any offending ones.[32] The remaining blocks, boot scrapes, and horse ties are protected by the city's preservation laws for posterity.

Products for Equines

Horses were consumers who required satellite industries to support their dietary, care, and harness needs.[33] Tanners, harness makers, and saddlers fabricated and repaired the driving lines, saddles, bridles, collars, and other pieces of tack for urban equines. Harness makers had to understand equine composition because ill-fitting pieces would cause a horse discomfort and possible injury. A loose or tight collar, for example, could chafe and excoriate a horse's withers or shoulders and leave painful sores. Age and skin sensitivity, bone structure and musculature, and type of work further influenced harness design.[34] The 1880 *Harness Maker's Illustrated Manual,* allegedly the first trade guide in English, provided tables for the lengths and widths of various harness pieces and extolled the importance of proper fitting for the horse's well-being: "a very large percentage of all the harness makers in this country look upon the idea of measuring a horse as unworthy their consideration, but the experience and observation of the most enterprising men in the custom trade has convinced them that the reason why there are so many ill-fitting harness in use is because of the failure of so large a number in the trade to adopt the same common-sense rules which govern other mechanics."[35]

Saddles were customized to horse size, spinal shape, riding discipline (hunting, pleasure riding, racing), and a potential client's budget. The saddling trade required brass working skills and leather working expertise. Saddlers like John Antonio (active from at least 1769 until 1816) repaired saddles, made tack, and imported finished pieces from England for resale.[36] Saddler Jeremiah Hawes's invoices show the variety of tack available in early Charleston: hunting saddles, quilted saddles with and without pads, girths, and cruppers (a strap running from a riding saddle and under a horse's tail, which prevents the saddle from sliding forward.)[37] The sign of the "Saddle and Cap," operated by London-trained John Whiting on Meeting Street, sold bits and snaffles, postilion whips, "English hollies" (coach whips), and offered "saddles fitted to horses with the utmost exactness" for sale.[38]

Archeologists located several pieces of saddle hardware, bits, and other horse equipment during an excavation of the Charleston Place Hotel site, where harness and saddlery shops had operated in the nineteenth century. Bits and other metal pieces of tack are common on downtown dig sites.[39] A block away, Institute Hall Saddlery made saddles and harness for stage, coach, gig, and buggy work, and sold halters and other accoutrements.[40] McKensie and Company at Church and Chalmers Streets was the largest tack shop, with over $30,000

1882 *City Directory* advertisement for Alvin Thomlinson's saddle and harness factory on Meeting Street.

of invested capital and 25 employees in 1860.[41] Alvin Thomlinson operated a saddle, bridle, and harness factory after the Civil War at 137 Meeting Street.[42] Love and Wienges Saddlery and Harnesses imported English saddles, harness, and "military work" equestrian items at 45 Broad Street.[43] The Cudworth and Company harness and saddle shop's 1880s cash book lists diverse equine merchandise from horse care products and tack repair parts: curry combs, buggy whips, curb chains, martingales, pole straps, team harness, saddle soap, harness oil, ankle boots, traces, hame straps, collars, stirrup leathers, and multiple McClellan saddles, a versatile all-purpose saddle popular during and after the Civil War.[44]

City horses wore tacks customized for use in urban environments, such as blinders attached to horses' bridles to prevent them from seeing activity in their peripheral vision which might frighten them. Horses are color blind, have semi-lateral vision, and a concave retina that reflects light differently from human eyes, traits that meant they could easily startle at puddles or unfamiliar shiny surfaces.[45] Grooms covered horses with blankets and tarpaulins on rainy or cold days, and straw hats were used as sunshades in the early twentieth century, before being replaced with lighter cloth or lace bonnets that became commercially available later. Southern Ice Company driver Willie Clark made an improvised shade screen for his horse Robbie out of a pasteboard box in which he cut holes for his ears to pass through.[46] Carriage horses today take their breaks in front of auto-water troughs or under sunscreens and misting fans.

Farriery

Horseshoeing is physically demanding and highly-skilled work, because hooves are delicate structures crucial to a horse's conformation, comfort, and workability. Farriers undertook hoof repair and corrective shoeing, and also acted as equine surgeons before the rise of veterinary licensing.[47] London-born farrier John Bryan, who operated a Church Street shop called the Three Horse Shoes, advertised in 1734 that he could

> make a sound cure of the following distempers . . . poll evil and fistulas, if not inveterate, Impostumes [abscesses] in the head, falling Evil, Mad Staggers, Glanders, Canker in the mouth, Kernels in the throat, strangles,

strains in the shoulder, windgall or Navel gall, stopping of a scouring [diarrhea], hurts in the Cronat [coronet] of the foot, quarter bone, horses that have been overridden and the Grease melted down . . . all cutting and burning the Lampards, bleeding, Paring the feet and shoeing after the best man.[48]

Large shoeing firms employed several full-time farriers, like WC McElheran near Anson Street who had several "first rate horse shoers" tending forges.[49] Timothy J. Kennedy operated a popular business at the Sign of the Gilt Horseshoe on Church Street. He later moved to Pinckney Street at the site of Pinckney Inn today, where he offered farrier services, general blacksmithing, and wheelwright work. His ads assured customers, "horses and mules treated good."[50]

Scottish blacksmith and master farrier Benjamin McInnes (1811–1897) offers a glimpse into the business practices of local horseshoers. McInnes constructed a three-and-one-half story brick building at 34 Chalmers Street in 1850, where he and his descendants operated a forge and stable until the twentieth century. The family still owns the building today, and the original arched carriage openings still adorn the facade.[51] McInnes owned at least eleven enslaved people; his granddaughter recalled that he "did not like slavery but needed a strong man to help him in his blacksmith work. A young Black man whom he purchased made such a ruckus . . . that he was being separated from his sister who had been sold into slavery. Grandfather went out and borrowed money to keep them together." They and

T. J. Kennedy's Horse Shoeing, Wheel Wright, and General Blacksmith Shop on Pinckney Street, photographed in 1890. The building is now the Andrew Pinckney Inn. Charleston Museum.

their descendants worked with the McInnes family for three generations.[52] An 1884 publication described McInnes as "a practical and experienced workman, and nowhere in the city is such finished and good work done as in his establishment. He employs four to five competent and experienced hands. His reputation as an experienced blacksmith has ever been first class, and the best class of people have their horses shod at his place. For exactness of fit, smooth finish, perfect adjustment, and durability, the shoeing done at his establishment cannot be surpassed, if even equaled, by any in the country."[53] McInnes even shod General P. G. T. Beauregard's horse while he stayed at the Mills House Stable during the American Civil War.[54]

Benjamin's son Peter McGregor McInnes (1839–1914) was a farrier, as was Peter's son John B. McInnes (1868–1918), who had a blacksmith shop on State Street.[55] Another of Benjamin's sons, Benjamin McInnes Jr. (1852–1937), studied veterinary medicine in Edinburgh and practiced in Charleston for sixty years at his "veterinarian and horse shoeing shop" at 57 Queen Street.[56] Benjamin Jr.'s sons George Fleming McInnes and B. Kater McInnes (1885–1977) were also medical doctors, and Kater was veterinarian for the city's equines. He earned a DVM from University of Pennsylvania in 1911 and was the first licensed veterinary surgeon in South Carolina. While his "avocation was the love and care of animals," he raised show horses and bred Scottish Terriers; he was also interested in public health, working part time for over fifty years with the County Health Board conducting meat and dairy inspections.[57]

1897 invoice from Dr. John B. McInnes for four horseshoes. McInnes had a shop on State Street and a branch location on Sullivans Island. Author's Collection.

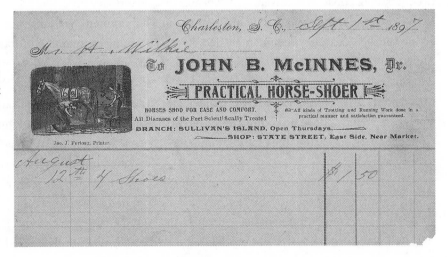

City farriers purchased blanks which they reheated to customize into shoes for each hoof. By the late nineteenth century, shoe manufactories offered pre-sized shoes for horses and mules, in standardized sizes still in use today. The Charleston City Railway used Goodenough brand "caulked" horseshoes that were fitted with small spikes at the base of the shoe next to the frog for traction, purchased from Anvil Shoe and Nail Co. at 65–69 Washington Street.[58] Patented Goodenough shoes were purported to cure contraction, corns, toe and quarter cracks, bent knees, thrush, cocked ankles, interfering, quarter cutting, "overreaching, speedy cutting, and all diseases incident to the feet." The shoes had pre-punched nail holes and were pre-shaped to allow cold shoeing. Farriers debated their efficacy; the calks prevented slipping, but proper fitting required the heels to be rasped considerably "[which] has frequently caused lameness by aggravating old corns. Further, the calks wore quickly, causing slipping, especially "among tired horses or those over driven."[59] Advocates in the horse rail industry called them, "a most economical shoe, as they require no fitting."[60] A Goodenough representative offered practical demonstrations in 1875 at the Enterprise Streetcar Stables, Charleston City Streetcar Stables, Calvitt's Shoeing shop at 602 King Street, and at Citadel Square, indicating the brand's popularity for city work.[61]

Located throughout the city, shoeing shops would have sung with the musical rhythm of shoes and harness accoutrement being formed on the anvil, resonating industry and productivity.

Several farrier businesses were found in the East Side and in Ansonborough near the livery, ice, and beer company stables. The 1904 *City Directory* listed approximately 20 horseshoers working as independent operators and for larger establishments, including the multigenerational McInnes, Phillips, and Sigwald family businesses. Black farrier Fred R. Blanchard had at least two other Black shoers at his Spring Street business.[62] Blacksmith Charles M. English operated from a shop at 22 Pinckney Street, where he also offered horses and wagons for hire. His son C. M. Junior was a blacksmith, whose work trajectory followed the decline of equine occupations as a whole; by the time of his death, he was a janitor for the Citadel.[63]

Ailments and Veterinary Care

Despite humans and equines coexisting for millennia, veterinary care was folk-based and rudimentary until the seventeenth century. Veterinary medicine advanced during the Enlightenment, yielding more scientific practices, training programs, and standardized protocols for equine care. Early veterinary medicine focused on horses rather than pets because of their importance in military affairs, agricultural practices, and transportation.[64] Pioneering veterinary surgeon Claude Bourgelat (1712–1779) founded one of the first veterinary schools in 1762 (in Lyon), while Farrier Edward Snape opened a ground-breaking horse infirmary with equine veterinary study courses in London in 1778, where pupils studied both well animals, "to preserve the parts of a healthy machine" and learned to diagnose and treat ailments and compound pharmaceuticals."[65] Knowledge of English veterinary advances first arrived in South Carolina in print when late eighteenth-century Charleston newspapers published articles reviewing the latest veterinary colleges in London.[66] There were no veterinary schools in the United States until the nineteenth century, however, so farriers continued to provide veterinary services. Livery stable operators also advertised their so-called medical skills, such as Richard Bettely, who "undertook all curable diseases in horses, either internal or external" and supplied medicines at John Jackson's stable, formerly operated by Greensword.[67]

Abdominal pain brought on by a variety of causes, collectively called colic, was and remains the most common equine symptom or illness. Some equines are susceptible due to genetic predisposition, but colic is aggravated by weather and temperature fluctuations, dietary changes, and poor-quality feed. Horses cannot vomit, so stomach ailments can be fatal. Lameness, the second most common ailment, is a general term for a change in gait caused by pain; this usually indicates an underlying injury, hoof damage, or neurological issues. Lameness can render a horse unable to work and can be a single occurrence or that of a chronic nature. It was a leading cause of equine death because a chronically lame horse might be shot to end his suffering or because he could no longer work.[68]

Common after long periods of idleness, working equines might suffer from azoturia, a semi paralysis from over feeding and underworking; this is avoided by providing them with regular exercise while they are not working over a long period of time. Other ailments included glanders, a contagious lymph node disease causing jaw swelling and mucous discharge from the nostrils; influenzas; "big head," swelling caused by a calcium deficiency, often caused by horses grazing on tropical pastures[69]; emphysema from moldy food or bad ventilation; founder, also called laminitis, which is an inflammation of the soft tissues around the coffin and pedal bone in the foot and hoof wall; and splints, a bony growth below the knee, triggered by working on hard surfaces.

Early treatments for equine diseases included the same marginally effective practices used on humans: enemas, blistering, digitalis, bleeding, purging of excess fluids by draining or syphoning, and poisonous medicines with high concentrations of metals which were as likely to kill as cure.[70] The city railway purchased a host of organic and chemical treatments for its equines: flax seed, peppermint, physaleae flowers, gentian root; they also purchased belladonna from the Aimar Drug Company. Powdered gentian root was used to cure glanders, and laudanum was diluted to kill botflies in the intestines; these treatments, as with belladonna, could be fatal if overprescribed.[71]

Charleston's equines were mostly spared in the great Epizootic of 1872, which brought American cities to a standstill. The virulent spate of equine influenza began in Toronto, Canada and spread across the continent, infecting equines in thirty-three states and Mexico. The fatality rate was below two percent, but with a recovery time of 10 to 15 days, freight and delivery, fire departments, and public transportation were crippled. The epizootic was a frightening reminder of how much cities relied upon their equines for every facet of daily life.[72] In its wake, Charleston passed ordinances to quell infectious equine diseases. The city council granted the Department of Health the power to euthanize equines stricken with glanders, "for the safety of the community in the ownership of valuable horses and mules." Though rare, glanders can infect humans when equine nasal discharge is ingested or enters the eye.[73]

Despite centuries of urban equine presence, horse skeletons are rarely found in Charleston archeology because their remains were recycled for industrial biproducts, or were removed for disposal outside city limits.[74] Old horses were commonly turned to pasture, abandoned in parks or rural areas, or shot and their carcasses sold to rendering firms.[75] Knackers used bones and hooves to produce gelatin, hides were used as leather, bones became weapon handles or were boiled to produce lime and fertilizer, upholsterers used manes and tails for furniture stuffing, and horse hair was a common binder in plaster.[76] John Lambert painted a grim picture on the periphery of the city in the early nineteenth century:

> Another very extraordinary, indolent, and parsimonious neglect of [Charlestonians'] own health and comfort is, the filthy and brutal practice of dragging dying horses, or the carcasses of dead ones, to a field in the outskirts of town, near the high road, and leaving them to be devoured by a crowd of ravenous dogs and turkey buzzards . . . I have frequently seen half a dozen dogs and above a hundred turkey buzzards barking and hissing in fierce contention for the *entrails, eyes,* and other *delicate morsels* of a poor unfortunate horse, whose carcase [sic] would perhaps lie so near the side of the road, that unless passengers were to windward, they ran no little risk from the infectious vapors that assailed their olfactory nerves. A part of the common at the back of the town is a perfect *Golgotha;* where piles of horses' *bones* serve the negro-washerwomen to place their tubs on.[77]

Lewis Thorne, who advertised as a veterinary surgeon trained in England, opened a glue factory outside of town on Meeting Street and offered to collect dead horses and cattle free of charge for his enterprise. Solomon Levine erected another glue factory in Rikersville, today's Heriot Street, and made an arrangement with the city "for the disposal of all animals which may die" in town, and to collect remains from butcher pen areas.[78] Residents complained about horse carcasses attracting flies and creating stench, leading the city council to pass an 1884 ordinance, "relating to the dead carcasses of animals, that it shall be the duty of the owners of all horses, mules, cows, or large animals dying in the limits to the city" to remove them from the town proper.[79] R. G. Salomon, who was awarded the removal contract, partnered with a D. Schoenstein's new "hide-oil-bone factory" in 1890, to "use all the carcasses of horses, cows, goats, and dogs which die in the city limits," sending the hides to tanneries and rendering the rest. Instead of paying the average rate of five dollars to the city for having a horse removed, Charleston residents could report a dead animal to the city police, then Schoenstein would remove it for free. This was far less offensive than dumping the city's "defunct animal kingdom" on the rear portion of Rhett's Farm located at the west end of Huger Street along the marshes, where residents complained of the smell.[80] A new ordinance in 1900 required owners of deceased large animals to notify the superintendent of streets, whose workers then conveyed their bodies outside city limits, for fifty cents per carcass. The streets department garbage crew collected 129 horses and 36 mules in 1915 alone.[81]

Animal Welfare

Humans in the past often viewed horses as investments worthy of exploitation for maximum return. Eighteenth-century Europeans and Americans adopted Rene Descartes's philosophy that animals were soulless machines devoid of reason, intelligence, and feeling. Under the misguided beliefs that animals did not suffer and showed distress only to protect their bodies from mechanistic damage, society tacitly accepted their exploitation and maltreatment.[82] The anonymous author of *American Husbandry* (1775) criticized colonial farmers as

the most ignorant set of men in the world. Nor do I know any country in which animals are worse treated. Horses are in general, even valuable ones, worked hard, and starved: they plough, cart, and ride them to death, at the same time they give them very little heed to their food; after the hardest day's works, all the nourishment they are like to have is to be turned into a wood, where the shoots and weeds form the chief of the pasture; unless it be after the hay is in, when they get a share of the after-grass.[83]

In the American South, there were upsetting parallels between slave owners' attitudes toward enslaved people and working equines, especially mules, as livestock with little to no autonomy.[84]

Massachusetts passed the first law in the American colonies in 1641 to protect "any brute creature which are normally kept for man's use," the model for which came from the Old Testament—"a righteous man regardeth the life of his beast."[85] Early South Carolina, however, had no such equivalent. We know less about colonial era equines' lives than in later periods. Pre-modern life was "nasty, brutish, and short," with limited oversight of human or equine well-being.[86] Aid for poor people was left to religious entities, and horse care left to an owner's discretion. Complaints about the condition of working animals, though rare, did occur. In 1742, the constables of Charlestown presented a grievance against wood carter Thomas Brand "and others, for the cruel usage of working horses, in carts, hardly able to draw an empty carriage."[87]

By the late eighteenth century, overworked equines became the focus of a nascent animal welfare movement. Combining "traditional views of animal subservience with the theological defense of kindness," Englishman Rev. Dr. Humphrey Primatt's 1776 *Dissertation on the Duty of Mercy and Sin of Cruelty to Brute Animals* was groundbreaking in its assertion that inflicting pain upon animals was morally wrong.[88] British author Robert Beatson's 1796 essay extolled the importance of adequate stabling, arguing that work horses were worthy of the same comforts as a race horse:

> in general farmers are by far too negligent of the accommodation or comfort of their horses. They seem to think that any sort of hovel is sufficient for a work horse. Were they only to bring the case home to themselves . . . they would perhaps have some degree of compassion on that noble and useful animal, on whose labours and exertions their own comforts so much depend. Eager to obey the will of his (often) ungrateful master, the horse strains every nerve to accomplish his imperious commands. At the conclusion of the day, fatigued, perhaps till his strength is almost exhausted, how barbarous it is to put this faithful, valuable servant, into a miserable tottering hovel, where he can neither lay down to take a little rest, nor stand up to taste his scanty morsel without it being wet or besmeared.[89]

Charleston book seller S. Hart offered several "valuable works on agriculture" for sale in 1842, including John Lawrence's *Philosophical Treatise on Horses and on the Moral Duties of Man toward the Brute Creation,* demonstrating that local audiences were receptive to new works on equine welfare.[90] Charleston passed an ordinance to prevent cruelty to animals in June 1810, punishing "any driver of a carriage wagon or dray, who shall wantonly and cruelly beat, bruise, maim or wound his horse or horses or any animal he may have in use, in any of the streets within the bounds of Charleston."[91] This may be one of the earliest equine welfare ordinances in any American city, ahead of statewide laws later passed in the South, and decades before the emerging national animal welfare movement of the 1860s.[92] Charleston's well-intentioned ordinance lacked enforcement, however, and overworked equines remained common in the city.

Humane laws for better animal treatment became more frequent during the 1860s and 1870s and were emblematic of changing attitudes toward morality and kindness, and the belief that improving the lives of animals and one's fellow man had a positive moral impact on all members of society. Diplomat Henry Bergh founded the American Society for the Prevention and Cruelty to Animals (ASPCA) in New York City in 1866 to tackle a number of animal welfare issues, but his foremost concern was protecting horses from overwork and cruelty.[93] Anna Sewell's famous 1877 novel *Black Beauty,* which anthropomorphized a cast of race, cart, and carriage horses, and which she hoped would "induce kindness, sympathy, and an understanding of treatment of horses," brought equine

A Charleston Fireman stands proudly with his
prize-winning fire horse in front of the Mills House
Hotel ca. 1900. George Williams Collection,
Charleston Archive, CCPL.

welfare issues to an international audience and bolstered membership in ASPCA chapters. Teamsters increasingly named their horses, entered them in work horse parades, and relied more on positive reinforcement and treats, thus "sparing [them] the whip." [94] Draying companies also encouraged animal kindness in training, and teamsters recalled the advice, "know every horse as a mother knows her child . . . animals are a lot like people. Each of these horses has a different personality, but all of them need tender, loving care . . . they always remember the people who treat them right."[95]

The *Charleston Courier* serialized several chapters of John Solomon Rarey's new *Art of Taming Horses* in August 1859. "The present useful improved system" offered kinder methods of breaking horses and calming those who had become "vicious and fearful" of humans after abuse. Rarey tied one of the horse's legs so he could not kick or flee, laid him gently on the ground, and sat on and touched the horse to acclimate him to human interaction. He advised against the violent methods of lassoing a wild horse, cloaking his head, using a harsh bit, and riding him to exhaustion, which left horses "vicious and stupid," arguing instead that "the corner stone of the [Rarey] theory is the law of *kindness.*"[96] Two titles in the Charleston Library Society's collections further demonstrate the changing attitudes from cruelty and trauma to humane kindness in equine management, Dennis Magner's *Art of Taming and Educating the Horse* (1888) and *The Horse Educator,* by Charlestonian N. R. E. Mayer (1873). Magner,

whose training involved restraint methods which might be considered cruel today, but which were gentle by the standards of the times, proudly noted that Bergh had come to many of his demonstrations. The unattributed forward claimed, "there are 11 million horses in the United States, and not one man in a million who knows how to educate them to the highest degree of usefulness. We say educate, for the horse is an animal of high and spirited organization, endowed by his Creator with capabilities and faculties which sufficiently resemble man. Next to child training comes horse training; and which is the least understood, it were hard to say. The boys are shaken and whipped, and colts are yanked, kicked, and pounded." Magner recommended patience in addressing behavioral issues including excessive fear, kicking, balking, running away, and bad manners for the farrier. He advised against cruel training; "I have frequently found horses so extremely sensitive that punishment of any kind would immediately excite in them the greatest resentment."[97]

The Horse Educator went so far as to mention love and trust between horse and human: "I firmly believe that all the vicious habits horses have, are taught them through the ignorance of their owners or trainers. We call ourselves the horse's friend, because in the use of our instructions he is kindly taught what is required of him. He is first taught that he must succumb to the will of the master. He is then caressed. By showing him that only kindness towards him is intended, he is made to understand what is desired of him, and he is at once your obedient slave." Mayer described horses as

reasoning creatures, possessing a keen perception for right and wrong. Were it not so, they would not so readily refrain from doing that for which they have been punished, or to do the bidding of those they love . . . They possess strong affections, and in a degree, manifest them in accordance with the amount of affection demonstrated by their master. It is also true, they know by instinct, a good man from a cruel one. If a horse is in the habit of being petted and fondled by a lady, he soon learns to love and follow her, demonstrating the principle that for himself love is the reward. The effects of rude treatment are noticeable particularly on horses of a sensitive, ambitious nature; such either fret, or are dangerous when subjected to the management of an impulsive, irritable groom, though extremely docile and safe to a careful, patient person.[98]

The Charleston SPCA was founded in 1874. Their representatives, including long-time president J. L. Ancrum and secretary and treasurer J. Alwyn Ball, had the power to issue fines, citations, stop work orders, and to seize animals from their owners' neglect. The organization had at least one enforcement officer but like today, they relied on citizens' reports of mistreatment to intervene and prosecute. The Charleston Police Department (CPD) also enforced animal cruelty laws, even within its ranks.[99] Charleston's police, city veterinarians, and SPCA representatives had authority to shoot equines to end their suffering, which "paradoxically led to the SPCA becoming the primary horse killer in cities."[100] The ASPCA vice president visited Charleston in 1891 and "found the condition of the dumb animals excellent, their treatment kind and a good humane society, and almost everyone she met had either read or was going to read *Black Beauty*." Other visitors were less impressed with the city's animal welfare. Author John Bennett described the hack he hired on arriving at the Charleston rail station in 1898 as "a worn-out conveyance with the horse on the verge of death; harness looked like a fish net."[101]

An 1888 article highlighting an urban and a suburban incident is illustrative of the intervention tactics of the SPCA:

The horrible cruelty of a huckster to his horse- A colored man named Glover was driving around in his wagon a horse so injured in his stifle joint that he could scarcely put his feet to the ground. Mr. Chapeau states that these kinds of cases happen only too often and if anything, are more frequent in the country than in town, and that recently while attending a picnic at Otranto he found an animal with a broken hip being compelled by its owner to haul passengers to Goose Creek Church, about a mile. This unfortunate creature was in such a fearful condition from hard work and rough usage, that when taken out of the wagon that he lay down unable to move and presented a pitiable spectacle of suffering and misery. Charleston has long needed a "Bergh" in these matters, and the Society . . .

will promptly prosecute anyone without regard to station or color, whom they find either ill-treating animals or driving and using them in such a way as to cause needless pain and suffering. 'The merciful man is merciful to his beast' and the unmerciful man will be dealt with by the Society.[102]

The SPCA pulled lame horses and mules from service, seized underfed and overworked horses, and treated animals with sores from ill-fitting harness.[103] Country drivers were fined for working unshod animals on the city's hard paved streets. The owner of one such mule argued that "he only been in the city for a period of two hours, and that the driver had been instructed to return to St Andrews parish as soon as he had finished his business in the city. It was pointed out that the mule did not need shoes, as it lived in the country," though the city judge was not convinced.[104]

Delivery work exhausted equines because of frequent stops and starts, long days, heavy loads, and few breaks. A letter in 1895 recounted the cart equines' plight:

> any man of common sense excepting the owners will tell you that five bales of cotton to a dray hauled by one mule and making at least half a dozen trips a day from the railroad yards to the compresses, are too severe a strain upon the poor animals. It's more than simply overtaxing the animals; it's downright cruelty and it should be stopped by the SPCA. Just think of it! Each mule must pull over 2500

An early seal from the SPCA, which appeared in *Our Town and Civic Duty* by Jane Eayre Fryer in 1920, implored people to "Be kind to animals." Similar images appeared in Charleston newspapers.

pounds in addition to the heavy dray, and has to haul this weight over Belgian blocks, which are now worn so smooth that it is barely possible for him to hold his footing. It's simply torturing the animal to make him haul this great weight all through the day.[105]

Another writer watched a mule try in vain to pull a three-ton stone on a two wheeled cart, and implored drivers to

> give the mule a chance. There is one proverb that a good many Charleston draymen would do well to remember: don't burn a candle at both ends. They ought to know that it is not economy to overload a mule. In busy times

the streetcars are often so crowded that the horses almost fall as they walk along . . . it is base cruelty and foolishly insidious to overtax an animals' strength, but in the end the strain will tell, and the owners will regretfully look back and wish they had listened to the Tale.

Luckily for the mule struggling with the stone, a young physician intervened, unhitched the mule, and threatened to have the driver arrested for cruelty.[106]

Black equestrians had reputations as cruel drivers who worked their animals harshly. "*A Prominent Citizen*" urged "that an example be made of inhuman Negro drivers" after they

witnessed a black driver mercilessly whip a mule trying to pull an overloaded cart over a curb into the yard of Meeting Street residence. This same *Citizen* lamented, "if a horse or mule stumbles under a heavy load, over a badly paved street, the Negroes proceed to beat the animal and to jerk the lines sometimes until the mouth bleeds. Frequently exhibitions of the most heartless cruelty are given by these drivers, and it would be a good thing for the mayor to instruct the police department to arrest the offenders."[107] In 1893, a Black driver for Enterprise Railroad Company purposely hit a mule in the eye with a club and knocked it out of its socket; he was attended by a vet and eventually able to return to work, but the arresting officer admonished that "such cruelty could not be too severely punished."[108] Black delivery driver Jesse Pervis was arrested for purposefully injuring a meat delivery horse by leaving a stall fork in his stall which caused a severe hoof injury; the motive was "owing to a grievance he had against his employer" T. Weinberg.[109] An 1876 article even recommended swapping Chinese for African American labor in the state because "one good trait of [the Chinese] is kindness to animals, and a farmer may rely upon it that a Chinaman won't beat his mules."[110]

Jim Crow racial prejudices aside, white drivers were also arrested for cruelty. In 1910, German groceryman A. W. Hontze was arrested for driving a lame horse after SPCA officer Arnold had instructed him not to work the injured animal.[111] Charlie Williams, a hackman for Southern Furniture Company was charged with cruelty, for his horse "had been working day

An unflattering caricature of a shoeless Black driver with a small mule pulling a heavily loaded wood cart. "Sketches in Charleston," *Harper's Weekly*, 1875.

and night without proper food and attention" and was "made to rest in a manner with inflicted torture." The horse was seized, treated, and sold two months later, with the proceeds going to the SPCA.[112] New Street grocer John Ahrens was arrested after his horse was discovered weak and covered in bruises and sores. Dr. John Arnold, SPCA veterinarian, had operated on the horse several weeks prior, but noted that the injuries were not related to the surgical recovery. Ahrens had been ordered not to use the horse until he had recovered, but a policeman had found him fallen on the pavement while hitched to a cart for work the previous day. Ahrens was arrested, as "even the hardened policemen who were instructed to care for the horse [who was brought to the station stables], accustomed to sickening sights though they are, were moved to pity."[113] Only one cruelty case was found that involved a woman, an Eloise Logan who was charged with working a mule who was unfit.[114]

SPCA officers targeted company owners who set harsh workloads for equines and the courts weighed the motivation behind cruelty cases, fining more heavily for wanton cruelty than cases motivated by ignorance or an employer's instructions. In 1906, for example, a Black driver was initially fined ten dollars for driving an injured mule whose trace chains cut into her sides while hauling logs to Union Station, "but this was a case of cruelty of the owner of the animal, who insisted upon the driver working him but then left of the poor Darkey to the mercy of the court."[115] In a similar 1911 case, bystander Bessie Wilson complained of black youths racing overloaded timber company mules with full carts, while beating them with knotted ropes to make them run faster. The boys were warned, and the SPCA noted, "as regards the owner of these mules, you would find no doubt, that these 17-year-old boys were given instructions to 'deliver this wood quickly now and come back for another load or you will be discharged.' I would like to know who this wood dealer is, who pays $200 or $250 for mules and then turns them over to 17-year-old boys to drive and then complains that he does not get protection from the city or the Society."[116]

Summer heat presented another hazard for working equines. The streets department lost two mules during a hot spell after the Hurricane of 1911, and several otherwise healthy horses died during a severe heat wave in August 1918. The SPCA offered tips to prevent heat strokes, as it was "not only humane but also practical to treat animals with proper consideration in this torrid weather: Don't speed your horse. Don't overload the wagon. Use well-fitting light harness and loose collars. Allow periods of rest in the shade. At first sign of exhaustion stop and bathe the animal's head and neck in cold water." They also issued preemptive care notices following hurricanes, when the weather was hot and there would be much hauling and clearing work to do.[117]

Rental equines encountered more abuse than privately owned animals because their lessees had no vested interest in them, a situation similar to that of rental car drivers today. Such was the case for a thin horse covered in sores owned by wood yard owner Robert Lawless of

63 Beaufain Street, who sent him out for work that morning when the driver was stopped while pulling an overloaded manure cart. The officer unhitched the horse and sent him to Graham's Stables for feed and convalescence.[118] The 1908 SPCA annual report noted:

> the greater number of cases which were prosecuted were of poor colored people who will hire from heartless white men mules or horses which originally cost $35 or $50 each and a for a rental of 50 cents to a $1 a week is paid—more in a year than the original cost. The Society takes this opportunity of asking all those who are compelled to hire, to hire only animals in good condition for work . . .

and thereby save themselves from arrest and punishment.[119]

As cars began to replace horses on city streets, and with sentiments changing to people treating animals as pets rather than as commodities, cruelty cases began to diminish. By 1925, the SPCA's membership had dwindled from over 100 to just four due to the decline of horses in the city: "In years gone by, when horses were everywhere and automobiles rare things and somewhat a wealthy man's toy, the SPCA was an active organization in this community."[120] After 1925, there were almost no mention of equine cruelty in the papers, and the SPCA's shifted its mission toward domestic animal cruelty cases.

Equine Occupations
SPORT AND PRIVATE TRANSPORTATION

"[Charleston] is on the whole a rather gay place, there being public dances, assemblies and plays, with horse races about a mile off. Most people of property keep single horse chairs which are very numerous indeed in the town; but many of the genteeler sort keep handsome four wheeled carriages; and several carry their luxury so far as to have carriages, horses, coachmen and all, imported from England," wrote a visiting Englishman in 1774, when horses dominated entertainment and transportation.[1] Carriage ownership, fine horses, and accoutrement were status symbols for Charleston elites, a form of conspicuous consumption. Southern consumers preferred more ostentatious colors and insignia for their carriages than did their northern counterparts, emulating European landed gentry's state carriages.[2] Wealthy Charlestonians typically had several horses and carriages to suit

different occasions, such as Benjamin Smith, who owned three horses named York, Rhode Island, and English; a coach; and a chair in his townhouse inventory of 1770.[3]

Carolinians were generally good horsemen, "all partial to riding, and even in Charleston few ladies venture to walk. They are seldom seen out of doors, except in their coach or chaise."[4] Riding masters and stable owners like Thomas Gordon and Thomas Griffith taught, "young gentlemen and ladies to ride, with the same safety, ease, and gentility, as is now practiced in the best riding schools in London." Griffith had a "convenient piece of ground for the breaking of horses, either for the field, road, or thorough manage" and kept a boarding stable. Philadelphian William Walton also operated a diversified business with farrier services, livery, and training for riding, single, or double draft.[5]

A rider walks his saddle horse while a coachman passes at the new Roper Hospital campus in 1905. South Caroliniana Library Collections.

Horses pervaded entertainment through riding, racing, hunting, and even traveling equestrian circuses, which came through town periodically to the delight of children. Mr. Rickett erected a "circus on Tradd Street" where he gave "equestrian performances from December to early Spring, 1793–1794, followed by "Mr. Lailson, the Swedish Equestrian" and Mr. Langley, who traveled in a troop together, visiting in 1798. Langley remained in Charleston and opened a riding school at Vauxhall Garden on Broad Street.[6] "Messrs. Peppin and Breschard of the New York, Philadelphia, and Baltimore Circuses," visited in 1812 and 1814 "with a *complete company of equestrian performers,*" prepared

"to display new and extraordinary exercises of horsemanship."[7]

Charlestonians owned more private carriages than did their contemporaries in other cities, and visitors were often struck by the number of fine vehicles they saw. Large coaches were five times more prevalent in South Carolina than Massachusetts in the 1790s, with 45 coaches, 30 assorted vehicles, and 1,232 chaises recorded in the state's 1798 tax returns.[8] A French visitor to Charleston in 1817 remarked on "the rather large number of private carriages. One sees some

which are really elegant, as well as some cabriolets. The breed of horses is fine and beautiful."[9] In the 1820s, "it was the custom in Charleston for the gentlemen to go on Saturday morning to market. They drove usually in open carriages with their children around them."[10] Charleston resident Charles Fraser (1782–1860) recalled that as a young man, "the Sabbath was a day for formal visiting, and for the display of equipage and horses, for in that day carriages were not as common as now, and every carriage was known for its livery, some of which was very showy."[11]

An English visitor wondered in the 1850s at seeing at least 200 carriages at the Battery, more than he'd seen anywhere else in the United States, "more than even in Boston, Philadelphia, or New York though its population, including the suburbs, does not exceed 30,000. The practice of riding and driving is so general in this city," he exclaimed, "that a family is hardly deemed within the circle of genteel society, if they do not keep their own carriage."[12] Residents spent huge sums keeping their carriage fleets up to date. Ann Vanderhorst wrote in her diary in 1859 of a Mrs.

Lewis, who "resolves to appear in elegant style. She plans to get rid of the old carriage and sport a heavy city coach, servants in blue and silver but there's not a dollar in her pocket to pay Reynolds, the coach master. But on she goes, dashing off, meets Reynolds and bargains for the grand coach."[13]

Carriage ridership differentiated elites from the lower classes, literally and figuratively, elevating them above those passing on foot along the streets. Elite women recognized that carriages were a respectable, convenient, and clean way to travel. "Ladies rarely set foot in the streets" wrote a French visitor; working women, by contrast, could afford no option but to walk. Historian Marise Bachand notes that "conveyance also separated blacks from whites. In both Charleston and New Orleans, blacks—free and enslaved—were forbidden to drive, use, or ride in a coach, except as a servant. To elite women, carriages meant more than increasing their social capital or distances themselves from the poor and free blacks. They were, primarily, a means of transportation. For those living in suburban villas or in the rural areas at the periphery of town, a carriage meant inclusion instead of isolation."[14]

In cities where race was an important social stratifier, whites viewed Black carriage use as a threat to the social order. An editorial in the *Charleston Mercury* scathed,

> why Negroes, who are slaves, are permitted to carry on trades in their own names; to keep shops and places of trade; livery stables, where their associates have control of a large number of horses, and whose premises . . . may be dens of vice. Why our public hacks, in the hands of Negroes, aye and some white men, are daily filled with black and mulatto males and females, slaves and free, indulging in the privilege of taking the air, in violation of known sentiment, that are they permitted to attend balls, churches, and funerals in carriages, to assume themselves prerogatives and distinctions which have been, and ought to be, amongst the landmarks separating the classes?[15]

Enslaved men chauffeuring white employers, however, was completely acceptable and very common.

Racing and Entertainment

Horseracing reigned king in the Lowcountry as planters spent small fortunes importing horses from Europe for racing and breeding.[16] The earliest organized races took place at Bowling Green Plantation, known today as the Ansonborough neighborhood, just north of the original town boundary in 1734. In subsequent decades, races were held in Dorchester and on the Charleston Neck. A jockey club was established in Charleston by 1760.[17] Yorkshire native and saddler Thomas Nightingale established the Newmarket racetrack that year on land leased from the Blake family. He offered prizes for the fastest mounts owned by planters and merchants, and a "mechanick's purse" for tradesmen's horse racing heats. Newmarket closed in 1792 when the

Washington Racecourse, future site of Hampton Park, opened. It was the crown jewel of the ten Lowcountry racetracks that attracted competitors from up and down the east coast.[18]

Races were popular social events for white and Black Charlestonians of all classes. Planters brought their families and horses to the city for the winter social season of theatrical performances, concerts, and races, and some allowed their slaves to attend as a privilege. So popular was Race Week that courts and businesses closed.[19] John Lambert described the races in 1808:

> They have some excellent horses; but in general, they are badly broken in and will start and fly at almost any object they meet. Horse racing is a favourite amusement with the Carolinians, though more discountenanced, many families having suffered greatly by the gambling debts made at the races. The racecourse is about a mile and a half from the city, on a fine level piece of ground, a full mile in circumference. Mile heats are run by American raised horses, and generally performed in eight minutes . . . several large booths were fitted at one end of the racecourse, and handsome cold collections of meat, poultry, and salad, were laid out on long tables for the accommodations of those who chose to dine there after the races. The gentry then returned to town, and spent the day in dinner parties, and in the evening in balls and concerts. The middling and lower classes of the people remained on the ground, and diverted themselves with some hack races, after which they

repaired to the booths, and finished the day in humble imitation of their superiors. A number of sailors enjoyed themselves with their girls, in the smaller booths, and the Negroes with their dingy misses, came in for a share of the fun. At the night they all came reeling into town, well charged with wine, rum-punch, gin sling, and sangoree [sangria].[20]

"Crowds of the most promiscuous character . . . the sailor, retailer, stable boys in one dense mass" entered through the foot passenger gate, juxtaposed with "the beautiful and splendid equipages, with rich liveried coachmen and foot men."[21] Northern visitors were surprised by the number of enslaved people in attendance at Race Week but, as in so many aspects of South Carolina life, planters relied on the skills of enslaved grooms, trainers, and jockeys who worked with the horses at their home plantations and traveled the racing circuit with them. Breeding horses was an exacting science of fertility cycles and working with stallions was potentially dangerous, so horse owners entrusted the duties to their stable supervisors, many of whom were enslaved.[22] Benjamin Backhouse's 1767 Charleston inventory listed an enslaved man known as "White Caven a Horse Jockey." Wade Hampton the First hired a skilled trainer named Cornelius from Col. Richard Singleton, and John Chesnut also paid to have Cornelius train one of his slaves as a jockey. Cornelius' equestrian skills were so valued and respected that he was allowed to travel out of state to visit his wife, and he even carried a whip among the white attendees as

"They're Off- and They're Mules!" A 1936 race at St. John's Jockey Club, Eutawville. African American jockeys were only allowed to participate in a side race using mules during the Jim Crow era. Brailsford Collection, Charleston Museum.

he led his horses through the crowds at Race Week.[23] Hercules, the trainer owned by the Sinkler family and hired by breeder Major Jack Cantey, was famed for turning a recalcitrant mare named Albine into a prize-winning racehorse. Dubose Heyward later wrote, "what she would do for no white man she did for old Hercules." Albine's win against a thoroughbred named Planet in 1861 was one of the most famous races at the Washington course. "Old Herc was very proud of defeating Planet," bystanders recalled, and everyone acknowledged the win was all his.[24]

Jockeys' lives were grueling, with restrictive diets to maintain the desired weight for racing and with the ever-present threat of potential beatings for training-related failures. As a counterpoint to the physically demanding work, enslaved grooms and jockeys were often allowed to keep a portion of a stud fee or racing purse when their horses performed well. Their work garnered respect and enslaved men expressed pride in the horses they spent their lives caring for. The horsemen worked closely with their white owners and developed familiarity and perhaps even camaraderie, talking "face to face with masters, as few slaves were able to do."[25] Harriet Horry St. Julien Ravenel wrote, "nothing could exceed the enthusiasm of the Negro grooms and jockeys on these occasions. Identifying themselves with their masters, as they always did, it was 'my horse' to the trainer and rider, quite as much as the owner."[26]

The Civil War and Reconstruction curtailed Lowcountry horseracing temporarily but some traditions resurfaced after Reconstruction. As civic leaders worked to revive the city's economy and social calendar, horse races remained a part of festivities, parades, and other promotional events. The Jockey Club petitioned the Freedman's Bureau to get the Washington Racecourse back after it had been used as a Union prisoner of war camp and cemetery. Race Week 1875, the first since the conclusion of the war, drew thousands and was celebrated as a return to the "good old days."[27] Business leader and horse culture proponent Frederick W. Wagener founded the Charleston Driving Association in 1883 and established a half-mile track on his Lowndes Grove plantation on the Neck to satisfy his carriage driving passion. The inaugural race took place 1 January 1884 and included five trotting heats with over 400 visitors in attendance, including women.[28]

Wagener also helped reintroduce Gala Week. The 1887 gala included horse racing, a fire engine tournament which an estimated 30,000 people viewed (shouting "look out! Here she comes! When the thunder of the horses' hoofs and the rattle of the engine wheels were heard coming up the street"), and several parades with floats and carriages for civic dignitaries and business sponsors. Wagener's procession included white clerks and Black draymen riding in

wagons and carriages, and men on foot holding a large sign that read "don't wait for the millennium, help the boom along. You have tried war, cyclone, and earthquake, now try peace, prosperity, and plenty."[29] The Fall Festival of parades and floats for the 1890 Gala included a host of carriage entries that processed down Meeting and King Street. The "True Patriots All" Ambassadors of Trade group "turned out in full force" with forty open carriages carrying members and drummers. Wagener and Co. entered several vehicles followed by "forty-five colored men, the porters, draymen, and cotton house employees."[30] Horse and carriage were a key aspect of civic boosterism, company pride, and entertainment. The 1897 gala week included several carriage racing heats, which the *News and Courier* reported with great fanfare; "the long talked-of race meeting of the Driving Association will be opened at Wagener Park. The stables of the city are filled with the finest racing and trotting horses in this part of the country. The horsemen of the city are more than enthusiastic over the meet."[31]

Among the exhibits and events at the 1901 South Carolina Inter-state West Indian Exposition were horse and carriage races, planned by Wagner, who even gave the city free use of his property for part of the Exposition grounds; parades with "carriage upon carriage of dignitaries,

An 1891 broadside for the Gala Week races and events at Wagener Park. Duke University Libraries.

CHARLESTON'S GRAND GALA WEEK!

COMMENCING * MONDAY, * OCTOBER * 26th, * 1891.

PAIN'S GORGEOUS SPECTACLE,

PARIS, FROM EMPIRE TO COMMUNE.

ATHLETIC SPORTS AND SPECIAL PERFORMANCES OF ACROBATS, TIGHT WIRE WALKING, Etc.

BALLOON ASCENSION!   LADIES' MILITARY BAND!   TRADES AND FANTASTIC PARADE AND TORCHLIGHT PROCESSION!   HARBOR EXCURSION!

GRAND TOURNAMENT   AT WAGENER'S PARK!

COMMENCING WEDNESDAY, OCTOBER 28th, 1891,

And continuing until all the Knights have Ridden.

RULES.

Tournament open to Contestants from this or any other State, subject to the approval of the Committee.
Contestants to be in Costume, to use a Lance held Five Feet from Point under Right Arm, each to have Three Runs at Three Rings, Two Inches in Diameter, suspended Six Feet Nine Inches from the ground, and placed 125 Feet apart.   Time required from Starting to Terminal Flag, Eight Seconds.   Distance from Starting to Terminal Flag will be 276 Feet.

PRIZES.

First, $1,000.   ※   **Second, $500.**   ※   **Third, $250.**

A Tournament will also be given for Boys under 16 years of age, open to all.

PRIZES.

First, $125.   ※   **Second, $75.**   ※   **Third, $25.**

ENTRANCE FEES.

MEN, $20.   ※   BOYS, $10.

Persons intending to participate will apply by letter to **J. H. LOEB, Secretary,** on or before October 19, also stating character to be assumed.
All applications must be accompanied by half of the Entrance Fees.
If more than 100 Knights ride the Prizes will be increased; if less, reduced.

COMMITTEES.

T. W. PASSAILAIGUE, Chairman.

F. F. CHAPEAU,   Capt. S. G. STONEY,   T. S. SINKLER,   GEO. VON OHSEN,   Capt. F. W. WAGENER,

Capt. F. W. JESSEN,   J. L. ANCRUM, M. D.,   F. W. CAPPLEMAN,   E. W. HUGHES.

New and varied attractions every day and night.

Reduced Railroad rates from all points.

Ample accommodations for all visitors.

Exposition officers, and common laborers" leading from Marion Square to the fairgrounds; a Carriage Worker's Convention; and a permanent exhibit for "Jim Key, the educated horse," who wowed the crowds by counting and answering various questions in a horseshoe-shaped exhibit structure.[32] Ten thousand spectators watched as the Liberty Bell was offloaded from a railcar and carried to the fairgrounds by a special wagon pulled by 13 horses in white blankets with stars to commemorate the original thirteen states.[33]

Charlestonians remained committed to horse racing culture long after elites in other southern cities lost interest in the sport, and horse racing interest never fully ceased. After the Exposition, several local racehorse owners organized a three-day event in November 1902 on the grounds. The Exposition stables had been removed, so horsemen coming from Savannah and the rest of the state boarded their horses in the city and had them "sent out to the racecourse in the afternoon an hour before the racing was set to begin."[34] Palmetto Park had been established twelve miles from the city near the Navy Base by 1912, with stables for 1200 horses. The "Gentlemen's Driving Association" course was still extant on a 1915 plat, and the Jockey Club retained a small adjacent property.[35] Though a rural phenomenon, northern industrialists who purchased former plantations in the early twentieth century also embraced equestrian traditions. The hunt continues in the Lowcountry, as do polo competitions.[36] The South Carolina Jockey Club resurrected in 1984 and renewed

A team of French Percherons pull a parade float down a brick paved street in 1901 on opening day of the Charleston Exposition. Franklin Frost Sams Collection. Historic Charleston Foundation.

its charter, and the Steeplechase of Charleston races began in 1986 and continue annually, at Stono Ferry racetrack on Johns Island.[37]

Private Carriages

Carriages come in a wide variety of seating configurations and frame types. Phaetons are high-bodied, open, four-wheel vehicles designed for fast travel, and which were immensely popular in the eighteenth century. Chairs, traps, sulkies, curricles (pulled by a team), gigs, and kittereens are two-wheeled vehicles, typically with an open cab and seating for the driver and one other passenger. Chairs were the most common vehicles in colonial South Carolina inventories.[38] Charles Drayton commuted from Drayton Hall to the city in the 1790s in a phaeton when traveling with guests and took a chair with an attendant riding along on horseback when traveling alone.[39]

Chaises, which often came with convertibles or calash tops, were light and made for fast travel, with two or four wheels depending on the model. Coaches, carriages, chariots, and landaus had four wheels and usually had an enclosed or partially enclosed cab. Brougham carriages, named for Lord Brougham who popularized them in the late 1830s, had an enclosed hard bodied cab for two passengers and elevated driver seats that exposed drivers to outdoor elements. Light-frame Rockaway carriages, with four wheels, fixed sides and roofs, and a driver's seat aligned with passenger seats, were named for the town in New Jersey where they originated but they were manufactured nationwide, including in Charleston. M. H. Nathan and Son on Meeting Street imported rockaways from McLear and Kendall of Wilmington, Delaware after the Civil War.[40] Barouche or "vis a vis" carriages featured two bench seats facing each other with ample room for four adults in an open cab with a convertible top, and an elevated driver's seat. Barouches were extremely common in Charleston and were often sold with fancy plated horse harnesses. Their convertible tops made them ideal for the Lowcountry heat, where an enclosed cab could be stifling. Local manufacturers advertised custom barouches for sale with "curricle tops," convertible roofs typically found on two-wheeled carriages and fitted with elliptical springs; the Gayer firm at Meeting and Wentworth Street built barouches on site.[41]

Also popular was the buggy, a typology that changed over time and was first known as a slang term referring to either a chaise or phaeton. The early American version had four wheels and seating for two passengers. Most models manufactured after the 1850s had seating for four over a compact frame, which became the most common carriage type made in the United States.[42] Wagonettes had an awning-like roof, two seats running the length of the frame facing each other with space for six to eight passengers, and a forward-facing driver's seat. All of these were used in Charleston and could be pulled by a single horse, a team, or even driven four in hand for show.

Carriages are technologically advanced vehicles that require engineering knowledge to design and expertise in wheelwrighting, blacksmithing, joinery, frame construction, and finish work to construct. Makers must know the latest design trends and performance requirements. *Decorator and Furnisher* magazine reminded readers that carriages are,

> Essentially artistic manufactures. There is nothing intermediary between gracefulness and its opposite in these vehicles. Curves must be adjusted so as to harmonize. The artist in laying down his lines must foresee the results. The coachmaker in some respects, is the most conservative of men; in devising changes of style and minor improvements he moved cautiously if not timidly. The carriage

of today is a thing of beauty, an adornment to our streets, and a contribution in its moving grace to popular artistic taste. The skill exercised in body painting is of no ordinary character. Each carriage must have twelve to fifteen coats of paint and three coats of varnish. The mechanical design of springs and lamps and forge work make every carriage a fusion of many different trades working together to create a thing of elegance.[43]

The 1790s letters of Henry Laurens Jr. to William Ball of Philadelphia in which he sought a coachmaker to build a carriage for his wife highlight the level of artistic design and technical features elite consumers expected. Laurens requested "an open quarters with fine glass and venetian spring blinds, large handsome globe lamps, white broadcloth lining, and the coleur de puce [which he had seen on Governor Pinckney's new carriage], plated moulding all around with Suitable Brackets." He wanted a Japanned boot, a storage compartment below the driver's seat, painted "a handsome bright yellow;" with the letter L "made large and enameled to suit the colors of the carriage," to ornament the doors. The frame should be light without sacrificing safety, sprung high enough to require two steps to enter, and "the wheels broad, the reason of this, the carriage rolls, having such wheels, over our Sandy Streets, & Sinks not so much into them." Laurens ordered four sets of harness with pads and blinkers to be engraved with the letter L, and he even had instructions for the wheel nuts, to conceal "the extremities of axle trees

and the filth of the grease which in open nuts is always oozing out."[44]

Once the carriage arrived, Laurens found several issues with it and immediately ordered a replacement: "it is really too heavy even for my strong horses, so high from the ground that my wife can hardly step into it, and so very wide that a jolt strikes it against the wheels. The panels are disfigured by repeated shocks." He hired a Mr. Hunter, who had constructed three carriages for the Rutledge family, to build the new coach, which was "intended as much for use in the Country as in town, and vastly more for use than for Shew [sic]. The colour of the body or part in which persons Sit, a shining bottle green, the wheel bright yellow- the furniture & mouldings plated neat, not flashy or heavy. A single L the initial of my name with my crest over it, painted on the door panels, I send you an impression of my Seal, the Crest is two naked Arms proper supporting a green Wreath of Laurel with four Bouquets of Roses & flowers at equal distance from each other."[45] Laurens clearly intended his carriage to be an outward expression of his tastes and ample finances.

Buyers traveled from across the state for Charleston-made carriages known for their quality. Nathaniel Heyward sought a Charleston carriage in 1816 for his mother-in-law in Beaufort, having looked "in vain for a carriage which I supposed would suit you; nor is it possible to have one made without considerable expense, say $400, without the harness, which would be $50 more. I believe it would be possible to have a carriage made by an inferior workman at a lower rate, but these would be liable to be out of order, and the inconvenience of having them repaired would be so great in Beaufort, that I think it would be better to give $100 more and have it faithfully built. I think if you could manage to hold out a little longer, that Edward or myself might be successful in our next visit to Charleston."[46]

Philadelphia-born carriage maker Benjamin Casey's shop, active in Charleston from 1794 to 1819, speaks to the breadth of consumer options in that era.[47] Casey made carriages and sold vehicles, including "one of the handsomest coaches ever imported from the northward . . . [and] an English-built chariot, but little used, with lamps and plated harness for two horses complete," and a Windsor sulky made by George Bringhurst in Philadelphia. Casey also did carriage and harness repair work and offered painting and varnishing services.[48] He carried the latest parts to customize carriages for his customers: "cradle springs; folding steps; coach lamps with spare glasses to each pair; full plated gig lamps, full plated coach and chaise mounting for harness; brass mounting for chaise harness; plated bands; plated harness for chaises; collars. Also the best polished plated glass for carriages, and Wilton and Brussels carpeting." He also modified carriages: "A curricle and harness complete, built by Bloodgood of New York for lightness, room and elegance . . . composed of the frame of a half Salisbury Boat, covered with high varnished leather, barouche seat and driving box. The pole separates to form the shafts for tandem." Salisbury Boats were a rare type of

enclosed carriage with a curved wooden lower framework.[49] His shop contained light sulkies on steel springs, chaises, coaches with glazed doors, stage wagons, gigs, hickory and ash to make shafts and poles, oak for spokes, and poplar and cherry boards for coach paneling.[50]

Casey advertised in 1799 for a "good strong hand, black or white, for blowing and striking for the blacksmiths," and he sought to hire "three or four good hands to the coach and chairmaking business and a good blacksmith" for his growing company in 1801.[51] He employed several enslaved tradesmen including Lawyer, a painter; Charles and Natt, blacksmiths; and Polledor and Dick, both carpenters. Dick was born in the Ebo

Benjamin Casey's advertisement in the
City Gazette and Daily Advertiser, 2 June 1812.

B. CASEY,
Still carries on the COACH, CHAIR and HARNESS MAKING BUSINESS, in all its various branches ; and also returns his sincere thanks to the Citizens of Charleston, and the Public in general, for their liberal encouragement since in business, and hopes that they will continue their favors—and all orders entrusted to his care, will be punctually attended to on the shortest notice, and on the most reasonable terms, for cash or approved paper at short date ; and also request those Gentlemen that have left Carriages and Chairs in his hands for repairs, will come forward and pay for the same, or else he will be under the disagreeable necessity of selling them at Public Auction, to defray the expences on them.

region of Africa but was able to read and write English.[52] Competition for skilled workers could be fierce, and Casey took out an ad in rebuttal to a Mr. Plum who had attempted to poach his workers; In reply to the publication of Mr. Plum in *Timothy and Masons* paper,

> I have only to observe, that a few months ago he endeavored to inveigle some of my workmen from my employ, in consequence of which I went so far as to turn him out of my shop, for which he thought proper in his mighty valor to send me a challenge. I met the said gentlemen in Broad Street, and gave him a genteel horse whipping, which I thought he justly deserved. And now publicly declare that I hold the said Plum in the greatest contempt and think him beneath my notice. I should have inserted this before, but hurry of business prevented.[53]

Benjamin's son Thomas Casey continued the coach making business on Broad Street.[54]

Carriage fabricators formed partnerships to combine talents, tools, and capital needed to construct complicated vehicles. James Lynch partnered with George Hewet in the late eighteenth century at a shop at Meeting and Cumberland Streets. Laughton and Bookless ran a workshop on a court behind St. Philip's Church; Hawkins and Petrie also had a shop nearby. Hewet dissolved his partnership with Lynch in 1772 to open his own chairmaking business and erected "a large range of coach houses for the reception of gentlemen's carriages that may come to be repaired, to prevent their receiving

any injury from the weather," where customers could lease annual carriage storage.[55] Lynch sold imported London phaetons "which one horse may draw with ease, being made on the lightest construction" and Italian chaises, one-person, two-wheeled carriages with long shafts and seats located over the wheel axles and that faced slightly forward, popularized in the Georgian era.[56]

Hawes and Laughton manufactured several styles of carriage and chair, made harness "of the best leather, and will be found, on trial, superior to those imported," and employed a wheelwright, Uz Rogers, at their shop.[57] Benjamin Hawes carried out all branches of coach making on site, "not to be exceeded in quality of materials, goodness of work, or neatness, by any importation; they can make and finish, without any assistance, out of their own shop, all sorts of coaches, chariots, phaetons, post chaises, curricles, sedans, and sleighs in the most compleat [sic] and elegant manner, and afford them as more reasonable rates than they can be imported." The firm took bespoke orders and could copy any "pattern from England."[58]

Stevens, Ash, and Reynolds offered their shop for sale in 1807, providing a detailed glimpse into a coachmaker's facility of the period—the fifty-foot-wide and 259-foot-deep lot had a shop "two stories high, built of the best materials. Back on the lot are two forges with bellows fixed up, and a large building used as a painter's shop."[59] The firm continued as Reynolds and Ash into the 1810s. George N. Reynolds mortgaged his interest in the "machinery, tools

Saddle horses rest in front of McLeish's Vulcan Ironworks factory on Cumberland Street in 1865. Foundries and machine shops made various metal parts for carriages, including frames and leaf springs. Unmanned carriages and coaches are parked along the street awaiting repairs. Library of Congress.

and apparatus and implement," the lease for a Meeting Street shop, and an enslaved man named Ben, probably a tradesman in the shop, in April 1811 to raise capital for his own firm.[60] It became the largest carriage shop in the city and operated until the Civil War under his son Richard.[61] John Artman's rival factory produced sulkies, buggies, and formal carriages and employed forty journeymen and apprentices. It

was equipped with a six-forge blacksmith shop, machine shop, wheelwright's station, storerooms, packing rooms, trimming and upholstery department, and two paint shops.[62] E. W. Lloyd's short-lived antebellum carriage warehouse and repair business on Meeting Street carried out painting and varnishing services, framework, forge work and new bolts, altering springs and fifth wheels, tire repair, leather work, pole repairs, lamp installation, and axle repairs for wagons, buggies, and carriages. Lloyd did work for individual clients, such as cutting tires for Daniel Heyward's "family coach" and had several standing contract clients, including the Mills House Stable and Reynolds and Smith Company.[63]

Vehicles became cheaper with mass production while ever-expanding rail networks brought northern-made wagons and simple carriages to Charleston for workers and middle-class consumers. Northern companies advertised carriages and parts for sale in catalogs, ready to "ship to any part of the south."[64] James Redding offered five roofed buggies, four no-top buggies, two sporting wagons, and one delivery wagon at his warehouse in 1878, which he had shipped from Louis Cook's shop in Ohio.[65] The *News and Courier* ran a feature on local carriage factories in 1900, touting their modernity and the quality of their products:

> To a person knowing little of the industries at Charleston it would be natural to suppose that Charleston could not boast of even so much as a hand pushcart establishment, to say nothing of the wagon and carriage factories. A reporter for the *News and Courier* made it a point yesterday to visit the leading wagon factories . . . Firms that have been in existence long before the war and have built anything from a 'Christian pony' [handcart] to an ice wagon or undertaker's carriage. Firms that have kept apace [sic] with the times and improvements. There is under construction now

in one of these factories a delivery wagon for a firm in Savannah, which shows that the firm is heard of away from home, if not at home. As a rule, these manufactories are complete, from the well-stocked lumber yard to the varnishing room, with every convenience and facility for quick and first-class workmanship. The class of work turned out by these places cannot be excelled in any other city. While they do not lay especial claim to fancy work, they do lay claim to work of a durable and lasting nature. The best proof of their work are the delivery wagons, from the smallest uncovered ones to the larger and more elegant in design, which are seen on the streets daily.

The reporter estimated that around eighty percent of the wagons in the city were homemade and valued between $50 and $300.[66]

Prussian immigrant Charles D. Franke founded the largest and longest operating carriage supply and repair company in the city in 1859. The original factory was located at 38 Wentworth, with an office and show room at 225 Meeting Street. Services included repairing shafts, single trees, breeching, wheel replacement and alignment, and installing "anti-rattlers" on carriage springs. Firm partner Emil Jahnz built a three-story show room with a pressed brick façade with the company logo put into the stamped metal parapet in 1908 at 172 Meeting Street (renovated in 1989 and is now a law office). Franke and Jahnz also purchased 181 Church Street in 1890. The large brick building was built in 1850, used as Franke and Jahnz carriage shop from 1890–1918, and was reconstructed as a hotel in 1989. The firm later retooled the facility to include auto parts, offering services including "automobile bodies, buggies, wagons, trucks and drays built, repaired, and repainted." They erected the elaborate Franke-Jahnz Carriage Works building at 171 Church Street in 1909, renovated as an office complex in 1981.[67] The building retains its company logo and carriage doors on the façades.

Coachmen

Carriage and riding horses required a network of humans to care for them. Grooms and hostlers brushed, cleaned, and fed them; mucked their stalls; and cleaned their tack under the management of a coachman or stable manager. A senior stable hand might oversee harnessing and drive occasionally.[68] Coachmen for private families were often responsible for horse care, chauffeuring services, vehicle cleaning and maintenance, and simple gardening services or general labor at the house of employment. There were white grooms like an unnamed "young man who understands driving a coach, chariot, or post-chaise, taking care of horses, and would be willing to wait on a gentleman," but most were of African descent.[69] Riding and driving horses are status symbols with medieval roots, which carried to the New World and pervaded in a slave society where elevating oneself over grueling manual labor through a trade or trusted position in the household had obvious

benefits.[70] Alabamian Daniel Robinson Hundley wrote in 1860 that enslaved men's "chief ambitions" were to become a groom, valet, or carriage driver, "this last is considered a post of great honor, even to be a wagoner, to drive the plantation mules and oxen, often becomes a fruitful source of rivalries and ill-feeling."[71]

South Carolina laws restricted the movement and personal freedoms of the enslaved, with exceptions for those working with horses. A 1735 sumptuary law prohibited fine clothing, except as part of a uniform, slaves could not leave a plantation without a pass "unless in livery," and they were forbidden from owning horses, though they could ride or drive them as part of their work.[72] Enslaved coachmen had more freedom of movement and unsupervised time than did other enslaved residents of the city. A complaint in the *Charleston Courier* in 1823 about "negroes congregating" on the Charleston Neck on Sundays, "guilty of riotous and disorderly conduct, to the great disturbance of the worshiping congregations," alludes to Black drivers taking advantage of a few hours' privacy while their owners were at church. The writer pitied "those gentlemen, who, during the term of Divine Service, entrust their carriages to the care and discretion of Negro Coachmen and footboys [who] little imagine how much their horses and carriages are at times jeopardized, by the carelessness and desertion of those to whom they are entrusted. Last Sunday we saw an elegant chariot, that was driven on speed by a small mulatto boy—the usual driver, we believe, having restored with some of his companions to

The 1800 "View in Charleston Taken from Savage's Green" by Charles Fraser shows a stately Georgian House fronting the Ashley River marshes on the west side of the peninsula. A driver and carriage wait in front of the hipped roof carriage house, which would have had residential quarters above. Gibbes Museum of Art.

a tippling house in the neighborhood—dashed to pieces."[73]

Enslaved grooms and coachmen typically lived within the confines of the house complex where they worked, sleeping in rooms within the carriage house or stable.[74] Some were hired out by their owners as chauffeurs, living off site and turning in all or part of their earnings to pay for their horse, carriage, and rent. For example, "a very good house servant, who is also an experienced coachman and accustomed to the management of horses; soberly and honest" was advertised for hire in 1802.[75] L. J. Moses offered for hire an enslaved coachmen and hostler, "a very intelligent young fellow employed several years in a livery stable."[76] Hercules, the Pringle family's respected enslaved coachman, lived in the outbuildings of the Miles Brewton house. He dressed in livery and had an enviable annual clothing allotment of two shirts, three pairs of pants, a livery vest, a thin vest, and a formal coat. Hercules drove the coach and hearse carrying John C. Calhoun to his grave at St. Philip's Church in 1850.[77] Ironic though it was that an enslaved man had the honor of driving the hearse of a vehement supporter of slavery and nullification, his selection speaks to Hercules' talent as a coachman.

Samuel Gourdin Gaillard (1853–1936) grew up on a plantation near Charleston and his family had enslaved coachmen and stable hands to tend their 24 work horses and mules and ten carriage and saddle horses, including four "heavy carriage horses" for the coach. A "superior Negro" named London was the stable manager, while William, Samuel's grandfather's elderly driver, "was considered to be the best coachman in the neighborhood, and perfect in the care of horses." Tradition held that William had driven four horses into the Black Oak clubhouse, around the dining table, and out again. Gaillard wrote that "this splendid old man was addicted to sleeping on the 'box' [the driver's seat] and I have often seen him taking a nap there, and I have in fact taken the reins from him and driven the horses a short distance before he woke up. Yet he was never known to have had an accident."[78]

After the Civil War, free Black coachmen continued living in the outbuildings of the main houses that previously houses enslaved equestrian workers, for convenience. A few examples from the 1880 census include Ben Hiatt, a 45-year-old mulatto coachman who lived at 18 King Street behind his employer, and 70-year-old coachman Jacob Jordan who lived at 43 Meeting Street and drove for banker Henry Griggs. Lawyer H. E. Jenny lived at 14 Legare Street and his servants lived in the historic carriage house—servants, cooks, a nurse, and Samuel Campbell, the 20-year-old coachman. Black coachman R. James lived behind the merchant Laurens Chisolm at 35 Meeting Street, while coachman Charles Wigg (age 58); his wife, the household cook; and a nurse and nanny, all of them Black, lived at 25 Legare Street behind the Smyth family who employed them.[79] Black coachmen endured in the minds of white southerners as a symbol of the plantation past. John Thomas Wightman Flint reminisced about the "'well to do' planter with the old black coachman on the box with the spirited high bred steeds 'well in hand' for the safety of 'mausa and missus'" in 1927 in a piece about the "romantic heroes" of South Carolina.[80] Nostalgia and stereotypes of the reminiscence aside, Black coachmen were known for their skills from the earliest days of Carolina until well after the horseless carriage was introduced.

Commercial Transit and Livery

The number of miles one could travel was limited before widespread auto use, and modes of travel were divided along socioeconomic lines. Residents who could not afford their own carriages simply walked or hired a ride when they could. Hackneys offered single-fare taxi service in urban areas; hack was also a general term for a horse available for hire for riding and light carriage work. Stagecoaches serviced longer point-to-point trips connected by stages or stops between communities as bus services operate today. White Charlestonians also had access to omnibuses, an early form of public transportation in which a horse or a team pulled a large vehicle with bench seating for six to eighteen people, starting in 1833. Omnibuses were operated by private franchises and arrived in Charleston after successful introduction in Paris and New York City. Unlike the later streetcar lines

that operated in Charleston after the Civil War, omnibuses did not operate on fixed tracks.[1]

Getting to the City

The parish level Commissioners of High Roads maintained carriage paths for overland travel in the colonial era, and South Carolina's stagecoaches became a popular way to travel from town to town.[2] Compared to 2 miles an hour on foot or 4–6 on horseback at a walk or trot, coach horses traveled up to ten miles per hour, pulling vehicles with luggage storage space for long trips. Stage wagons between Charleston and the town of Monck's Corner ran several days a week "for the frequent, safe and expeditious conveyance of passengers and goods."[3] Long haul stagecoaches stopped every fifteen to twenty miles to pick up passengers and rest their horses or switch teams.

The Charleston and Savannah Mail Coach operated biweekly between Mr. Brockway's Tavern in King Street and a coffee house in Savannah, with two dining stops along the way. The base fare allowed up to fourteen pounds of baggage, beyond which a fee was imposed per additional pound.[4] Support communities equipped with stables, pastures, inns, and horse shoeing services developed along coach roads.[5] These hubs survive as place names, such as Six Mile in Mount Pleasant east of the Cooper River.

Charleston also had private ferries operating under public charters to bring pedestrians, goods, horses, and carriages across rivers to the city. Horses and mules powered some of the ferries working as tow animals walking on a path alongside the boat to pull it along a placid river, or operated treadmills or windlasses for turning paddle wheels to drive the ferries. Joseph Scott operated a horse boat ferry to convey passengers "from country to town" in 1765. Andrew Hibben operated a flat bottom horse boat, and later, a "team boat" equipped with two horses operating a circular treadmill for propulsion from Mount Pleasant to Charleston in the 1820s.[6]

Charleston became a leader in rail development when the South Carolina Canal and Railroad Company began operating the "Best Friend of Charleston," the first passenger steam locomotive in the United States, to transport commuters and freight between Charleston and Hamburg in 1831. Horses played a key role in the rail transportation revolution, providing the labor for grading land and laying rail track, and transporting the materials needed for building the state's web of rail lines. They also bridged the transportation gaps to areas not serviced by rail via stagecoaches, and carted passenger luggage for transfer companies. The last leg of the rail journey into most cities was completed quietly and safely by horses, which pulled passenger and freight cars into city depots until well after the Civil War.[7]

In Town: Omnibuses and Equine-Powered Streetcars

Urban horsecars, which provided early mass transportation, were "path-breaking technology, setting in motion far-reaching changes in urban spatial structure. The horse retained its animal nature, but in its relationship to the streetcar, it had become a machine and a critical source for transforming power."[8] Horsecars allowed residents to live further from the dense and congested areas of cities without owning their own vehicle.[9] Single equines or teams pulled omnibuses along predetermined routes for set fares, but the absence of track allowed flexibility if needed. The vehicles had at least two axles and four wheels, and seating for a minimum of six passengers on benches running the length of the vehicle frame (similar to a wagonette carriage still used in the carriage tourism industry). New York City coachbuilder John Stephenson

perfected a four-horse car that sat up to thirty passengers, while Jack Slawson of New Orleans developed a light "bobtail" omnibus with seating for twelve, which could be pulled by one horse.[10]

In 1833, the *Southern Patriot* reported that "a few enterprising gentlemen of this city have ventured on the experiment of introducing omnibuses for the accommodation of the citizens for conveyance to and from the Railroad. Two of these vehicles arrived here yesterday from New York. We wish the enterprise every success."[11] Charleston's routes ran north to south, with east-west spurs crossing the narrow peninsular city. Competing companies operated lines from White Point Garden to the Washington Racecourse, and from the East Bay wharves to residential areas on the peninsula's west side, taking commuters to business, residential, and civic districts. The city set fare caps and required omnibus operators to purchase annual licenses to offset road maintenance costs; vehicles with wheels four inches wide or greater received a discount. The maximum allowed speed was 6 miles per hour and drivers were required to slow their horses to a walk when making turns.[12]

R. Douglass and Company, which began as a mail stage line from Greenville to Charleston in 1837, expanded into the urban market in the 1850s. They operated several routes "stocked with well broke horses, good coaches, sober polite careful and experienced drivers."[13] The company opened a line to Magnolia Cemetery in 1855 "to afford many advantages to all who wish to easily and cheaply imbibe the fresh rural air or visit the "silent city" where the dead repose in a quiet

A petite mule pulls a "horse car" for the "Broad-Meeting-Calhoun Line" in "Sketches in Charleston," *Harper's Weekly* 1875.

state."[14] In 1858 they petitioned the city council to extend their routes further down Meeting Street. By 1861 the Douglass company owned the Charleston Hotel Stable at 29 Pinckney near the market and the lot at 13/15 Shepard Street on the Neck, where the company's large wooden omnibus stable was located. The occupants of 15 Shepard Street were listed in the 1861 *City Census* as "slaves," probably drivers and hostlers who worked for the transportation company. The firm operated their omnibuses in the early years of the Civil War before permanently going out of business in 1863.[15]

Streetcars ran on tracks installed flush with the street surface, which allowed equines to produce four times more power compared with pulling along cobblestone pavements, making trolleys a vast improvement in efficiency.[16] New York City debuted the first streetcar of the nation in 1832, and by the 1850s many cities had invested in streetcar lines to replace omnibuses

as, for instance, Boston in 1856, followed by Philadelphia, Cincinnati, Baltimore, and Chicago. Streetcar systems revolutionized city planning, allowing sprawling suburban development while reducing urban traffic congestion. Investors formed the Charleston City Railway Company in November 1859 to introduce streetcars to the city. They raised capital by selling stock, secured permission from the city to lay track on Shepard, Line, Meeting, and Hasell Streets, and received a corporate charter in January 1861, but planning ground to a halt until after the American Civil War.

Residents suggested resuming the streetcar plans in September 1865—"the importance of such an enterprise is as great now as it was then. The considerations of convenience and economy in travel and transportation, of inconvenience resulting from drays and other wheel[ed] vehicles in our crowded streets, the noise, dust, and damage to the streets, all operate now as they did before, and as a measure of public interest, therefore, there can be little question, we presume, as to its utility."[17] The city council re-approved the company's operating plan in late fall.[18] Workers installed tracks in the roadbeds and paved around them with stone block or brick. The Charleston City Railway received estimates for twelve cars with 33-inch diameter wheels, alleged by the builder to be "lighter, stronger, and more durable than any other now in use . . . saving 40 per cent in horse flesh resulting in the fact that the car can be easily pulled on the track by one hand."[19] The company instead ordered tried-and-true Stephenson cars with "richly gilt letters on the upper panels of either side" indicating the car's route. The Charleston Railway purchased new cars as needed from Stephenson and shipped cars back to New York for repairs and retrofitting.[20] The heavy cars glided quietly along the tracks, the traces jingling only when the equines started and stopped at predetermined points every few blocks. The tracks ran along Meeting and King Streets to service the commercial area and the elite residential district to the south. Later cross tracks ran east-west on Calhoun, Wentworth, Broad, Spring, and Columbus Streets, and another line ran from Spring Street to Broad Street along Rutledge Avenue, servicing several new residential areas.[21]

The cars took their inaugural run in December 1866 against a backdrop of racial tension and societal change. Streetcars created freedom of movement and autonomy previously only available to elite city dwellers, but they also challenged racial and gender mores because of their public accessibility. Black customers tested their new-found civil liberties by trying to ride the streetcars and were denied service. One operator tried to throw the car from its track before unhitching his horses from the car rather than transport Black passengers.[22] The Black riders filed a formal complaint with the Freedmen's Bureau. Major General/Assistant Commissioner N. K. Scott wrote to the city railway regarding Mary P. Bowers's complaint:

> that she was told by the conductor that she couldn't ride. In consideration of the general number of colored residents of this city it seems to be unwise and unjust on the part of your company to deny to them a privilege which the laws of the United States will surely and eventually grant them . . . I am convinced that the fears of many, that the cars would be crowded with colored people who wish to take advantage of this new privilege, are imaginary as but few colored people would feel disfavored to at once break down the social barriers of this community and thus acquire an unpleasant notoriety.

A city railway representative replied, "I beg to convey to you the assurance that I have not individually nor has any of the directors of the company any desire or purpose to deny any portion of the population of the city the right or privileges to which any or all of them may be entitled."[23] Streetcar and omnibus operators in Charleston solved the ridership issue by designating segregated "colored" compartments, as did New Orleans.[24] Though they could only ride in segregated cars, many of the city's streetcars and omnibuses were operated by Black drivers. Don Doyle notes that the streetcars "were met with defiant 'prejudice' and conservative people [who] preferred to go on foot, even under considerable discomfort from heat and rain, rather than patronize public conveyances that were so democratic."[25]

A rival company called the Enterprise Street Railway began operating in 1871. The firm, already unique for its all-Black board of directors in that none of them came from the city's free Black elite, was even more groundbreaking

The inset on the *Bird's Eye View of Charleston*, 1872, shows streetcars drawn by single horses and teams at the intersection of Broad and Meeting Street. A carriage pulled by a single horse also passes by. Library of Congress.

because all, but one, had been enslaved before the Civil War. Enterprise competed with dray companies by offering freight shipping and passenger transfers from the Ann Street rail depots to the Cooper River wharves along East Bay Street. Despite the company's Black leadership, draymen in the city, three quarters of whom were Black, unsuccessfully protested the rail for fear that it would reduce their business. As the Jim Crow era began, however, the company "was in the hands of whites" by the 1880s.[26]

Enterprise's Act of Incorporation granted them the authority to lay tracks at White Point Garden northward on Meeting, then east to East Bay at Broad Street, then through Wragg-borough and Hampstead on the east side of the peninsula, "and thence along Meeting and the State Road to Ten Mile Hill to such a point as they may deem most advantageous."[27] As the suburbs burgeoned on the Neck and surrounding islands, Enterprise expanded its routes. In 1892 they purchased eight two-horse cars from Boston to service the new Suburban Extension, which ran "four miles up the road, through the most beautifully picturesque outlying district in the South. It passes through the truck farming section of the Charleston suburbs and through beautiful woods and thickets overgrown with artistic clinging moss and fragrant jessamine [sic] and honeysuckle." There was a "ladies reception room and hostelry" with refreshments at the northern end of the line.[28] By 1895 the lines reached new Chicora Park community in today's North Charleston.[29] Because of the flexibility of operating off track, horse-drawn omnibuses continued to serve areas not on the streetcar routes and were available for private charter for special events like picnics at Magnolia Cemetery.[30]

Public transportation was hard work for the animals, regardless of whether the streets had tracks or not, because they not only had to pull heavy vehicles, but also passengers, and their parcels. Horses and mules typically worked just five years in mass transit, before being depreciated, similar to the treatment of modern automobile fleets, since they slowed and were more likely to become lame as they aged. Private owners or delivery businesses often purchased them after that.[31] Streetcar companies were large outfits that streamlined management practices and optimized animal care for efficiency. They replaced shoes on schedule even if not fully worn, set five-hour workdays, and employed "helper" animals for steep inclines and bad weather. Joel Tarr notes that these "practices were defended in economic, not humane terms, and an 1893 survey in London showed other equine shifts varying from 6 to 16 hours a day for other jobs."[32] Pulling uphill or in snow could stress and damage joints, but fortunately, Charleston's equines worked on flat terrain and snow was a rarity.

The Charleston Rail company purchased horses and mules from Robert Graham's Mills

House Stables, including 8 horses for $75 each, 4 more horses for $150 each, "warranted sound and delivered," and 8 mules for around $215 each in April 1873. The company purchased several more horses in July 1875 to replace thirteen mules they had sold.[33] The company's annual operating receipts included equipment; equines and harness; car and road repairs and iron castings; stable improvements; horseshoes; forage; and payroll for conductors, drivers, hostlers, and laborers.[34] The city railway purchased several kegs of horseshoes, farrier files and knives, nails, and various gauges of iron for wheels each month from the C. D. Franke Co.[35] Railway equines' feed included bran, oats, corn, and salt supplements purchased from Rohde Brothers on King Street, a large firm with six delivery vehicles, and from Hermann Bulwinkle. The animals slept on sawdust bedding purchased from Devereux wood mill.[36]

Livery and Sale Businesses

Livery stables rented equines, vehicles, and drivers for hire on a short-term or seasonal basis, and frequently offered stall boarding and carriage parking to local horse owners.[37] Larger liveries also provided training, farrier services, and pasturage. Liveries were often associated with inns and taverns, such as the Crown Inn in the 1740s, which had seven rooms, a shop, kitchen, hay house, store, straw rooms, an additional hay loft, and a stable to accommodate forty horses.[38] Even taverns in the densest part of town, such as a facility near King and Broad Streets with its arched carriageway, had boarding facilities in the rear.[39]

Joseph Marley ran a longstanding livery stable in Stoll's Alley, from which he leased and sold horses and coaches. Marley boarded horses by the month, quarter, or year. He advertised that "each horse has a standing to himself, and shall be well cleaned and curried every morning, and fed night and morning with corn, and plenty of corn blades at all times."[40] Francis Greensword purchased Marley's facility in 1768 and had "a number of white men to attend his yard, and himself no other employment to take him off from that business," to take in boarders or prepare chairs and horses for hire "at any hour of the night." He trained horses for saddle and driving and reminded potential customers "that he was the person who cured almost all the horses that had distemper the past winter, that were sent to the said yard, without receiving any benefit to himself, which he hopes will be sufficient to recommend him."[41]

Thomas Adamson, formerly groom to wealthy Santee plantation owner and colonel of the Light Dragoons Daniel Horry, opened a livery stable on Meeting Street at the Sign of the Horse Mask, where he trained horses and carried out simple veterinary procedures for "curable disorders."[42] Thomas Eustace's King Street stable at the Sign of the Horse and Chair offered horses and carriages for rent by the day.[43] John Russell's establishment near Bank Square, now Washington Park, which he bought from John Gell's estate in 1815, had "large and commodious stables" and employed a farrier who

could correct "the bad habits of horses (whether in body or disposition)."[44] F. Campbell offered "accommodation of citizens and strangers' carriages, buggies, and carriage horses," and offered new vehicles "of the finest make and latest style, together with gentle horses and careful and honest drivers" for hire.[45]

Now occupied by a later building, 113 Church Street held the Billings livery stable, which was in operation from 1816 until the mid-twentieth century under various owners. Edward Francis took over after John Billings died in 1825, advertising that:

> said stables are continued by him, and shall be conducted with the utmost attention; good grooms are provided, and the best grain and forage will be furnished. From the long experience he has had in such business, he hopes to be able to render satisfaction. NB—drove horses will be stabled on accommodating terms. Horses, gigs and carriages will be kept for hire, and carriage horses broke to both double and single draft at a moderate price.[46]

Following Francis's death, George Fryer took over the Church Street stable or "old stand, next to Carolina Hotel," which today is part of the grounds of the Confederate Home located at 62–64 Broad Street.[47] It was later operated by Charles D. McCoy, and then by Charles Crull, who also sold equines, including thirty-five horses and mules in the summer of 1918 from the Remount Station who were being sold after their war service.[48]

Transfer companies conveyed baggage,

passengers, and goods from the rail depots to hotels or other accommodations as airport taxi services do today. Geraghty's City Express hauled freight and luggage in the 1860s, and Hoffman Livery Stables advertised in the 1890s that their "vehicles meet all trains. Carriages and buggies for hire at moderate rates."[49] The Charleston Transfer Company's various sized vehicles were pulled by "horses selected as well for beauty as for working power, and the company therefore maintains the best services of the kind in the United States," from their Hayne Street stables behind Charleston Hotel.[50] The Jackson and Pickett firm operated the Charleston Hotel Stables and the Charleston Transfer Company, which provided omnibuses and baggage wagons for transporting residents to and from the hotels and rail depots, offered transport to funerals within the city or at Magnolia Cemetery, scenic rides to Magnolia Cemetery, and offered general city carriage rentals at a rate of $2 per hour, with discounted rates for three hours or longer, in the 1890s. The company had licenses to operate eleven team vehicles, five single wagons, and four omnibuses.[51] Co-owner Merritt Pickett lived next to the stables on Pinckney Street and was a well-known and kindhearted horseman. When he died suddenly of apoplexy in his carriage house in 1899, his son-in-law and a stable hand recounted his final hours:

> in the rear end of the [livery] stable were two box stalls, where at night Mr. Pickett kept his own private team, a pair of pet horses, of which he thought a great deal. He went back

to see them, as was his custom, petted and led them out to the water trough. When the horses finished drinking, he led them to their day stalls, spoke to them kindly, and went on his rounds about the stable. In a few minutes he got up and went into the carriage barn, opened the door to a carriage and sat in it. A negro stable boy, looking toward the carriage a short while later, saw the vehicle shaking violently.[52]

For the final ride, undertakers provided horse drawn hearses to Magnolia and other city graveyards and cemeteries. County Antrim native John McAlister (1865–1920) was one of the first licensed embalmers in the state and operated the premier funeral parlor and undertaker firm in late nineteenth-century Charleston. He had four team hearses and "shared with other Southerners a love of fine horses, and in the horse-drawn days his matched teams were among the finest in the city."[53] J. M. Connelly operated a large Richardsonian Romanesque funeral parlor at 309–313 Meeting Street in 1894, alongside his large residence, a coffin factory and greenhouse with garden, and a wood frame stable for the hearse horses.[54]

Most antebellum stables were white owned; Samuel D. Holloway was the only free man of color to own a livery stable business before emancipation, located on Legare Street.[56] Samuel's nephew James H. Holloway (1849–1913) ran a harness shop in his residence at 39 Beaufain Street, later demolished to extend Market Street. His calling cards read:

A brougham funeral carriage manufactured by Flandrau & Co., New York, purchased by the McAlister Brothers Undertakers and Embalmers in 1884 and used "well into the 20th century" to convey families of the deceased behind the hearse in funeral processions.[55] Charleston Museum.

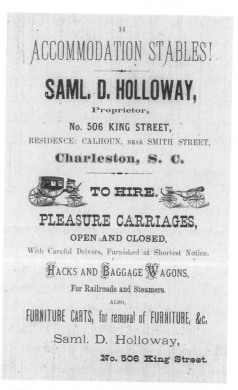

A *City Directory* advertisement for Samuel Holloway's Accommodation Stables, which furnished pleasure carriages, hacks, and baggage wagons.

18th-19th-20th century. A colored family to own and occupy the same lands and residence and business stand in three centuries. J.H. Holloway Harness Shop. Faithful work guaranteed." The reverse states, "centennial home of the Holloways. Richard Holloway built the home on land he got from his father-in-law. Know old Charleston? Hope you do! Born there—don't say so—I was too. Born in a house with a shingle roof, standing still if you must have proof.[57]

During Reconstruction, freedmen operated their own livery businesses, capitalizing on equine management skills learned while enslaved. Among these was Stephney B. Riley, a carriage driver from Wadmalaw Island whose

hack stable and livery service catered to a white clientele. He became one of the richest Black men in the city, with property valued at $3,750 in 1870 that included his stables at the southeast corner of Smith and Bull Streets.[58] English abolitionist Sir George Campbell wrote that Riley "stuck to the whites in bad times amid persecution of his own race, and is now a prosperous stable owner, and a friend of the party in power."[59] When he ran for city council in 1875, the press quipped, "Democrat Riley . . . would be a non-entity, unless he were required to drive a coach and four through some city ordinance."[60] In October 1885, Riley was shot by Amos Bellinger, a white physician, in an argument that allegedly escalated after Bellinger rebuked Riley for abusing his horses. Bellinger testified that as he was returning home around 9 p.m.,

> his attention was attracted by the noise of a furious lashing going on some distance ahead of him. On reaching Smith Street he found that someone was brutally whipping a pair of horses attached to a carriage in front of him. In the darkness he was unable to distinguish who was the diver, but pitying the animals, and thinking that there were being made the victims of needles cruelty, he called out to the diver not to beat his horses so unmercifully. His remonstrances seemed to infuriate the already angry driver, who turned from the horses to assail Dr Bellinger with a torrent of vile epithets. For the first time recognizing the driver as Riley, whom he had always previously been on very pleasant terms, Dr Bellinger renewed his expostulations against his maltreatment of the poor dumb horses.[61]

Bellinger alleged that as he was passing Riley's house the next day, the two argued again and Riley came at him with the knife, prompting Bellinger to shoot him several times. Riley's body was moved to his carriage house for an inquisition. Bellinger was found not guilty by an all-white jury.[62]

Black stableman John Jones furnished "fine carriages and careful drivers at reasonable prices" at the Jones Hack Stable at 131 Coming, no longer extant, from 1867 to 1893.[63] Three of the nine livery stables listed in the *City Directories* were operated by Black men in 1870; three of twelve hack, livery, feed, and sale stables in 1900; and three of nine in 1920. Celia Minort, a 39-year-old Black widow, operated a stable at her house at 138 Spring Street in 1900 and had three-team vehicles available for hire.[64]

Livery staff typically lived at the stables, which were hives of activity day and night as customers called for carriages at all hours. Chalmers Street was home to several of them in 1880 namely, James Devoe, James Washington, and Theodore Goff, Black stable boys, aged 21, 20, and 19 respectively, who were all illiterate. Robert James, an 11-year-old stable boy, lived at 30 Chalmers. Jason and Eugene Brown lived at their hack stable at 12 Chalmers, and Black stable hands Jeff Johnson and John Rodgers resided next door. The Browns ran an additional hack stable behind 30 Meeting Street, where Fritz Martin (a harness maker from Germany), William Jenkins (a Black stable hand), and Chris Gibson (a mulatto hostler born in the West Indies) lived and worked.[65] Four Black livery stablemen in their early twenties, all illiterate, lived at the Jones Hack Stable, and others lived next door with German grocer John Oetjen and his Norwegian wife.[66] C. R. Holmes Junior, a 34-year-old white draymaster, lived with his uncle in a large house at 33 East Bay, now 2 Water Street. The rear buildings were home to 15 Black tenants whose relationships to the head of the household were listed in the census as servants.

These tenants included four draymen who worked at the large brick stable on the back of the property.[87] Of the 107 men listed as hostlers in the 1890 *City Directory,* all but four were identified as "colored." They worked for the city railway and for the Enterprise Rail Company, for livery and sale stables (which sold equines newly arrived in the city and resident animals, and which might be standalone businesses or part of a livery business), and approximately half were likely employed by private families. William Aiken was the only hostler identified with a specific family; he worked for Andrew Simonds and lived behind his Villa Margherita mansion at 4 South Battery Street.[68]

Hackmen

Hackmen hired their time to take passengers from point to point, to and from hotels and passenger depots, home from running errands during the day, or to appointments, like a cab or Uber would do today. Some worked for hack stable companies and others owned their own modest conveyances. The work was sporadic and the hours long, but hack driving was profitable, and on a busy shift, drivers might have back-to-back customers.[69] Some drivers catered to high-end clientele, including chauffeuring families to church on Sundays. "Night hawk" evening taxies attracted the opposite type of clientele—drunken, sometimes aggressive revelers needing rides after an evening out. Night hawking was considered the lowest type of driving occupation. When Black hackman John

Fraser died in 1906 of a sudden heart attack, the newspaper noted that "in the days of the old volunteer fire department he was a driver for the German Fire Engine Company. He was well liked by all classes and at one time was in a prosperous condition and had a good business. Reversal brought him down and of recent years he has only been a night hack but worked hard and made a living honestly."[70]

The brief biography of Jerry Rhodes, an "old Faginay [Virginia] Nigger," published in the *News and Courier* in 1895 provides a rare personal story of an enslaved man who worked with horses before and after freedom; the details of so many other Charleston drivers are lost to time. Jerry worked as a night hackmen for over fifty years, a witness to the "gas-lit side of Charleston life" and to the debauchery and drunken ramblings of generations of residents. "He and his hack have dodged about town after dark for half a century, and all they have seen and heard is as lost to record as though it never happened. Into the glare of the saloon light, dodging up and down alley ways, jogging through the main streets and creeping about the slums, his rickety vehicle totters ever onward . . . the men who had 'a night out with the boys' in the fifties were carried home in Jerry's hack." Jerry was brought to Charleston from Virginia for sale as a young man, and after three months, was still unsold and living in a stable yard on Pinckney Street. The trader was about to send him back to Virginia when "one fine morning a well-known Charleston gentleman came into the yard and bought him for $50. And that his how Jerry came to the city, and having driven hacks for his master before the war, when freedom came, took to driving for himself."[71]

Drivers who serviced rough parts of the city often ended up in police court as witnesses to crimes. While awaiting a fare, a hackman named Manning witnessed a fatal stabbing on Market Street in front of Vincent Chicco's New York House pool hall in 1909; he fled the scene and the coroner tracked him down later at his stable of employment on Spring Street, most likely that of Celia Minort, for his statement.[72] Drivers also faced the ever-present possibility of altercations, especially Black drivers who had little recourse in the Jim Crow era. Jerry Rhodes, for example, donned a white felt hat with dents and rents "bestowed upon it by Jerry's patron's" over the years.[73] Black hackman Charles Brown was arrested in 1899 for blocking Dr. William H. Huger's driveway at the west end of Broad Street. Brown was "waiting on a colored funeral and stopped his vehicle directly in front of the carriage gate and when requested to move to one side, he refused," for which he was arrested and sent to police court. A rowdy would-be passenger who was drunk on election day tried to cut an unnamed hackman with a knife when the driver refused to "haul him about town without remuneration."[74] Hackmen Isaac T. Williams ran afoul of the law when he unwittingly chauffeured a murderer. Williams was near West Street, a known speakeasy district, when a white electrician named William Schaffhauer shot and killed Joseph D. Rivers, also white. He, in one statement, claimed he was driving past as

shots were fired and that Schaffhauer jumped in his carriage and told him to "drive like hell" away from the scene; "Between 2 and 3 o clock I came from King to Beaufain, and drove through Archdale, Magazine, and Logan to West Street. I saw a white gentleman lying on the sidewalk and another standing up. This gentleman Schaffhauer, jumped in the hack and said "drive, nigger, or I will kill you" and I drove fast to save my life. At the corner of West and Archdale streets I saw a policeman and he asked where the shooting was. I said this man wants to kill me." Williams testified in court that the assailant was already in the hack, jumped out and committed the crime, and then insisted Williams drive him from the scene.[75]

Hack drivers had reputations for being rowdy, overcharging passengers, and keeping bad company. A visitor quipped in 1864 that Charleston hackmen were "the most profane in the world."[76] Irishman James Morgan who worked for Mills House stables was caught and prosecuted for quadrupling the length of a trip to charge excessive baggage fees to a visiting Frenchman in 1856.[77] Hackmen "owned the city" after the hurricane of 1911 immobilized the streetcar system, and "prices for hacks skyrocketed until an ordinary mortal had to draw on his bank account in order to ride home."[78] The 1880 census for Chalmers Street where several livery stables were located and Warren Street, which was home to wood frame single houses and "negro tenements," enumerated Black and mulatto tenants working as carriage drivers, "drivers of jobbing carts," stable hands, draymen, fishermen, tailors, spouses and children, laborers, and several prostitutes. Helen Murry, a 25-year-old white prostitute born in Georgia, rented a room with one of the stable hands.[79] Cohabitation with prostitutes was no true reflection of equine workers' characters, or that of the women themselves, but in Victorian-era Charleston, households with fallen women as residents would have scandalized elite and middle-class Charlestonians.

Hackmen also had a reputation for animal cruelty. Driver William Lee was arrested for abandoning a horse on a vacant lot on Cooper Street, who had been "starved, beaten until it was sore and worked without shoes." Five men lifted the horse and brought him to convalesce at a hack stable on America Street since he was too poorly to make the trek to the police stationhouse stable. Lee had supposedly traded for the horse recently and "disappointed with the deal, left the animal to fend for himself."[80] George Joseph was arrested in 1902 when he was found "dead drunk in his vehicle on King Street in the early morning . . . in blissful ignorance as he lay on the back seat of his carriage curled up. His old horse was taking things very easy, glad of the opportunity, no doubt, to rest his weary bones."[81] The SPCA admonished nighthawk drivers for treating their horses poorly; some drivers had their equines pulling loads for wood yards all day before starting a second work shift without resting or feeding the horses. They operated from "11 pm to daylight to prowl around bar rooms and gambling dens, picking up drunken men and others and carrying them home after a night of debauchery." The society urged potential clients to avoid hiring ill-treated animals, in hopes of pushing cruel drivers out of business.[82] Two years later, they reported that nighthawk drivers were buying a "better class of horses" and providing better care, and working conditions had also improved for postal service wagon horses.[83]

Charleston's livery businesses began integrating autos into their hack fleets to chauffeur passengers and their baggage around the city in the early twentieth century. Jitney Motor Company advertised "quick, clean and reliable" taxi and bus service to the train station in 1916.[84] Cities regulated the new vehicles as they had with hack carriages, requiring that drivers pay for licenses and that they queue in specific areas so as to reduce traffic congestion around hotels and transportation depots. A police order said that auto taxis were to park on the north side of Hayne Street and that carriages should do so on the south side of Pinckney Street while waiting for passengers from the Charleston Hotel.[85] The shift from equine to auto travel was gradual, with horse delivery and transport vehicles outnumbering autos by nearly five to one in 1926, but at that time, the number of business carriages already dropped from 473 in the previous year to 370.[86] Livery and hack stable business subsided until after World War II, when a new form of horse travel business called pay-by-the-ride emerged through carriage tours, discussed in the final chapter.

Carting, Draying, Machine Work, and Deliveries

Horses and mules hauled materials, food, and fuel to keep the city running. They powered machines that pumped water, sawed wood, winched material, and removed manure piles. They drove the mechanisms that operated mortars and pestles on plantations, and grinding wheels used at rice and grist mills.[1] Planter Thomas Caw's 1773 inventory counted eight head of machine horses and Benjamin Williamson had "several machine horses" on his plantation.[2] A visitor to Charleston in 1817 observed a "newly invented machine for separating cotton from its seeds [the cotton gin]. Several men are needed to power the machine but a horse or a waterfall can also be used."[3] Antebellum millwrights sold rice mills that could be powered by "hand, horse, or other powers."[4] Horses walked on treadmills to drive belts that pulled railcars for the Charleston and Hamburg line in the 1830s when steam engines were barred from the city for safety reasons.[5] They also toiled on the wharves alongside dockworkers by turning screws that pressed cotton tightly into bales for shipping and operating hoists used for loading and offloading cotton and other bulk goods from ships. Rigger John Symons hired out hoisting horses and enslaved drivers at his antebellum outfit.[6] The Dunneman Company stevedores and horseshoers on Linguard Street had licenses for seven single animal wagons.[7] Prominent merchant and wharf owner James Adger kept horses for hoist work and used them for hauling steam engine pumps to his ships.[8] City grain mills used horsepower for grinding well into the late nineteenth century.[9]

Horses pulled a variety of hauling vehicles including wagons, carts, and drays. Carts are single axle, two-wheeled vehicles that could be

Workers unload cabbages brought by a horse with a two-wheeled vegetable cart and repack them for shipping at the Atlantic Coast Dispatch rail. South Carolina Historical Society.

unhooked from the harness and tipped back for unloading goods, the original dump trucks of that day. They were common for city carting until the early nineteenth century. Drivers usually walked alongside the vehicle.[10] Two wheeled carts with a bench seat for the driver were in use in Charleston into the 1910s.[11] Sturdy four-wheeled vehicles such as wagons and drays had to be manually offloaded but were safer for heavy cargo such as cotton bales, beer kegs, or barrels of rice. Wagons had a bench seat for the driver and an enclosed cargo bed. Drays usually were flat bedded with little to no sidewall. Vehicle builders and harness makers needed to be intimately familiar with equine composition and principles of draft, because unbalanced vehicles or putting traces on the wrong angle from the collar to the carriage could lift a horse off the ground, thus reducing his draft power and potentially injuring him.

John Marley, John Braund, and Michael Kalteisen's carting, wood selling, and boating partnership of the 1760s gives an indication of the vehicles and facilities that colonial companies used. They owned several carts and drays, horses with their own fitted harness sets, and a schooner large enough to carry ninety barrels of rice or twelve cords of wood. They leased a pasture outside of town and had a city lot with a thirty-horse stable, corn house, harness house, chair house, water shed and well, "and a small dwelling house with four rooms and a convenient site for carrying on the carting and watering business."[12]

The colonial and municipal government regulated drayage by setting rates, routes, and rules of operation. A 1764 act required draymen and carters to obtain licenses, and set a penalty of a twenty-shilling fine for overcharging and speeding and, "if a white person [they] shall be put in the public stocks for four hours."[13] The city government made the act permanent as of 1783. An 1805 ordinance established twelve cartage and three drayage zones with 61 routes, most of which ended at the wharves, where dray work was an integral part of the shipping industry. Michael Thompson argues that regulatory practices "confirmed not only the ubiquity of draymen and carters on the wharves, but also the central and indispensable role these workers played in the smooth and efficient flow of goods through the port." Drays for hire queued in designated areas and charged rates that varied by distance and type of freight.[14]

American city councils debated in the 1830s on whether to allow rail lines through the heart of cities because early steam engines were loud and potentially dangerous.[15] The high expense of early engines and their massive weight, which crushed brick paving and damaged road beds, led some engineers and municipalities to deem horses more cost-effective for city freighting; horse teams were more efficient for short distances in any case.[16] Charleston's politicians were divided between allowing railroads through the city to the wharves for fostering greater economic growth, or preventing their encroachment for safety reasons and thereby protecting property owner interests, maintaining good road conditions, and preserving the city's residential character. Charleston ultimately barred rail lines from the city proper, thus preventing goods from going directly to and from the wharves and making horses indispensable in Charleston's international shipping industry. Crops steamed into the rail depots above the city limits, where they were off-loaded and repacked onto carts and drays

The Cooper River wharves teem with dock workers and draymen loading and offloading goods into carts and drays. *Harpers Weekly*, January 1878. National Park Service.

to be taken to the wharves and reloaded onto ships for export. The process occurred in reverse for goods shipped into the city. While this extra equine step added 12–20 percent to the cost of transporting cotton from plantation to ship, it protected the city from unchecked industrial development, created hundreds for jobs for hostlers and drivers, and reinforced equines' vital role in Charleston commerce.[17] Shipping and transfer companies and dray firms owned the horses and mules that carted goods to and from the wharves, rather than the rail companies. but relatively few stables were located directly on the wharves where storage space was at a premium. The equines who worked on the docks typically lived a few blocks away in livery and company stables on high ground, as storage space was at a

premium on the industrial waterfront.[18] One key exception was the long, one story "mule sheds" and neighboring addition stable of Robertson, Taylor, and Company, located at the southeast corner of East Bay and Hasell Streets, which processed cotton brought to Charleston from the plantations for shipment.[19]

Antebellum drivers operating a "vehicle, cart (including farm and phosphate), dray, hack, or wagon" paid annual licensing fees which varied for different vehicle types–one-horse carts, wagons, or trucks; livery stable buggies or carriages; one-horse buggies and carriages drawn for hire, namely, hacks; omnibuses; and for the same categories of vehicles that equine teams pulled.[20] The city stamped 415 dray and 145 cart badges in 1850, an increase from 206 drays and

Horses and mules pulling cotton drays, carts, and closed-body vehicles line East Bay Street near Vendue Range as they await the next round of deliveries from wholesale, maritime, and warehouse businesses in the late nineteenth century. Cook Collection, The Valentine.

81 carts in 1831 and up from 311 drays and 127 carts in 1845.[21] This increase in number reveals the city's growth and expanding maritime and rail trade. The assessor issued 777 licenses in 1896, mostly for single-animal delivery vehicles.[22]

Equines delivered products for every type of business. Cannonsborough Rice Mills paid drivers monthly for carting rice to market and rice offal, or chaff, away to be sold for fill material.[23] Breweries such as Germania and Jessen's Anheuser-Busch, building material suppliers, and wholesalers such as Welch and Eason owned delivery horses or mules. The William Johnson coal shipping company had thirteen vehicles, Consumer Coal located at the Central Wharf had six, and the P. Broderick coal and wood distributors on Concord Street had ten.[24] Livery owner Charles D. McCoy kept "constantly on hand all kinds of saddle and harness horses. Also dray, timber, turpentine, and plantation mules." He allowed customers sixty days to try and return horses, charging them a fee plus interest during the trial period. A reporter noted that McCoy was "always ready to sell at moderate prices, and as all of his stock is brought out direct from the West, he can be depended upon to furnish you with the best horses at the cheapest prices. His stables are well ventilated and well-kept, and you could not find a better place to board your horse if you are fortunate enough to have one."[25]

Before electric refrigeration, ice was first a luxury and then an indispensable commodity utilized by butchers, grocers, restaurants, and residents. There were a series of short-lived and long-standing ice companies operating in the city from 1841 onward that retailed both natural ice from the North and, later, locally made "artificial ice."[26] Palmetto Ice was the first to offer deliveries by mule and horse wagon in 1873. The company sold its assets the following year to another investor—3 spring wagons, 7 ice wagons, 1 city cart, 1 dray, 12 complete sets of harness, 8 "large prime mules, and one fine mare," which another outfit purchased to continue local ice deliveries.[27]

Eureka Ice House at 182 Meeting Street had a brick Roman Revival office facing the street with ice storage facilities behind it and two wooden stables for delivery equines in the back of the lot. The rear yard was accessed by a narrow passageway between the ice house facilities and the row of brick shops and grocery store-owned wood stables at the corner of Market and Meeting Streets.[28] The office and part of the rear storage buildings are still extant. The company's ice "was hoisted by mule power from the holds of schooners landed at Central Wharf."[29] Equine teams also hauled bulk ice to refrigerator rail cars for shipment to the rest of the state and beyond.[30]

The Charleston Ice Company used both horse and mule teams for deliveries, including "one large brown or dark bay known as the City Ice Company horse. One black mare mule named 'Jenny'. One black mule named 'Nigger,' both of these mules about 10 years old."[31] The Mutual Manufacturing Company constructed an ice plant on Inspection Street near the Cooper River in 1898 and was "getting its stables ready

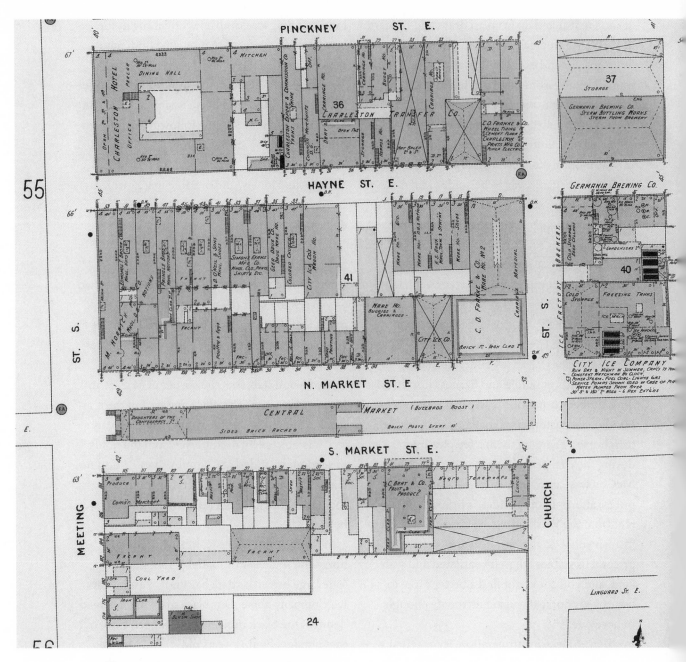

Stables in the Market area housed the equines who delivered for Germania Brewing, the Charleston Transfer Company, the City Ice Company, Bart & Co. Fruit and Produce, and others. 1902 *Sanborn Insurance Map*, sheet 57.

for delivery wagons, horses, &c.," while Arctic Ice built a factory on Columbus Street near the Southern Railway tracks to supply the shipping industry and locals on the Neck, via wagon delivery.[32] The Consumer Ice Company advertised their "polite drivers" to bring blocks directly to one's home with their draft mule teams while the Southern Ice Company, established in 1924, quickly purchased equine fleets from smaller local companies, rebranded ice wagons with their logo, and ran mule deliveries into the early 1950s.[33]

City butchers and meat dealers, such as Armour Packing; sausage maker and butcher Louis Seel, who had three wagons; and George Cunningham who had two vehicles for delivering goods from his market stall, made deliveries with mules.[34] Butchers' stables were clustered near tidal creeks on the outskirts of the city, "a short distance from the slaughtering. They are sometimes united in one long continuous row, or else separate and distinct. Here the carts and animals are quartered and taken care of, so that at any time the meats can be rapidly transferred to the market and offered for sale."[35]

The Simons-Mayrant engineering and construction company owned several horses and rented additional equines in busy seasons. The company's records include monthly invoices for hauling brick, stone, cement, lumber, nails by the keg, roofing shingles by the cart load, iron by the bale, and coal. They paid "Lockwood's Sale and Feed Stables, Summerville SC" for hauling sundry construction materials and had a standing contract with "T.B. Miles, Carts, buggies,

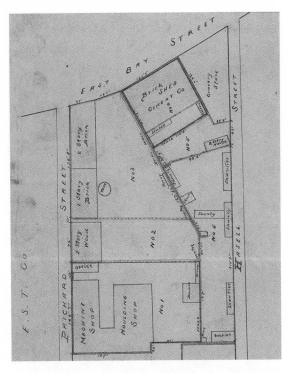

The small stable behind the Cement Company's brick building at the eastern end of Hasell Street offered simple and typical housing, and a small yard for construction industry delivery equines. McCrady plat 410. Charleston County Register of Deeds.

wagons, and saddle horses" for freight work. As late as 1926, they had sixteen single-animal wagons for carting materials.[36] Lumber mill mules carted materials to and from wharf side businesses; Anderson Lumber alone had nine delivery vehicles and Halsey Lumber had six.[37]

King Street was lined with two- and three-story wood framed and brick veneered bakeries, offices, trade shops, pharmacies, restaurants, and clothing stores; several of these businesses kept

Horses and uniformed drivers pose with their closed body delivery wagons in front of Lloyd Laundry and Shirt Manufactory at 161 Meeting Street in 1901. Library of Congress.

an equine and wagon for deliveries. Delivery drivers for grocers, such as Fincken and Jordan Grocers located on East Bay Street, operated delivery routes all the way to the city limit, approximately three miles away.[38] The Charleston Teapot grocery and wholesale company on King Street owned three wagons, five horses, and four sets of harnesses.[39] Having more horses than harnesses might indicate that the firm regularly gave their equines scheduled days off from work. The telegraph cable company, laundries, and furniture businesses also relied on delivery equines.[40]

Charleston's grocery, ice, laundry, and milk delivery wagons were fully enclosed by a wooden or metal roof and side walls with painted company logos. As gas-fueled delivery vans became more common, companies shifted to smaller wagons pulled by a single equine, "which could be maneuvered more easily through increasingly crowded streets and the long heavy tongue of a doubled rigged carriage

A deliveryman smiles with his well-groomed Charleston Ice Company horse. The wood-bodied wagon had a stretched canvas top. Taken in 1946 on Calhoun Street near Emanual A. M. E. Church. *Time Life.*

had a disturbing habit of basing into the rear of automobiles with a battering ram effect when a team stopped too suddenly in traffic."[41]

Carters and Draymen

Some drivers owned their vehicles and contracted with clients, while others worked as employees for larger companies. Drivers' lives could be dangerous and difficult and involved long hours in all weather. They, like grooms, were often disparaged as lower class and "rowdy," with the "odor of the horse blanket clinging to them always."[42]

Enslaved draymen frequently worked on the hire out system. Wage arrangements included flat weekly or monthly payments as well as payment per job. They had greater freedom of movement rarely afforded by other occupations, and some could keep part of their profits or work on the side for extra cash.[43] An antebellum visitor noted "the streets are thronged with them. They are the draymen, the market tenders, the carriers of burdens." The city required enslaved workers to wear badges demonstrating that they were permitted to work independently. The treasurer issued 700 draymen and 400 carter badges in 1851 alone.[44]

White Charlestonians feared the autonomy of hire-out slaves, especially after the Denmark Vesey insurrection plot was exposed in 1822. The alleged plan to take arms, kill white slave owners, and sail for Haiti had purportedly been organized by Black carters, draymen, sawyers, stevedores, and mechanics who would then enlist hundreds more seamen and draymen to the cause.[45] Horses played a key role in the plot; enslaved handlers would allegedly form a cavalry to subdue the town and to recruit "country people", or enslaved people living on plantations, to fight. A slave named Bacchus testified that participants planned to "have mounted horsemen . . . many draymen belonged to [the plot] who had horses."[46] Others attested that the Billings Church Street Stable and another livery stable behind Flynn's Church (also called the Second Presbyterian church) on Meeting Street, had been gathering places for planning the insurrection. An 1822 *Narrative of the Conspiracy* alleged four means to supply the mounted troop: "numbers of draymen and carters of the city, who are all persons of color, and many of whom have their horses both day and night under their control, were to act as horsemen," while butcher boys would take their delivery horses, livery stable hands "would open the stable doors, and thus provide their comrades with horses," and others would simply steal their owners' cavalry horses.[47]

Contemporaries, including Governor Thomas Bennett, questioned the way the trial was conducted, and some historians argue that the insurrection plot was inflated by white imagination. The confessions were obtained by coercion, torture, and even promises of freedom or lighter sentences. The trials led to the conviction of 67 slaves and free people of color, 35 of whom were executed by hanging. Among the convicted were Elias Horry's coachman John; a coachman owned by a Mrs. Bryan, whose name was not recorded; Charles "a coachman and horsier . . . of excellent character" in his mid-20s who belonged to Samuel Billings and worked in his stable; Monday Gell, who worked at Gell's Stables; Caesar, a 25-year-old drayman who belonged to Naomi Smith and who supported her with his hire-out income; Prince Graham, a free drayman of Coming Street; Dr. Simons' coachman; Isaac, coachman to lumber merchant William Barth, whose death sentence was reduced to transportation out of the state, perhaps for his cooperation in the trial inquiries; Smart, a draymen owned by Robert Anderson; and drayman William who was owned by Martha Garner, who had hired his time "with an understanding that he could eventually buy his freedom" from her.[48]

The rebellion caused a wave of paranoia and resulted in legislation ranging from outlawing manumissions, to prohibiting free people from leaving the state, and to the Negro Seaman's Act of 1822.[49] White tradesmen and politicians alike criticized hiring out practices for creating labor competition and potentially putting the community at risk by giving Black Charlestonians the opportunity to meet clandestinely or plot another rebellion.[50] Most regulations controlling hiring out practices, especially those related to draying, went unenforced. Wealthy white Charlestonians profited too much from their enslaved equestrian workers and garnered enough benefits from their services that they accepted the increased risk of them running away or getting into mischief.

Labor competition between white and Black draymen, mechanics, and day workers accelerated as the city's immigrant population grew in the 1840s and 1850s. Several unnamed merchants wrote a letter to the editor in 1844 decrying the rail companies' hire out practices that they viewed as detrimental to local interests, and criticizing the carelessness of the enslaved delivery drivers who brought goods from rail to ship: "for if a package of goods, however valuable, is lost in the hurry of receiving from alongside the ship and carrying it to the R. Road Depository (and in the nature of this case, nothing is more likely, for our black draymen as all irresponsible) or damaged and not discovered by the drayman," who would be liable?[51] Some employers actively sought Black drivers, such as Felix Meetze who solicited "four colored draymen" for his railroad transfer company.[52] Similarly, a livery company advertised to hire eight black draymen with good character recommendations.[53] Black draymen earned approximately one dollar per day compared to the two dollars per day that white drivers earned; this created an incentive for businesses to hire enslaved workers.[54] Enslaved men also had an employment advantage due to their perceived immunity to yellow fever. When a yellow fever epidemic broke out in the city, Mayor Miles issued a resolution that maritime goods "shall be delivered by acclimated negro draymen to be conveyed on drays to their proper destination in the city."[55] This enraged the city's Irish, German, and native white drivers and exacerbated racial tensions.[56]

The Irish flocked to carting and draying jobs in antebellum Charleston, New York City, and New Orleans. Charleston's Irish population increased between 1850 and 1860, glutting the labor market and heightening the competition for dock work and dray jobs. Of the free draymen in 1850, 37 percent were white; the percentage of white draymen increased to 83 by 1860.[57] Violence occasionally erupted over labor competition. Diarist Jacob Schirmer wrote of an enslaved draymen named Sam who drove for Southern Wharf, who "got a severe beating from an Irish drayman."[58] A judge that same year observed that "the great proportion of those we receive in Charleston from Ireland, manifest a proclivity for turbulence. I am afraid there is an inclination to make war upon the Negro."[59] Several Irish draymen were incarcerated in the Charleston jail for violent waterfront crimes in the 1850s and early 1860s.[60]

The Reconstruction era brought sweeping changes to Charleston's social order and altered

---

OVERLEAF: Clerks and drivers pose with their delivery mules in front of the F. W. Wagener & Co. building at 161 East Bay Street for Gala Week in 1887. The delivery mules lived in a long wooden stable behind the stately shop front, accessed from State Street. Founder Frederick Wagener was an avid horseman who enjoyed cart racing. South Caroliniana Library Collections.

Two Black delivery drivers pose with an enclosed delivery wagon and an open-bodied vehicle alongside the Heinsohn family and clerks in front of Heinsohn Grocery at 129 Broad Street, ca. 1900. Historic Charleston Foundation.

labor demographics. Freed people who had farmed by force on plantations and plowed with mules flocked to the city looking for work as drivers and laborers, thus saturating the equine labor market. Highly skilled enslaved workers had dominated equine-related support trades, workers such as saddlers, harness makers, and wheelwrights. Now, as freedmen, they competed with whites for jobs since whites could no longer rely on enslaved labor.

Germans and German-Americans cornered the Charleston grocery and bakery markets, employing hundreds of Charlestonians of diverse races and ethnicities. Oskar Aichel's Broad Street grocery business had two German clerks, a Black porter, and a Black driver. J. C. H. Claussen's bakery staff was integrated, with five white

drivers, three Black drivers, and a Black hostler. All twenty-two of Frederick Wagener's grocery drivers were listed as "colored."[61] Otto Tiedeman and Son's "grocery and provision dealers" at 172 East Bay Street employed four drivers in 1890, three of them Black. The company had a standing contract with Northeastern Railroad Company at that time for a drayman to deliver around 50 cords of wood per month.[62]

Fifteen men, all white, identified as dray masters in 1882, a supervisory role that included scheduling deliveries for multiple drivers, calculating freight charges, driving, and managing equines. John Danehay worked for Wilburn and Peper grocery and liquor purveyors; Thomas Jordan, William Easterby, John Bischoff, and Gourdin Pinckney worked for Atlantic Wharf;

William Huger, Alexander Oliver, and Peter Carroll worked for Chaffee and O'Brien Wholesale and Liquor; and others managed firms of which the names are no longer known. The 1896 city assessor's vehicle license ledger listed several dray masters: Peter Carroll had three single wagons, Peter Galvin had five, Robert Holmes had three, C. R. Holmes had three, and James Kinloch had twenty.[63] That year, approximately 179 Black and 54 white men were drivers for city fire and police departments, lumber companies, ice yards, the City of Charleston's stables for its working equines, grocers, street rail companies, fruit merchants, funeral parlors, fuel dealers, breweries, and for express wagon companies.[64]

Ninety percent of Charleston's draymen, hackmen, and teamsters were listed as "Negro" in the 1900 census, 574 out of 636 total, and 57 of the city's 62 hostlers were Black. Equine-related occupations remained among the most common jobs for African American men throughout the New South.[65] An article describing the busy shipping season described, "a very large and respectable class of colored men in Charleston who follow this occupation [draymen] . . . on East Bay and Broad Streets, at any hour of the day now, is a busy scene, a long line of cotton-laden drays rolling along between the car tracks, getting in the way of the carts, and making their presence generally felt and seen."[66]

Charleston's Black carters founded a fraternal group called the Draymen's Benevolent Association, which existed for at least fifty years. The organization purchased a lot on Rose Lane in 1875, the earliest reference to their existence,

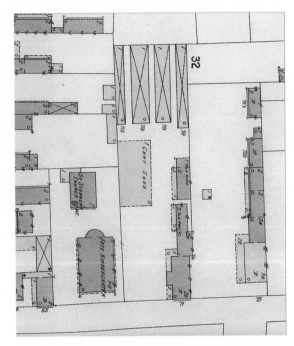

A series of one–story wooden stables for Kinloch's delivery horses and a cart shed lie behind his brick house at 71 Anson Street. 1902 *Sanborn Map,* sheet 45.

and published a funeral notice for one of their brethren, Scipio Martin, in 1925. W. H. Washington, president of the association, and the association's secretary, Robert Doctor, were listed in in the Charleston *City Directories* of the 1920s as laborers.[67]

The William M. Bird hardware and construction supply company opened in 1865 to sell paint, glass, cement, and whale oil, offers a glimpse into horse-powered delivery and supply chain logistics in changing times. The company purchased a schooner in 1884 for transporting

A mule rolls down Tradd Street ca. 1910, pulling a simple wooden vending cart with misaligned wheels, open sides, no business logo, and fitted with an umbrella to shade the driver. Morton Brailsford Paine Collection, Charleston Museum.

lumber and naval stores for Charleston, Savannah, and Boston clients. Mr. Bird "was proud of his hauling equipment and would be seen traveling around Charleston in one of his two drays which were always kept beautifully painted in Brewster green with gold leaf lettering."[68] The company's board voted to stop using horse-drawn delivery equipment and purchased the first Bird Company truck for $3,100 in May 1919. A note on the photo of the first truck reads, "it was a hard break for Mr. Bird, for he was very fond of horse flesh and did not like to change, but he realized that to keep up with the trend of business, horse drawn equipment was too slow."[69]

Public Services and the City of Charleston Fleets

Equines provided public services necessary to keep the city clean and safe. Trusty equine staff toiled alongside their human counterparts as members of a pseudo-police force and as part of the city sanitation crew, starting in the early eighteenth century. As the city expanded its services to include street maintenance and fire suppression, the equine fleet grew correspondingly. Lesser-known city departments and facilities also relied on horses and mules: inmates at the House of Correction farm plowed with a mule, the Colored Industrial School had horses and mules, and the Pleasure Grounds department had a horse and two mules for maintaining Hampton Park.[1] Even the city inspector, affiliated with the engineering department, had a horse for his rounds.[2]

Horses pulled ambulances for the city hospital and Roper Hospital and brought board of health and city physicians to their house calls. Underscoring the importance of the horse-drawn ambulance service, the Commissioners of Roper Hospital requested additional equines in 1909 to keep up with the growing demand. The ambulance service consisted of, "but one horse and driver, who are required to respond to the general calls in this department. These calls consist of conveying the pauper dead of the city and county to their place of burial, hauling clothing and bedding for disinfection to and from the hospital, conveying coroner's cases to the morgue, conveying patients to the hospital, and when necessary, returning them to their homes after discharge."[3]

The city government published municipal yearbooks from 1881 to 1949, offering insight into the numbers, duties, and types of equines employed in various city departments. The fire,

"1915 Election shooting scene" offers a rare photo of a horse-drawn ambulance. A white Percheron waits patiently with the Roper Hospital "crash wagon" while onlookers gather at the scene of Sidney Cohen's shooting, a *News and Courier* reporter who was caught in the crossfire at the contested mayoral election. Charleston Museum.

streets, and police departments had the largest equine fleets and meticulous care of the horses and mules ensured that they performed well and maintained their value. City employees who worked with equines included mounted policemen and patrol wagon drivers, fire engine drivers, carters and drivers for the streets department, park maintenance crews, grooms, and hostlers. Many remain nameless in the records as was the case for the equines with which they worked. The *Charleston City Yearbooks* occasionally recorded certain city employees by name for injury, merit, or long careers in city service. M. O. Brown, for example, was only 46 when he died suddenly of heart failure in the police

department stable at King and Hutson Street. Brown had been a hostler for many years, drove for the department, and cared for the officer's horses, meriting a brief obituary in the *News and Courier,* an uncommon occurrence for Black Charlestonians.[4]

Fire Horses

For two hundred years, firefighting was a dual government and volunteer effort, with the town or city providing equipment and passing fire prevention legislation, and civilians fighting fires when they occurred. As of 1698, a group of commissioners provided fire suppression equipment to the public. Citizens formed bucket brigades and hand pumped steam or suction engines to quell fires, drawing water from public fire wells.[5] Several volunteer companies were founded after Charleston officially was incorporated as a city, including the Vigilant Company in 1793, in all likelihood the first one, whose role was that of fire suppression and "removing goods and effects of the citizens, which shall be endangered by fire."[6] The early companies relied on manpower, but an 1826 letter to the the *Citizen Gazette* suggested substituting horses for humans: "it is worthy of experiment whether horses may not be beneficially substituted. In London and other large cities of Europe, they are advantageously employed. The harness is simple, and easily fitted, and the whole operation of attaching the horse, and moving the engine to a point proximate to the fire, would not consume a moiety of time now given to that object."[7]

Two weeks later, "A Charlestonian" suggested that a fire engine be kept at the ready at the main Guard House, "a place most likely to be first informed from the man in St. Michael's steeple, where a fire may happen, with two horses with proper harness for them, and a driver." The horses could stay in an adjacent stable, and "one or more of our draymen might be prevailed on to sleep in or near the Guard House for this purpose. We have some white draymen, should blacks be objected to. Could some horses and drays be also attached to our other engines for the purpose of conveying them and hogsheads of water, with promptness, to fires, the advantage would be great."[8]

New steam fire engines developed in the 1830s proved too cumbersome for men to pull, and companies across the United States began introducing horses into their firefighting services.[9] Charleston's volunteer companies opposed steam engines into the early 1860s and relied instead on pump or suction engines until the shortage of fire fighters during the American Civil War led the companies and city authorities to adopt steam engines, which required far fewer men to operate.[10] The volunteer companies used engines provided by a Board of Fire Masters or bought their own, and some had their own engine houses and stables, later incorporated into the city fire department.[11] After the Civil War, the city counted 11 horse-drawn steam engines, 2 ladder trucks, 800 white volunteers, and dozens of Black men who manned seven hand-pumped engines.[12]

The Charleston Fire Department (CFD) was founded as a paid, professional company in 1881, equipped with a fleet of six steam engines, two reserve engines, two hook and ladder trucks, and a fleet of horses to pull the equipment. Each engine house employed engine, truck, and supply wagon drivers.[13] The nascent department purchased four horses from Graham and Company, sixteen from Charles D. McCoy in 1881, and a horse for the fire chief. The CFD also purchased an engine and pair of reel horses (who pulled hose reel wagons) from the German Fire Company, bought a team from the Vigilant Fire Company, and paid McCoy for stall boarding while new engine houses were under construction.[14] Black firefighters drove and manned the hook and ladder trucks.[15]

The CFD owned an average of 28 horses per year from 1882 to 1918, employing horses rather than mules due to the heavy weight of their vehicles. The CFD sought American-bred French Percheron geldings between 5 and 6 years old, weighing at least 1,400 pounds. Fire work required calm dispositions and strength; "a good fire horse is one that never balks in the engine traces, who flattens out with the engine in the sand and tugs her through, who learns quickly to leave his stall and take his position under the harness when there is an alarm, who gets the atmosphere of the department quickly in his heart." Fire horses were trained to patiently wait curbside as their engines were deployed at a fiery scene.[16] Teams were selected for strength and appearance, "with an eye for some speed as well as for endurance and soundness."[17] Because fire work was physically difficult, the department sold older animals or placed them on a reserve list to limit their working days.

Firemen worked with new horses to teach them to leave their stalls and take their place in front of the engine at the sound of an alarm and stand as their harnesses were lowered into place with ropes and pullies from above, before they were hooked to engine wagons. Horses were

A team of Percherons race down Cannon Street while competing during the Firemen's Tournament. The event offered a chance to show off the teams' prowess while providing conditioning and training. Morton Brailsford Paine Collection, Charleston Museum.

then tested under various loads and acclimated to having loud, heavy engines behind them. A veteran CFD fireman explained that training one horse took two men, one to holding a horse's halter to guide him and the other ringing the alarm and then tapping said horse on the rump when the alarm sounded. "At this the animal pranced forward, the cheekpiece man guiding the horse to a position behind the tongue. After about a week, the animals jumped at the sounds of a mere telephone bell and sometimes a "smart" horse even learned the locations of [fire call] boxes."[18] Firemen exercised the horses for two hours per day as a way of keeping them in shape between calls. Veteran horses knew their jobs well, and firemen in the 1930s shared memories of a driver who fell from his seat as the rear fireman was clinging to the back of the wagon. The horses continued their run, following the directions of bystanders; "they even turned several times from one street into another. Upon reaching the scene of the fire, the rear man shouted whoa to the horses and they drew up closely to the nearest hydrant."[19]

Engine house employees took meticulous care of their horses and facilities, compiling expense ledgers with itemized columns for payroll, forage, gas, wood, coal, and oil charges along with those for other supplies, such as new harnesses, hoses, bedding, stable utensils, heaters, and other new apparatuses. They also recorded charges for repairs, shoeing and veterinary services, along with how much they paid for new horses. Each engine house bought dozens of mane brushes, curry combs, and horse blankets each year.[20] The Halsey lumber yard supplied sawdust for bedding, the Bennett and Company supplied hay, W. Bennister and Company brought cracked corn, oats, and bran feed, A. R. Thomlinson provided sets of harnesses, and E. H. Gadsden received payment for delivering stall bedding. Benjamin McInnes billed for horseshoe and veterinary services.[21] The CFD kept a journal of how many calls the engine houses answered each day. Horses were sometimes mentioned by name, such as when J. Campbell was "out of station from 11:00 to 12:40 to get Joe Horse to blacksmith. J Campbell taking Horse Burns Lane to headquarters."[22]

The Superintendent of Horses was responsible for the fire department equines' care and his duties included scheduling and reporting their veterinary care, inspecting the engine houses and resident horses every two days, "buying and trying of horses for the Fire Department," and selecting fodder types and quantities.[23] Irishman Michael Hogan (1842–1913) who came to the United States as an infant and fought in a Confederate cavalry unit, and later served as Superintendent of Horses from 1881 until his death in 1913. Fire Chief Louis Behrens said that "[Hogan's] judgement in the selection of horses was most excellent, and during his long service, he never once failed to respond to a call of duty. At every fire where his presence was necessary, he was on hand to see that the horses received the best of care."[24] Veterinary surgeon Charles Dudley Hasbrouck who replaced Hogan already had experience with the city's equine practices, having serviced the streets department's mules previously.[25] Dr. Leo James Hogan, DVM, was the last fleet superintendent, caring for the remaining reserve horses until their final retirement in the 1930s, when he noted that the fire horses "are in excellent condition—even better than most farm horses hereabouts."[26]

The superintendents kept lists of horses at each engine house, their job, whether they be wagon, engine, or hose reel horses, along with any ailments. They listed horse injuries and treatments, as for instance, engine horses Dany, Colonel, and Russia at Engine House 1 were treated for lameness, founder, and a sore leg in 1898; McKinley at House 2 for lameness and founder; Longfellow for colic; and Hampton at House 4 had a nail removed from his foot. Other common ailments included thrush, a hoof fungus; loss of appetite; coughs; stifle injuries; abscess; bruises; staggers (a temporary ailment caused by mineral imablence or toxcitiy in feed); swollen legs; fistula; worms; diarrhea; and sprains.[27]

Serving as a fire horse was a dangerous job, and the work was strenuous. Horses were roused from their stalls for harnessing and then rushed at break-neck speed, pulling a multi-ton engine to the scene of a fire. This is similar to when a sprinter begins a race without having already stretched and warmed up. Pavements were slippery, and the momentum of the engines they pulled could crush horses if they happened to fall. Rufus was killed in 1910, for example, when he lost his balance while responding to a fire on Smith Street. He tripped in a pothole while the engine kept moving, and his neck was broken.

Another apparatus had to respond to the fire because he was lodged under his engine and jacks were required to remove him.[28] False alarms endangered horses, firemen, and citizens alike. Every call was exhilarating and exhausting, and the horses returned to the station "tired and jittery . . . and usually too frazzled if another alarm was sounded too soon after the false bonging."[29] A "perverted humorist" went on a spate of false alarm calls in the summer of 1911, prompting the CFD Chief Behrens to offer a $50 reward for any information on the culprit.[30]

Robert, a large bay horse with eight years of service, died enroute to a fire at 196 Spring Street, "probably due to over exertion" in 1914. Robert "could always be depended upon. This tribute, in the prose of a eulogy, was paid the animal by one of the members of the department, who, very fond of the horse, frequently fed him sugar."[31] His partner Tom, a "big, black horse, went to join Robert" after Dr. Hasbrouck, over a six-month period, was unable to treat his leg injury. The newspaper noted that the sixteen-year-old horse had been in service for nine years and "with his mate Robert, made a fine showing on the streets of Charleston. Many persons knew the big black animal well."[32] Francis, in service for twenty years and on the reserve list, was called to action when another horse lost a shoe and dropped dead while answering a false alarm call on Longitude Lane. He "was held in deep affection by all the members of the department."[33] Firemen were also sustained injuries while working with horses, beyond those acquired in the already-dangerous line of duty. Driver J. Gibbes was thrown from his horse and broke his leg, entitling him to two months and twelve days off to recover.[34] Driver C. Bowen was thrown from his engine horse while on exercise and bruised himself. Fire engineer E.C. Myatt was kicked and received four days off pay.[35]

The firemen and their horses developed deep bonds as they worked and lived together in the engine houses and answered dangerous calls day and night. An observer in 1907 noted, "there is affection that is always strong between the fire horse and his master. Where is the department without its fund of stories about 'old Jack' or 'George,' long since dead, shot perhaps after a broken leg suffered in a brave run on a sleety night, and where is the department house whose men do not lovingly point out the virtues and beauties of the gently, powerful, sweet natured beasts that draw their own particular beloved engine?"[36] Russia was a department favorite who served from 1895 to 1907. His story speaks to the personalities of fire horses and their relationships with their human handlers:

> There are 28 horses in the Charleston fire department, all handsome fellows, of good weight and sound bodies . . . [Bryan's] record is excellent. Burns Lane is also a good horse. Bob, Charley, Dewey, Mack, in fact all the horses in the service are well liked by the firemen with whom they are associated. The oldest, the horse with the most memorial record, the animal that weighs the most that cost the least, is big, black, satin coated Russia [who] now spends his days in a roomy box stall all his own, in the yard at the Wentworth Street station. When he was bought from a Western dealer, he looked his name. He was a great, shaggy beast with hair three inches long, and presented so much the appearance of a long-haired Russian that [Lt.] Bicaise promptly named him Russia and took the new fire horse into his affections. And it was a splendid animal that was bought for a mere song. The driver with the carload of horses was anxious to get away from the city. He did not like Russia and offered him for almost nothing. Worth $300 easily, and weighing 1620 pounds, the big horse sold for $125. He has never been on the sick list, never been victim of an accident, and has developed the keenest intelligence of any animals in the service. He marked his entrance to the station by attending three fires on his first night. His proclivity for innocent mischief only serves to endear him to the hearts of his fellow firefighters. At station 1 he learned to lift his stall rope and leave the station at will. Combined with his ability to get under the ropes was a fondness for apples, and so when ladies at the St. John Hotel offered him fruit from across the street Russia would . . . watch his opportunity when the firemen were absent, and quietly work his big body out of the stable. Then across the street he would go pay a special call, eat apples, and return to his stall.[37]

The fire horses lived in stalls in the engine houses dispersed throughout the city, where firemen also slept in upstairs dormitories, or in attached rear stables. Several fire houses survive, some adaptively reused while others are still in service. These houses were dispersed in various parts of the city to respond to fires in a large geographic area. Some locations included:

- 8 Chalmers Street (German Volunteer Company 1851–1887, later CFD, now a museum)
- 27 Anson Street (Palmetto Engine Company 1850–1887, later CFD, now a residence)
- 5 Cannon Street (CFD, 1888 to present)
- 242 Meeting Street (CFD double house, 1887 to present)
- 116 Meeting Street (CFD 1887, now an office)
- 370 Huger Street (CFD, 1910 to present)
- 1095 King Street (CFD, 1933–1981, now an office)
- 33 State (1849–1882, Vigilant Company, later CFD, now a residence.)[38]

The 242 Meeting Street firehouse was erected after the earthquake of 1886 and designed by architect Daniel G. Wayne using the latest technology, which included, among other things, a Silsbee heat system for keeping engines steam-ready and an automatic call system that sounded the gong for the horses to assume their positions at the engine wagon tongue for hitching.[39] The city constructed a rear stable "large enough to have a good space for a hospital for sick horses and a yard to run loose in" behind the station.[40] The facility had stalls for 13 horses in the brick firehouse, plus reserve stalls to the rear in 1902.[41] 242 Meeting Street is still a fire station and is the most intact house to date. It retains its upstairs dormitory, stall

Firemen and their horses pose with an engine and ladder truck in front of the newly constructed Fire Station No. 8 at 370 Huger Street in 1913. This station is still in use. Historic Charleston Foundation.

ghost marks can be seen on the floor, and it still has the characteristic arched carriage doors and grooved pavement in the hitching area, which allowed the engine horses to get traction as they pulled out of the house. The Huger Street engine house, built in 1910, has traction grooves in the floor as well, while the 162 Coming Street house, built in 1945, was clearly constructed for automotive trucks—it has wider, square doors and no interior concessions for equines.[42]

The CFD purchased its first motorized engine in 1910. The department's holdings had dropped to 21 horses by 1919, and down again to 13 by 1923 when the CFD put its first motorized ladder truck into service.[43] The department retired most of its equines in September 1926. They attempted to sell off the fleet and received only one low bid, which was denied, so the SPCA, mayor, and the CFD board recommended the horses be "pensioned" and not "sold to someone who would mistreat or slave them."[44] Three of the seven retirees died within the year and the *News and Courier* noted, "there are not a few who think that homesickness for the mad dash of action and the acrid fumes of smoke were a greater contributing factor to their deaths than age or illness."[45] The four remaining retirees, Martin and Sigwald, gray horses aged 21 and 23, a 22-year-old bay called George, and Courtney, "an aristocratic black" lived out their remaining years in "ease and luxury" at Runnymede Plantation. The department retained four horses in reserve for emergencies: Blocker a 12-year-old, purchased in 1925; Gus and Myers, aged 14 and 17 respectively, who were bought together as a team in 1918; and Henry, a black 19-year-old purchased in 1917. They were "still made ready every time the gasoline trucks go out, and they champ and fidget with the zeal of old when they hear the gong which used to send them snorting down the street with the populace gaping in awe behind them."[46]

The reserve horses were listed in 1932 as "old, and past the years of reliable service, but necessary until a city service truck is purchased."[47] In 1936, the *News and Courier* ran a detailed story about Gus, Blocker, and Myers' final call:

> Last of city's fire horses had nice gallop to recent waterfront blaze. If animals could talk, Charleston's only fire horses—three healthy old geldings—in the John Street truck house,

still would be buzzing about their spectacular run to the Clyde-Mallory pier last September. Blocker, the youngest, a 20-year-old bay, would listen to Gus, 24, and Myers, 23, the two iron gray horses that drew the antiquated hook and ladder wagon down Meeting Street on the afternoon of the fire. Blocker, a reserve animal, didn't get to work during the big fire. It was the first run in more than four years, and it was almost a matter of luck that Gus and Myers once again felt the excitement of racing to a fire. At the time, the motor truck was under repair, so the negro firemen at the John Street station harnessed the two veteran fire horses to the old hook and ladder wagon in the garage and hurried to the eastern waterfront. Despite their age and more than 17 years of service, Gus and Myers performed their duty well. There was no hesitation and the two animals galloped as confidently as though they had been on active duty every day. Of course, they puffed a little bit after the run, but they seemed to like it. The three animals, once trained to leap from their stalls to the truck tongue at the sound of a bell, no longer jump and because of their age the firemen no longer keep them trained. Gus and Myers are kept in stalls in the wagon garage. Blocker remains in a stall in the rear of the garage. Today the three are given the best of care. Twice daily they are exercised on John Street. They are fed at 5 a.m., noon, and 5:45 p.m.[48]

The three were still in town in 1939 when the department mentioned plans "to pasture them at some reliable place." The next year they went to pasture on city land for retirement. Myers died at age 27 on 6 May 1940. Gus' death date was not noted, but Blocker lived until 1943.[49]

Scavengers and the Streets Department

A 1710 Act regulating the market provides the earliest reference to the position of scavenger, also known as a garbage collector, whose duties expanded by 1750 to include "the cleansing, filling up or repairing of streets, lanes, alleys, drains or common sewers," while the Commissioners of Streets oversaw the creation of new roads in the town.[50] The city council absorbed both the scavengers and the streets department as municipal entities in 1783, revising their duties and renaming the departments periodically. Both departments relied on equines to cart trash away and bring in construction materials. Equines helped create hundreds of buildable lots out of the peninsula's lowlands as they hauled city refuse to designated dumping areas, marshes, and depressions in the city's streets to raise them as a way of preventing floods.[51] The Commissioners of Streets employed trash collectors equipped with horses and red wagons that were marked "Scavenger's cart" in large white letters. The city's garbage cart drivers and laborers were almost always Black, as they had been in the colonial era. They removed refuse, unclogged drains and gutters, raked and leveled street surfaces, and performed street maintenance as needed.[52] After the Civil War, the division was called the Department of Streets or the Public Works

Department. While the department name fluctuated depending on the current mayor and his administration, their duties remained the same; they were tasked with trash collecting, including the removal of street sweepings and manure, and street maintenance.[53]

The Streets/Public Works Department owned an average of 45 mules and 3 horses, divided between scavenger/garbage collection, street sweeping, and highway sub-departments from 1880 onward. The fleet pulled wooden or metal carts and wagons of various sizes, street sweepers, and lawn mowers. The city purchased carts from the Ernest W. Hill Company in New York, which manufactured two-wheel dump carts for a single animal ranging from a capacity of 1 to 7.5 cubic yards and four-wheeled team wagons, with a ten-yard payload.[54] George Marx and Company provided "short-turn" team dump wagons with a fifth wheel to improve tighter turning radiuses on narrow streets.[55] The superintendent of streets had standing contracts with equine service providers, including M. M. McInnes and T. J. Kennedy, who shod for the department during the 1880s; followed by George J. Philips in the early 1900s; and after that by Leonard and Magrath.[56] H. Steenken was the contracted wheelwright, A. R. Thomlinson provided new harnesses, and John Ogren repaired harnesses in the 1910s and 1920s.[57] The department bought feed in bulk—73 bushels of white corn and 438 batches of oats, coming in 32-pound bushel increments, in one order alone, and 17,000 pounds of prime timothy hay and 516 bushels of oats in another.[58]

The streets department mules were constantly at work in the growing city, hauling 114 loads of sawdust for their own bedding and a total of 50,076 cart loads of garbage, tree trimmings, and grass cuttings to the lowlands for fill in a single year.[59] The city purchased a lot at the corner of America and Lee Streets and constructed the first city incinerator, or "garbage destructor," on the site in 1917. The mules carted the garbage up a long, straight ramp to a platform, where the waste was gravity-fed into hoppers to be burned.[60] Even after the department began adding motorized sweepers and garbage trucks in 1921, mules kept working alongside bagmen on foot because they were more effective for large street debris, which damaged the motorized sweeper, and for working around parked cars.[61]

Like the CFD, the streets department rotated older animals and those "unfit for continuous service on paved streets" out of the fleet and replaced them with younger mules. The Superintendent recommended selling eight mules and one horse "while some return can be obtained for them. These animals would probably furnish excellent service in the country but their days of usefulness on paved streets have nearly passed."[62] The department bought replacement mules early in the year to acclimate them to the heat and city work before summer and supplemented their fleet by renting mules for heavy work seasons or to relieve injured or older animals who could only work a few days per week.[63] Of the 43 mules in the fleet, 12 were "incapacitated for work" in 1904, possibly due

to age or a difficult work streak.[64] The superintendent reported purchasing five new mules to replace "some who have literally been worn out in service." in 1905.[65]

Dr. Charles Dudley Hasbrouck was veterinarian for the department from 1910 to 1917 and was credited for the "excellent health of the stock at the city stables," and for his "constant and intelligent advice," which included adding a cooling shed and wash stall to the stable facility.[66] He treated mules for common occupational illnesses including tetanus, lameness, poor appetite, sores, and nails in the feet, and pulled animals from service for health issues and injuries including foundering; mules with wind gone, meaning that they were short of breath or lacked stamina; and mules up on toes—this is when they try to keep weight off their heels due to lameness, navicular disease, or other hoof discomforts.[67] Dr. B. Kater McInnes became the department veterinarian in 1918, and recommended condemning and replacing a lame mule named Rebecca and an older lame mule called Daisy.[68] At least one incurably lame mule was sent to live out the rest of their life on J. A. Mellard's farm in Goose Creek.[69] The city also employed a Superintendent of the City Stables, a position held by Joseph McInerny in the early 1920s.[70]

The fleet size peaked to a height 50 mules in 1917 but the number remained fairly consistent with at least 42 mules until 1933 when the city began phasing out equines for a motorized fleet.[71] A December 1932 article reported nostalgically on the mules' retirement:

The days of the Charleston garbage cart mule, long a familiar sight on city streets, are numbered. Like his once haughtier contemporary, the noble fire horse, he is scheduled to fall before the advancing tide of the machine age. The motorization . . . will be accomplished gradually, a few of the mules being replaced at [a] time, but it is conceded that all these mules must go. With the passing of the mules will go one of the most picturesque of the municipal services. Marching forward slowly or stopping lazily at the command of the negro driver, the mules pass through the city streets in the collection of garbage. When the cart is full and headed toward the dump, the mules assume a livelier gate [sic], however, and joggle along at a fair speed.[72]

The city offered 42 mules for sale in January 1933, to be delivered to their buyers after the city's new garbage trucks arrived.[73] The last "garbage mules" made their final trip in April 1934, and returned to the city stables, "now properly the city garage, twitching their long ears and occasionally bellowing a long hee-haw as they await the arrival of their purchasers." The newspaper spoke of the mules' relationships with their drivers in saying that,

A strange sort of attachment has grown up between the mules and the negroes who drove them. One has been a mule driver for forty years, and others also have worked for long periods of time. Most of the negroes had their favorite mules, and there also are mules which had the reputation of being 'tricky.' Practically all the drivers adorned the harness of the animals with flashy articles picked out of the trash from Charleston's best homes. These adornments might include a bit of tinsel, a Christmas bell, a battered cowbell, a bent silver spoon, or anything else which might attract attention. On their part, the mules showed their affection by tranquilly plodding along the street, regardless of heat, cold or flies, responding with almost human intelligence to the barely audible words of the driver.[74]

The city stable, a two-story wood building with a one-story shed roofed porch on the rear at 133–139 Line Street, was torn down and its lumber used for enclosing the adjacent wagon shed in 1936.[75] The Enston Homes for the Elderly purchased one of the retired Street Department mules to replace Elizabeth Enston, their work mule. Elizabeth was known for her "tameness and propensity for following people [and] was a general favorite at the home," until she was euthanized at age 23 for painful seizures. The newly purchased Street Department "homing mule . . . refused to stay in its new home, got lonely and broke loose, returning to its old home at the city stables," before being returned to Enston Homes.[76] Sadie, the city's last mule, was offered for sale in January 1938. "Not a young mule, but a good worker," she had pulled the grass mower at Hampton Park for years, as Charles Webb, the city clerk, explained. Sadie was purchased by a Greeleyville farmer, whose cousin wrote to the city two months later to let Mr. Webb know that she "is now doing fine as a plow animal" in the country.[77]

Police Horses

Horses were employed in the protection of the town and colony by 1673, when the Grand Council (a colonial era governing body that was the forerunner to the state General Assembly, and which passed colony-wide legislation before individual cities like Charleston were incorporated) instructed John Godfrey and Maurice Mathews to launch an attack on horseback against a hostile band of Native Americans near Charlestown.[78] Charleston's police force expanded in breadth and scope as the town's boundaries and population increased. In the colonial era, an unpaid paramilitary unit called the Night Watch comprised of free white male inhabitants aged 16 to 60 policed the town limits primarily on foot.[79] To keep order in the rest of St. Philip's Parish and the Neck, the General Assembly passed an "Act to settle a patrol [sic]" in 1704 to create another militia unit. A captain equipped with a "good horse" led the Patrol in times of active duty.[80]

In the colonial era, there were separate but similar pseudo-police entities with mounted contingents to protect the colony in general, and Charlestown, the colony capital. From 1696 onward, the governor had authority to call a Horse Troop or Horse Guard unit to serve as his personal sentry.[81] The Horse Guard included approximately forty free men living in or near

Charlestown who were periodically active by 1708. While they did not directly police the town, they traveled between Charlestown and the rest of the colony's settlements in service to the governor and in times of unrest, such as during the Yemassee War.[82] John Lawson, surveyor general of North Carolina, described the horse Guards as, "a well-disciplin'd Militia; their [troops of] Horse are [mostly] Gentlemen, and well mounted, and the best in America, and may equalize any in other Parts." The year 1736 shows the earliest evidence of a standing or permanent guard.[83]

After incorporation, the city council replaced the Night Watch (a colonial-era urban policing entity separate from the Horse Guard which functioned as a militia unit) with the City Guard, a similar body of mounted and footmen to patrol the city and nearby unincorporated areas.[84] The City Guard was a standing municipal entity that used horses as part of their regularly nightly patrols in the city limits. The thwarted 1822 Denmark Vesey plot led the government to more tightly police the enslaved population in and around Charleston, especially on the Neck where they might try to pass as free.[85] The state passed an "Act to authorize the formation of a mounted corps in Charleston," similar to the colonial era Governor's Troop of Horse but serving as an urban militia. The Charleston Horse Guard included up to 100 men led by a captain who would perform duty in times of alarm. The "Troop of Horse" equines were exempted from annual taxes levied on other horses, and were separate from the City Guard.[86]

By the 1820s, the City Guard included six mounted men, increasing to eight by 1833. Duties included raising the alarm for fire or unrest, and apprehending persons committing crimes or violating the town's curfews, such as Peter, a "daring Negro" who assaulted a mounted officer on the Neck while trying to run away.[87] In 1846 the city government reorganized the City Guard and expanded the mounted unit to cover large territories more effectively. The mayor at the time was "struck with the efficiency of a Horse Guard," so at his request, the city council passed an ordinance to reorganize the city guard into separate foot patrol and Horse Guard units that year.[88] The Horse Guard committee purchased "six young and strong horses at an average cost of $72.00, that have been furnished with saddles, bridles etc. and are now on duty," and recommended "that the horses be kept on livery, and that they be authorized to advertise for contracts to keep the horses at the guard house, the contractors to furnish corn, oats, hay, bedding, etc."[89] Until 1850, the lands north of Boundary Street were outside the City of Charleston and were protected by a county Patrol. With the annexation that year, the upper peninsula gained a Police Guard of the Upper Wards (a new unit of the city police department) to replace the Patrol, and it was to be equipped with 46 privates, 26 of whom were mounted.[90]

The Charleston Police Department (CPD) was organized as a uniformed, paid municipal entity in 1856 to replace the various earlier policing bodies. The Committee on the Reorganization of the City Guard noted the Savannah's police force's success with mounted men, who could "go over a larger beat, are more on the alert, and [are] fresher after pursuit. A large, mounted force is destined to prove of great value to us. The growing custom of Negros assembling by night on farms out of the city proper but within corporate limits, requires imperatively to be looked after. This can only be done by a horse patrol."[91] The city passed an ordinance to begin purchasing horses for the sergeants and privates. Other officers would furnish their own horses and would be reimbursed for feed expenses.[92] The force was divided between a main station and stable, namely, the Guard House at Meeting and Broad Streets, and an upper ward station. The department purchased hay, grain, and oats from Campsen and Company. They quickly bought more equines from Ross Spriggs, increasing the fleet size to 43 horses.[93]

The CPD purchased five additional horses in 1893 to patrol a territory "extending from river to river" of underdeveloped suburban tracts above Cooper and Shephard Streets, and to ride in "parades and large assemblages."[94] Several years later, the CPD requested funds to buy horses for all of their sergeants and justified it by citing the fifty percent decrease in robberies along routes serviced by mounted officers.[95] A new headquarters opened at King and Hutson Streets equipped with adjacent stables to replace the city guardhouse after it was damaged in the earthquake of 1886, and, in turn, a facility was erected at Vanderhorst and St. Philip Streets in 1907 to replace the King Street station.[96]

The CPD also employed chauffeurs, also called drivers, and a stable foreman.[97] The force used patrol wagons drawn by "well trained"[98] horses to transport persons detained for crimes and to respond to service calls. They later remodeled the wagons to make them lighter, thus reducing the construction cost and making easier work for department horses, especially on dirt streets.[99] The CPD regularly collected horses and mules wandering at large, as well as abandoned or stolen carriages and drays, which were brought to the station house to be reclaimed or sold.[100]

Police horses needed calm dispositions to tolerate loud noise, crowds, chaos, drunken revelers, and violent criminals. They were gaited and could switch leads (alternating between leading a gait with the right or left leg) and were trained to side pass (moving sideways by cris crossing the legs to move to the side without moving forward) in order to push and contain crowds. It could take over a year to train a police horse for the complexities of city work.[101] Equine police work was difficult and stressful, and accidents and injury were an ever-present threat. A dramatic incident occurred in 1909 when Brandy "became unmanageable" and threw several policemen from the patrol wagon to which he was harnessed. Brandy got the bit between his teeth so his driver no longer had control of the reins for steering him, and pulled a tight corner from St. Philip Street onto Spring Street, having become "greatly excited" when he heard the sounds of the fire bells and the "clattering hoofs of the fire horses" coming up

behind him. Several officers sustained bruises and broken bones, Brandy was bruised, and the wagon sustained considerable damage.[102]

Mounted officers were responsible for the health, appearance, grooming, tacking, and general care of their horses, and, in so doing, formed bonds with them as they served together. Lieutenant Homer D. Waller Jr. in charge of training police horses in the late twentieth century explained, "you've got to really like horses, because rider and horse work together. It's one officer and one horse, and strong attachments are formed. The horse learns to obey his partner. Horses are like children, they have good days and bad, just like people. Some are more high-strung than others, but they learn their job, they calm down."[103] The officers' attachment shows in a 1914 article about the death of a veteran police horse:

> There is sorrow in the stable at the police station. Dayman, the big fine black horse, was killed yesterday morning, after an illness of some time. Dayman entered the police department slightly more than ten years ago and had been a favorite. During his time at the barracks, he had been used as a patrol wagon horse and had responded to calls, going to fires at breakneck speed, and hauling injured and sick persons to hospitals. Dayman had been on the sick list for some time. Although he was given treatment, his malady was of a serious nature and his recovery was doubtful. Yesterday it was decided to send him out, hauling the patrol wagon on its round

gathering lanterns. When the horse reached Clifford and Archdale Street he fell. Investigation proved that he was all in. He was a victim of a severe stroke. JR Arnold, special officer for the Society for the Prevention of Cruelty to Animals, was called and he decided that Dayman should die to save him from pain.[104]

The CPD invested in their equine fleet alongside their new auto and motorcycle patrols. They purchased seven young horses in 1917 and reported that, "the Department can be proud in saying that we have the best equipped stable of patrol horses in the Southern States." The new purchases included a draft horse for the patrol wagon and saddle horses for street sergeants, so they would no longer have to procure their own mounts.[105] The department had eleven horses "of a superior quality and in fine condition" in 1920.[106] No ordinance or city council discussion was found to determine when the CPD retired its horses, but a retrospective article claimed that mayor Thomas P. Stoney instigated the end of the mounted police unit, following his inauguration in 1923,

> Mounted Police Abolished. Joint campaign meetings were held in Marion Square, where the rival candidates [for mayor] and their supporters hurled epithets, jeers, and cheers. Mounted police jostled the crowds, including the newly franchised [female] voters. It is said that this caused Mr. Stoney to abolish the mounted police when he went into office.

From that day on, there have been no horses in the police department.[107]

Despite that report, the CPD had horses at least until 1941, when they were given a month off because of the summer heat and their officers switched to a bicycle patrol.[108]

The police station stables were gone by 1944.[109] Retiring officers reminisced about the good old days when horses were part of the force. Sergeant Anthony P. Langan, a County Mayo native who retired in 1949 with 42 years of the service in the CPD, said that when he enlisted in April 1906, all officers were either mounted or foot patrol, "I'd rather have a horse. You could get around better."[110] Chief Detective John Healy's obituary after he was killed in an automotive accident in 1937 noted his "strong admiration for fine horses. His early police days when he was a mounted policeman were among his most treasured memories."[111]

After years of a horseless force, Mayor Joe Riley reestablished Charleston's mounted police unit in 1978 for crowd control and to promote a friendly police presence in the city. The city constructed a police horse stable in Hampton Park for its fourteen-horse fleet. The mounted unit had Arabians, palominos, and draft horses that they purchased or received as donations.[112] The mounted police rode in parades and appeared at city events, including summer camps, where children had the opportunity to pet and groom the police horses.[113] Corporal Barbara Majeske described the efficacy of police horses in giving the officers a commanding view,

visibility, and respect. Private Debbie Fitts called her horse "the definitive tool for crowd control." A mounted officer "can move a crowd without even having to touch anyone. They just back away from us."[114]

The city again disbanded its mounted police force in 2011, citing budget cuts. "It hurt," said Master Patrol Officer Ed Davis, who had been with the mounted unit since 1997. Davis told reporters that,

> horses were powerful and effective in police work. He remembers the day he decided to get involved in the mounted patrol. He was in a training session on crowd control. About 40 officers were told to go outside and, like protesters, form a line standing shoulder to shoulder. Then four officers rode up on horseback and were able to break up the line quickly. He saw how effective horses could be in police work. At the end of that day, he submitted a request to become a mounted officer. In just one day, "I had a career change."

The last six police horses, which included Napoleon and a Clydesdale-Belgian cross named Moose, were retired.[115]

Municipalities across the country including Tulsa; Boston; Camden, New Jersey; and San Diego also cut their equine force for cost savings in 2011. The decisions were largely unpopular with the public; "romantics have a nostalgic attachment to police horses, and many police officials value them, saying that when dealing with crowds, one mounted officer is as effective as 7 to 10 officers on foot. They are highly visible, these officials say, and can deter crime, and their popularity with the public is a welcome change from the mistrust that many departments battle."[116] The CPD reinstated its mounted police in October 2021, following a decade of requests from its own force and the community. Palmetto Carriage Works donated Holmes and Watson, two carriage horses already acclimated to the city, as the first new equine members of the force. Their first day in service was April 2, the day of the 2022 Bridge Run.[117]

Holmes and Watson, the first of the CPD's reinstated mounted police unit, walk down Guignard Street in March 2022 after finishing their training. Photo by Sophia Old.

The Buildings Where
Equines Lived and Worked

Stables are dwellings for horses, often equipped with storage for hay, tack, and harness, and living space for human attendants. They came in a variety of sizes, materials, and layouts reflecting the wealth of the property's owner, ranging from grand stables to glorified shacks.[1] Stables had earth, packed clay, brick paved, or concrete floors and frames and varied from having a simple lean-to wood construction to being grand masonry buildings with pressed brick facades and architectural ornamentation. The Horlbeck Brothers contractors' daybooks contain plans and programmatic statements of the size and scope of antebellum stables. One measured 23 feet 6 inches by 17 feet 6 inches wide, with tuck pointing on the façade and flat pointing on the other elevations, indicating a high-profile, street facing location. Specifications for a square, brick

stable in 1845 included interior paving and a slate roof next to a 10-foot by 12-foot carriage house. An 1847 stable plan called for one of 22 feet long by 14 feet wide, with tin cladding over a wood frame structure, with room for two standing stalls approximately 7 by 10 feet, and a carriage.[2] Carriage houses, also called chair houses and coach houses, used primarily for parking vehicles, might incorporate a stable under the same roof, or in an attached bay. Carriage houses had the requisite large, hinged doors to allow vehicle ingress, while dedicated stables only needed doors large enough for a horse to pass through, making carriage houses easier to spot as former equine buildings after they had been converted for adaptive uses.

Stables and carriage houses were the lifelong habitats of the equines that resided in them. The

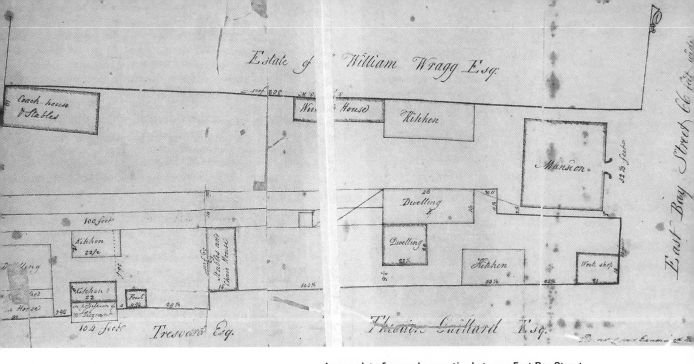

Estate of William Wragg Esq.

Coach-house & Stables

Kitchen
22½

Dwelling

Kitchen
22

Fowl

Tresvant Esq.

Kitchen

Mansion

Dwelling

Dwelling

Kitchen

Work shop

Theodore Guillard Esq.

East Bay Street 66 feet wide

A 1794 plat of several properties between East Bay Street and Union, now State, Street shows stables and carriage houses on lots of varying sizes, placed behind workshops and small houses as well as on large parcels with stately "mansions" fronting the street. Deed book K6, pg. 374. Charleston County Register of Deeds.

condition of a stable conveyed information about a human's values and relationship with his horse, for keeping a clean, well-maintained stable was not expensive but made a real difference in the health and comfort of the equines living there. There were parallels in human housing and equine stabling reforms, and health experts recognized that both species thrived with well-ventilated, well-lit, clean quarters. Equine authorities admonished that,

> badly constructed, badly kept, and badly managed stables are the contributing causes of most of the illnesses that horses suffer from. As nine stables out of ten in America are bad in all three regards, I am confirmed in the belief that horses are very hardy animals instead of the delicate creatures we think they are. Why a stable should be dark and the living room of a human light, I cannot conceive. There is no good reason why a stable should not be as clean as any other part of a gentleman's establishment.

Health experts recommended ceilings should be high, the stalls cool and shaded in summer, and kept warm and dry in winter. Equestrians debated on the optimum stall size, some favored box stalls large enough for a horse to lay down while others preferred standing stalls, but most agreed that working animals should have comfort and refuge from the weather.[3]

Residential Equine Buildings

Buildings in the oldest part of the city on Elliott Street, Tradd Street, and East Bay Street's Rainbow Row often occupied the entire frontage of residential lots, a common practice in European cities that was brought to Charlestown. Arched passageways through the façade of such a building led to courtyard space in the rear.[4] Josiah Smith's upscale residential tenements constructed in 1795 at 85 Broad Street, for example, featured two symmetrical units framing an arched carriage drive to access the stables and outbuildings in the rear yard. The layout is reminiscent of the neoclassical hotels constructed in Paris during the eighteenth century, but is also found in buildings used by the working-class people of the city, where stables and workshops were tucked behind the street-facing residence. 40 Tradd Street, built ca. 1718, had a breezeway which Dubose Heyward widened when he purchased the property in 1919, connecting it to the rear yard of the Heyward Washington House on Church Street.[5] The masonry Arch Building at 85 Calhoun Street, built in 1800, and a nearby dwelling and bakery at 77 Calhoun, no longer extant, also had arched passageways that led to stables and tenements in the rear yard, as did the Inglis Arch house at 91 East Bay Street on Rainbow Row.[6]

By the mid-eighteenth century, builders responded to the Lowcountry's climate by constructing detached residences to prevent fire and promote air circulation, which also allowed for driveways located down the side of lots between neighboring houses. Connected buildings, however, endured in the oldest, most dense part of the city, and were found in commercial areas where lot frontage was at a premium. The ten-foot-wide Unity Alley had been created between East Bay Street and State (formerly Union) Street by 1739. An additional, unnamed eight-foot passageway was cut to provide access from Unity Alley to the rear of the large lots along East Bay Street. The waterfront had been devastated by fire in 1796, but instead of taking the opportunity to redevelop the crowded area, both Unity Alley and the passageway were retained in the rebuilding. The passage led to a large, square carriage house fronting the large rear work yard and stables of an East Bay residential property that would otherwise not have been accessible. A later plat after this area's redevelopment into commercial antebellum buildings shows that the small passageway remained intact. The new commercial buildings between Unity Alley and Queen Street, as in other dense commercial areas of the city, had party walls (structural walls shared by two adjoining units), so that small passageways off smaller side streets (as, for example, Unity Alley) remained the only way to access the back of the lots. At the time, the passageway led to a large stable 80 feet long by 25 feet wide, facing into a small work yard behind F. W. Wagener's stores.[7]

Equine building placement changed over time but was usually determined by the depth and width of the lot, the plan and size of the principal building, and what the owners could afford. Elite property owners desired fine horses, carriage houses, stables, and a contingent of employees, the majority of whom were enslaved and lived on site in the second stories of carriage houses or stables prior to 1865. Elite townhouse properties allowed room for a host of outbuildings, such as kitchens, washhouses, slave quarters, stables, carriage houses, livestock sheds, privies, and wells with "relatively spacious configuration", placing "crowded, dirty, noisy" work yards away from the house," while middle- and working-class properties were often subdivided and became increasingly congested.[8]

Regardless of building width, a practical hierarchy governed building placement on urban lots, with kitchen houses located closest to the main residence while stables, privies, and other animal buildings along with their accompanying stench, were relegated to the back of the property. Where kitchen houses were usually constructed of brick, stables and carriage houses might be made from wood or masonry. Most Charleston lots are narrow and deep, so the most common building placement pattern was a single house, a narrow vernacular residential form running one bay wide facing the street that is usually placed along the sidewalk with no front yard and a narrow drive running parallel so as to access rear buildings, arranged in a row behind the main residence.[9] The 1785 Elihu Hall house located at the intersection of Meeting Street and St. Michael's Alley offers a prime example. A large garden and carriage drive ran beside the narrow single house, behind which was a carriage house with a wood frame upper loft,

a one-story wood stable next to a work yard, well, and one-story privy. The extant stable, now a dwelling, originally featured four standing stalls.[10] The carriage house behind 33 Hasell Street, which survived the fire of 1838 and predates the current single house, contained space for two vehicles and stabling for three horses. It was converted to a dwelling by 1884, but retains its carriage entry doors.[11] The Christopher Schutt house, a stately single house constructed in 1800 situated at 51 East Bay Street, maintains its complete range of outbuildings—kitchen, carriage house, quarters, and stables. The narrow carriage house is placed behind the kitchen house. It is constructed of local brick laid in Flemish bond and has a hipped tile roof and interior chimneys along the north wall, which provided heat for the enslaved grooms who lived there. The building retains four wide, arched doors that open into the back yard. The two-story, hip-roofed stable projects from the carriage house to create an ell. The first floor contained stalls, a storage room, and stairs to access the upper dwelling space.[12] Placing stables behind and in line with a single house or in the rear corner of a narrow lot remained a common practice throughout the centuries.[13]

The one-story brick stable and carriage house behind the Heyward Washington House on Church Street, constructed ca. 1772, predates the main residence, having survived from an earlier iteration of buildings made by gunsmith John Milner following the fire of 1740. It is likely one of the earliest extant equine buildings on the peninsula. Thomas Heyward cleared part of the lot to erect his grand Flemish-bonded brick Georgian double house, leaving Milner's kitchen house, located close to the main dwelling and the stable, halfway down the southern lot line in front of the formal garden, in situ. The long one-story brick hip-roofed stable was divided into three bays. The bay closest to the house was used for carriage parking and has a large door. A central windowless bay accessed by a wide door from the work yard was the tack room, and the stable was in the largest bay toward the rear of the building. The stall area had a window and two doors wide enough for a horse to pass. Ventilation shafts kept air moving to carry the ammonia-like smell of horse urine away from the main house and kept the animals comfortable and cool. The floors were likely wood plank or made of packed dirt. The Heyward Washington House was rented out as tenements and the stable converted to a dwelling space, with a new one-story wood stable on the opposite property line by 1902. When the Charleston Museum purchased the site in 1929, the partitions and walls in the stable were gone, but archeologists have confirmed its construction date as ca. 1740 and determined the interior layout through excavations.[14]

The Miles Brewton house, constructed in 1765 on lower King Street, has a series of stables, a kitchen/laundry, carriage house, and slave quarters that are now residences. The street-fronting carriage house retains its carriage doors and a second story Gothic window that lit the stable hands' quarters. William Alston added additional stables fitted with tack rooms for his racehorses behind the original outbuildings in 1820.[15] The urban estate was accessed by the gated carriage drive, or via a locked wrought-iron street gate. The brick single house at 14 Legare Street, built ca. 1800, which abuts the Brewton house lot to the west and retains a carriage house and stable, embodies the typical architecture of a federal-era wealthy person's house and outbuildings. The buildings are intact and have been converted to dwelling spaces.[16] George Edwards had a plat of the site made in 1838, which gave a detailed description:

> coach house and stables—a detached one and a half story brick building covered with slate, used as a stable, coach house, and loft. The whole premises are faced with high brick walls, except next the street from which the house recedes 6 feet 2 inches and is fenced with handsome iron railing having marble capping on driveway brick walls—a very handsome flight of double stairs to front entrance with a banister on each side. J Hyde, architect.[17]

Nathaniel Russell, a wealthy Bristol, Rhode Island merchant, constructed a grand town house at 51 Meeting Street in 1808 and placed the outbuildings behind in the usual fashion, but the property was unique in that it had a double lot. The house lacked piazzas and instead had a semi-octagonal projection with large windows and balconies that overlook garden paths and ancient magnolia trees. The Russell House features a formal foyer and merchant office, which visitors accessed via a hinged pedestrian gate on

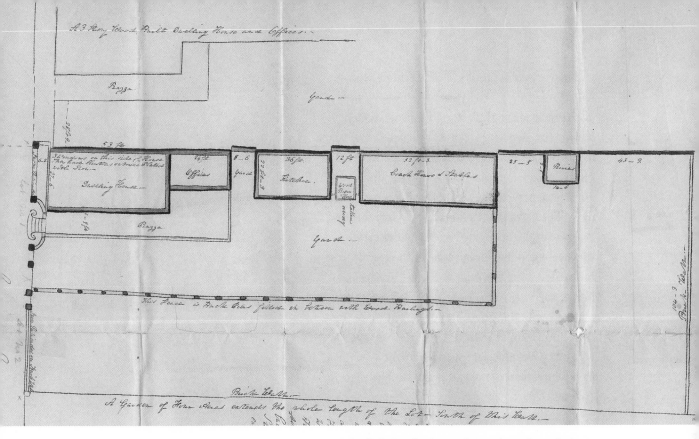

An 1838 plat of 14 Legare Street shows the typical arrangement for a single house lot. The brick residence fronts on the street, with piazzas and a side drive accessed by a gate. The rear yard holds a brick kitchen, coach house, and stables, which are all extant. Plat #33 121 01. South Carolina Historical Society.

Meeting Street. The rest of the house, separated from the business space by ornate glazed doors, was the private sanctum of this wealthy family. The carriage drive ran down the other side of the house, out of view from the garden-facing windows, and led directly to the now-lost carriage house and stables in the rear. A small exterior door tucked below the grand, free-flying, spiral staircase in the formal hall allowed members of the family to exit their carriages directly into the residence as their coachmen and horses continued on to the work yard. Archaeologist Martha Zierden notes that large lots allowed segregation of workspaces and formal gardens, but "these seemingly spacious yards became quickly cramped as a townhouse owner, his family, a retinue of 10–20 slaves, horses, and other livestock lived and worked within a circumscribed area."[18]

Social control and segregating spaces for the enslaved members of the household also influenced property layouts. Walls and formal entry gates surrounded urban residences to control people's access to the property, reinforcing "both the assertion of domestic authority and its very vulnerability."[19] The Pringle House constructed at 70 Tradd Street in 1774 is a single house recessed slightly from the street, which allowed for two access points—a gated sidewalk to the piazza, and a gated carriage way. Bernard Herman explained the motivation for this spatial arrangement when he stated that "servants entering by the carriage way literally passed beneath the gaze of the occupants of the main house as they went about their business at the rear of the house or among the outbuildings. Carriages or horses carrying social equals entered nearly at eye level with the pizza. The organization of the single house unit ran from street to backyard wall in a pattern of decreasing formality, declining architectural detail and finish, and increasing dirtiness."[20]

Stables were often placed toward the rear property line of the lot, adjacent to a garden or work yard for both double and single houses. The George Eveleigh house at 39 Church Street, built in 1759; the Daniel Elliott Huger house at 34 Meeting Street, constructed in 1760; and the Douxsaint house at 132 Church Street, built ca. 1800; and others followed this common pattern.[21] Peter Manigault's design for Ralph Izard's double house at 110 Broad Street, with stalls for six horses located behind the kitchen house to the north of the main house, "which will be part of the house used only for bed chambers."[22]

Large suburban lots afforded property owners with space for formal gardens and spacious equine outbuildings. Their remote setting away from the city center necessitated horse and carriage ownership, especially before omnibuses

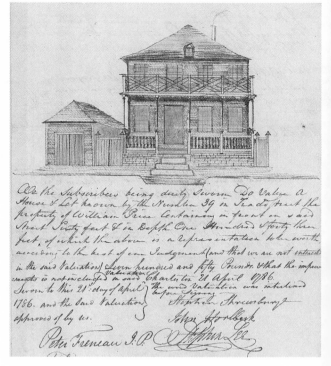

A 1786 elevation sketch of William Price's Tradd Street house shows a large house fronting an enclosed lot. The property was accessed via a gated side drive, and by ascending the stairs to the formal door on the front porch. A hip-roofed carriage house next to the main residence opened directly onto the street. SCDAH.

and streetcars. Willingness and the means to commute via horse and/or carriage gave wealthy residents more privacy, greater comfort, and an ability to maintain a greater distance from the hustle and bustle of the city. Samuel Adams's large property in the now-lost Village of Washington on Rutledge Avenue on the Neck provides an example of this kind of lot. In the

The grand Daniel Elliott Huger house at 34 Meeting Street is placed in the center of the lot along the street. Typical of a double house, the rear yard is flanked by a kitchen house and work room on one property line and by the carriage house and stable on the adjacent lot line, with a formal back garden behind. The house and its outbuildings have all survived. Plat book 2N, pg. 363. 1795. Charleston County Register of Deeds.

1790s, Adams would have traveled on horseback or carriage to Charleston proper via King Street, which was then mostly unpaved north of the city limit, and paved in the city proper to the south of Calhoun Street. The "mansion house" overlooked a side yard with a kitchen house, beyond which was a large stable building with a paddock or fenced turnout area. The two-story equine building had a stable bay in the center, flanked by shed-roofed side projections that likely stored harness, carriages, and fodder. To the rear of the house was a massive garden with a central walk lined by two rows of peach trees and a crossing walk covered by a grape arbor.[23]

Property owners with wide lots placed the big house in the center of the parcel along the street, with two banks of rear outbuildings on the opposite property lines and a large wall surrounding the whole compound to keep enslaved residents confined to the property, giving rise to the term "urban plantation."[24] Wharf owner

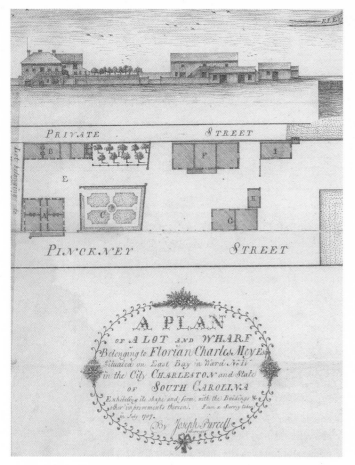

A highly detailed "Plan of a lot and wharf belonging to Florian Charles Mey" shows a plan view and elevation of Mey's property. The dwelling house (letter A) was flanked by a fenced side yard, with a "kitchen, washroom, carriage house, stable . . . two story brick and covered with tile" across the yard (letter B). A large arched carriage door is placed in the center of the south façade. The rest of the yard held a former garden, orchard, and store houses. McCrady plat 209. Charleston County Register of Deeds.

Florian C. Mey's residential estate at the foot of Pinckney Street adjacent to his East Bay commercial wharf had a stately double house fronting the street with a formal parterre garden alongside, and a two-story brick kitchen, carriage house and stable building with an adjoining orchard. Moving closer to the wharf, visitors found Mey's businesses buildings, including store houses and a scale house.

One of the best surviving urban plantations is the Aiken Rhett house.[25] The mansion was built by William Aiken Sr., who was one of the richest men in the state. A chief investor in early rail development in the city, Aiken ironically died of injuries when he was thrown from his carriage after his horse became frightened by the sound of a train engine at Aiken's Charleston depots.[26] William Aiken Jr. inherited the house and embarked on a grand renovation, modifying and enlarging the plan, and constructing several outbuildings. The complex retains a laundry and kitchen opposite a carriage house and stable with a large yard between, accessed via a carriage gate on the rear property line at Mary Street. The equine facility measures nineteen feet wide by seventy-one feet long, with parking for at least two carriages, standing stalls for six horses, a tack room on the first floor, with a hay loft and residential quarters above, replete with a windlass winching system to lift hay through a Gothic-arched opening. Grooms dropped hay through shafts into stall troughs below. The grand stalls have wooden Tuscan-columned supporting arches and dividers. Visitors can tour the entire estate, which is operated as a

The Aiken Rhett stable features Tuscan-columned stall dividers and original wooden feed troughs. Hay was dropped from the loft above.

house museum by the Historic Charleston Foundation.

When the Gothic Revival style became popular in the mid-nineteenth century, residents remodeled their carriage houses with Gothic-arched carriage openings and crenelated parapets reminiscent of castle battlements. The Aiken Rhett stable/carriage house is a prime example of the Gothic Revival style, with its Tudor-arched carriage doors, struck stucco render, and bricked-in Gothic window-like recesses along the exterior wall facing Elizabeth Street. Other examples are found at the Gaillard Bennett House's brick carriage house at 60 Montagu Street, built in the 1850s and now living space, which retains its original Tudor arched openings

and fenestration. The carriage house behind the Italianate style Patrick O'Donnell House (1850s, 21 King Street), also now a residence, runs perpendicular to the main house along the back property line and features large carriage door bays (the openings are now glazed) and a Gothic window and crenellation on the upper story.[27]

While most Charlestonians were struggling to recover financially after the Civil War, two wealthy residents, George Walton Williams and Francis Silas Rodgers, built grand Victorian homes on large lots along with fine carriage houses and stables that demonstrated the ongoing prestige and importance of equestrian amenities for Charleston elite. Williams was the richest man in postwar Charleston, having

Aiken Rhett's carriage house and stables are completely intact, with Gothic-arched carriage doors leading to stalls, a tack room, and carriage parking on the first floor, with living quarters above.

amassed great wealth through a self-built wholesale grocery empire, and who had converted his assets out of currency and into real estate, gold, and cotton in 1860. He purchased a lower Meeting Street lot that extended to Church Street, on which he erected what is still the largest house in Charleston, a grand brick edifice with stone trim and Italianate/Renaissance Revival details. The large, two-story brick coach house and stable was massive unto itself, measuring 44 feet by 47 feet, with a large central aisle, probably constructed for ventilation, stalls on one side and coach parking on the other, and dwelling space for the coachmen and grooms above.[28]

Merchant and civic leader Francis Silas Rodgers purchased a corner lot at Wentworth and Smith Streets in Harleston Village and commenced construction on Charleston's second-largest house in 1885, an imperial Second Empire brick mansion designed by architect David G. Wayne, with gardens and outbuildings behind and adjacent. Rodgers's Wentworth Mansion has an arched port cochere on the eastern side of the property with a wide carriage drive that leads to the rear yard. The quoined brick carriage house with its hip roof and reverse central gable features two large carriage doors on the first story and careful fenestration of the second story for the grooms' quarters. The house also had a stable opening onto Wentworth Street, a well-proportioned, one-story brick building with high ceilings in the stall area and a parapet obscuring the gable roof line.[29] The stable was connected to the carriage house via a series of service buildings along the coach drive. The stable has been converted to a shop space and the carriage house has been transformed into a restaurant, built ca. 1886.

The stable at 25 East Battery Street is one of the most intact in the city and reflects husbandry ideas that emphasized the importance of good ventilation. The recent restoration offers a rare glimpse into a historic stable interior. The brick and stucco building has a shed roof tied to a southern boundary wall behind the main residence. The standing stalls measure approximately -five feet six inches by nine feet in depth and have wooden hay troughs and grooved posts to receive horizontal partition boards, spaced to allow ventilation. Lath ghost marks on the rafters indicate that the building had interior plaster as well as a large fireplace. A rare, surviving tack house with a struck stucco facing and a louvered roundel vent located in the steep parapeted gable end stands nearby. A gate in the Atlantic Street wall, which has since been infilled, accessed the stable and backyard.[30]

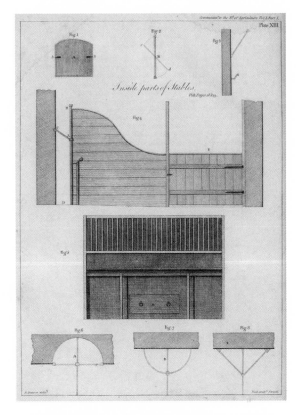

A plate from *Communications With the Board of Agriculture* (1796) showing plans for "the inside parts of stables," including partitions walls and doors.

The stable behind 31 Legare Street built ca. 1789 features similar stall partitions with a grooved channel for receiving vertical boards. Board partitions, often with a cyma curve that reduced the height of the stall partition wall from the feed trough toward the back of the stall "so strange horses may not see each other" were common by the late eighteenth century. Openings cut into the masonry exterior walls allow southerly cross breezes into the stall area.[31]

31 Legare Street's intact stable building, located to the rear of the property behind the kitchen house, with an upper dovecote and ventilation slats above the stall bays. Historic American Buildings Survey.

Livery, Sale, City, and Workhorse Stables

Before modern urban zoning became a common practice, businesses were interspersed throughout the city and small stables for delivery horses were tucked behind corner shops and houses, while industrial businesses had facilities for their delivery equines adjacent to their operations.

There were several delivery horse stables along King Street for dry goods companies, wholesalers, and other shops. Fleming and Devereux, a plaster and cement company found at the wharves on the east side of Hasell Street, had a large warehouse with a wood stable, cistern, and yard in the rear.[32] A mill house on Judith Street in the 1830s had a small stable attached for the mill horses; this was likely a water mill as the lot abutted a tidal creek.[33]

Taverns and houses of entertainment were usually equipped with stables and pastures. A house for sale on King Street in 1781 featured a brick-paved stable 45 feet long and 29.5 feet wide, the total width of the lot, with separate stalls for each horse and a central aisle for parking carriages, a large hay loft, and a stable yard. The owner noted that the location was ideal for a store or tavern, "King Street being the leading street from the country."[34] Robert Rawlins's "Sign of the Bear Inn" on King Street near Boundary Street had "commodious outhouses, a stable big enough for twenty horses, at present well supplied with corn blades and hay . . . the pasture adjoining to it, newly fenced in, and the only public pasture within Charles Town Walls . . . [with] room enough for 8 waggons [sic]." Philip Well's Cross Keys Inn stable on King Street was the largest advertised, with stalls for sixty horses.[35]

Chalmers, Queen, and Church Streets were livery stable hubs for the adjacent shopping, hotel, and business districts. A 90-foot by 35-foot wooden carriage house stood on Chalmers Street in the mid-nineteenth century and was located in a mixed residential and business area. There were three livery stables on Chalmers by 1861, in addition to the McInnes Farriers; the John M. Haley's stables at 14 Chalmers Street, Haley lived next to his rented facility; Planter's Hotel's brick stables and carriage house at 24 Chalmers Street; and Purcell's Stables at 30 Chalmers Street, which included three brick buildings.[36]

William Hockaday's facilities on Church and Anson Streets offered mules for sale or rent in the antebellum era. Hockaday also purchased a large lot on the south side of Pinckney Street in 1853 and built a stable with partner Ross Sprigg, which remained a livery facility long after their retirements.[37] Pinckney Street was home to several stables and carriage sheds associated with Meeting Street businesses. Many were leased, like Charles Siegnous's stable on the north side of Pinckney Street opposite the Charleston Hotel near Maiden Lane, which he rented out for a ten-year term to the Frederick Campbell

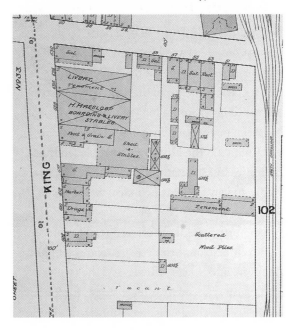

Henry Haesloop's large enterprise at 620 King Street shows a typical livery and sale stable of the 1880s. The two-story wooden livery stable had tenements on the second floor, probably for stable hands and drivers. Haesloop also had a boarding stable, a hay, grain, and grocery business, and additional stables and sheds next door. 1888 *Sanborn Map*, sheet 21.

Company. Curiously, part of the buildings was a bathing establishment, while a stable was operating on site.[38]

Hotels had livery stables to board their guests' horses and to provide horses and carriages for hire. Mr. F. Lamonde Jr. operated St. Mary's hotel and livery stable at 173 King Street, formerly Brockway's tavern, with space for fifty horses, and he hosted saddle and draft horse dealers. Lamonde even employed "an excellent cook and a good supply of liquors . . . every day from 11 to 2, there will be turtle or mock turtle soup, or oyster soup."[39] The long-operating American Hotel on East Bay near George Street had a facility in the rear for guests' horses and offered boarding by the month.[40] The Pavilion Hotel began operating in 1840 at the northwestern corner of Hasell and Meeting Streets. To the rear of the property facing Society Street was a large one-story 40-foot by 90-foot brick carriage house and stable accessed by a narrow "carriage way" running between two Society Street buildings. The neighboring lot held a "shed for old carr'ge," while the lot to the west had a narrow alley leading to a building with a series of small bays that might have been stalls for the delivery animals.[41] The hotel owners replaced those buildings by 1884 with a three-story brick livery stable and an adjacent two-story brick stable, while the wooden carriage shed remained. The three-story stable had been reduced to one story, with a three-story brick harness room and office opening onto Society Street, and the two-story stable also reduced to a single story "hack house" by 1888. A dwelling, cleaner's shop, and a large

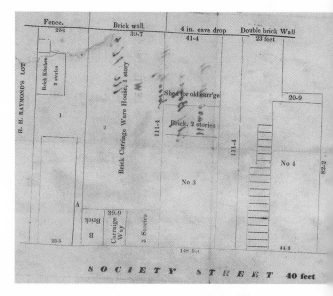

Behind the King Street commercial district, ancillary streets like Society held stables for delivery animals (note the standing stalls on lot No. 4). McCrady plat 3707. Charleston County Register of Deeds.

one-story square wood frame stable occupied by site by 1902.[42]

The Brown family were successful multigenerational African American stable owners at the turn of the twentieth century. Jason Brown and his wife Diana McCall moved to Charleston from the upstate of South Carolina in 1878 and ran a stable on Chalmers Street before establishing a livery and hack stable at 62 Queen Street that ran from 1881 until at least 1920. Jason's brother, Eugene, owned hack stables at 30 Meeting Street and at 87 Rutledge Street.[43] The current two-story wood frame building with its parapeted facade on Queen Street began as a one-story hack stable building. The Browns

Church Street looking north near Chalmers Street. McCoy's Sale Stable and Mule Yards on the left have been replaced, but the brick Builder's Depot on the right side of the street, with its large carriage delivery doors, remains. Library of Congress.

added a story ca. 1888 and built a rear stable addition on the north facade. A 1936 account stated that the "stable kept some of the very ancient carriages in which the aristocratic white people of Charleston used to enjoy such a delightful ride to church, joy riding, and often to business."[44] A Democrat, Brown offered free use of his carriages for Confederate Memorial Day and "had many white friends who learned with regret of his death" in 1926.[45] Diana assisted with the stable business by applying for licenses in her name for 2 two-horse wagons in 1896 and later became the first Black female antiques dealer in the city, operating the Queen Street shopfront from 1913 until her death in 1949. Ralph Muldrow notes, "the decision to repurpose 62 Queen into a formal antique shop coincided with her husband's retirement and the closure of the livery stable, a development possibly prompted by the increasing obsolescence of horse-drawn transportation amid the growing popularity and accessibility of the automobile.[46]

Charles McCoy's livery and sale stables at 111–115 Church Street was the longest running stable site in the city. McCoy purchased the Church Street property, "occupied by the late Rutherford Oakman as a livery and sale stable,"[47] and the neighboring lot, in 1879 and 1880, but there had been a livery stable at the site since 1825.[48] McCoy had rented the site as early as 1872 before building his new facility.[49] Richmond, Virginia native Charles E. Crull (1879–1966) took over McCoy's stable in 1917 and expanded, with a second building at the corner of 14/16 Cumberland Street and 53/55 State Street.[50]

The *Charleston Evening Post* reported in 1924 of Crull's business:

> thriving establishment [that] deals in horses and mules. Despite the phenomenal advance made in the automobile industry, the day of the horse is by no means over, and especially in the South, agricultural and industrial interests will be interested in animals for many years to come. In Charleston, prominence in this line of business has always been Crull's sale and exchange stable, located at 12–16 Cumberland Street. This business occupies a very large building which is very convenient to its trade. Mr. Crull had long experience in the sale of horses and livestock and during his residence in this city he has built a most satisfactory organization which now employs seven persons.[51]

Crull's stable fronted 75 feet on Cumberland Street and was over 100 feet deep. The facility survived a serious fire that started in the neighboring house in 1935, in which "the stables were roaring in a big blaze with pillars of smoke shooting skyward from the hay and straw in the stables and from neighboring buildings used to store lumber and antiques." Fortunately, a stable hand turned the animals out so there were no casualties.[52]

The Harper Brothers' massive stable, located at 155–159 Church Street on the corner of a large lot that they purchased from CD Franke, was a one-story building with a white sand brick facade measuring 180 feet by 115 feet with "roomy and sanitary pens and stalls, and the sick animals enjoy the advantages of a hospital. The arrangements for fresh drinking water and clean food are surprisingly simple and effective."[53] The stable was later converted into Smith Buick and

John McAlister Livery Stable, located on cobblestone paved Horlbeck Street near Meeting Street, offered boarding and livery services, ca. 1898–1912, Franklin Frost Sams Collection. Charleston Museum.

the site is now a parking lot. Robert Graham ran two large sale barns at 30 Chalmers Street and 60 Queen Street, later operated by H. J. Hickson and Co., who advertised horses, mules, ponies, buggies, surreys, delivery vehicles, and road carts for sale in 1901.[54] The Queen Street facility was a two-story wood building with a central aisle supported by brick posts and flanked by one-story side aisles, it was, essentially, a basilica plan tailored for industrial use. By 1888, Graham had added a brick facade along Queen Street and a low one-story ell-shaped "mule shed" (additional stabling for mules in a shed-roofed building) in the rear.[55] The building was converted to a storage shed between 1944 and 1951.[56] Most of the sale stables, including that of McAlister's

near the market and the F. Horres Stables at 105 Meeting Street (later relocated to 147 Spring Street), also offered boarding and livery services into the twentieth century.[57] There were still four sale stables in the city in 1929, Bennett and Messervy's facilities on Queen Street, Crull's Red Stable on Cumberland Street, and Simmons Stables on Church Street.[58]

City-owned stables were located near the neighborhoods their equines served. The CPD stable in the Central Police Station on Marion Square was equipped with "stalls (or nine houses, besides harness and feed rooms)," a granite paved courtyard, and dormitories above. The stable floor was artificial stone "provided with open grated small channel gutters, stench

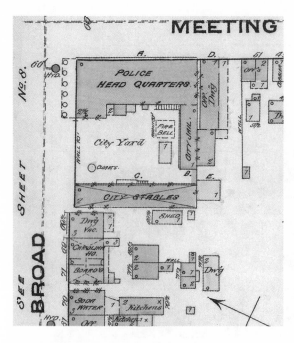

The Police Headquarters at the Four Corners of Law featured a large portico, a two-story brick "city stables" for the police horses, likely with dormitory space above, and a work yard. 1884 *Sanborn Map*, sheet 20.

traps, and an improved mode of carrying the drainage from stalls to properly trapped cesspools, which can be readily emptied, deodorized, and disinfected. Upon the stone is laid a stout flooring of planks" that provided softer footing.[59] In 1892 the department purchased an existing building next to their headquarters at the northeast corner of Hutson and King Street with the intention of converting it into additional stalls for the police horses.[60] By 1893, "the rear portion of this property has been remodeled and fitted up as a stable and wagon house. This gives the much-needed room at the Main Station for

the construction of new cells for the prisoners."[61] Contractor Henry Oliver completed the renovation work.[62] In 1898, the department converted the rest of the building into additional stalls for the sergeants' horses.[63]

The city erected "new quarters for the police horses and vehicles" at Vanderhorst and St. Philips Streets in 1902, noting, "the new stable building will be a credit to the city and to the police branch of the municipal service, and will be in keeping with the headquarters structure erected some years ago. The stables will be ready for occupancy within the next few months. The building will be constructed of the best available material and will be an excellent specimen of architecture."[64] Following a small fire in 1905, the CPD hired H. T. Zacharias to make repairs. His contract gives details for the finishes of these modern stables—operable window sashes in the loft area, canvas-covered sliding bay doors, a tinned roof with dormers for ventilation, sliding windows on the lower/stall story of the stable, and the interior walls and ceilings painted with high grade linseed oil paint. The J. T. Nelson Contracting Company updated the CPD stalls in 1907 with new feed boxes, cast-iron mangers, hitching rings, and saddle brackets.[65]

The streets department replaced its upper King Street stable with a new facility on Line Street near Rutledge Avenue in 1889 that was home to roughly 45 mules. The city stable was open to the public, and the streets department prided itself on keeping the premises "neat and clean."[66] In 1909 workers installed new stall partitions and flooring, whitewashed the interior and exterior, and painted the tin roof, although the Superintendent advised that "the present stable facilities are somewhat limited and in the near future will prove inadequate to the increased demands which the growth of the City will surely impose upon the Department."[67] In 1915 they advised the city council that, "the safety of the stock and the comfort of the employees demands a new brick stable at the earliest possible convenience," although the city instead made periodic renovations to the existing Line Street facility.[68] The city stable became redundant when the mules were replaced with motorized equipment, and it was removed in 1937.[69]

Stables in the Twentieth Century

The *Sanborn Fire Insurance Maps* provide a snapshot in time of every building standing in the city during a given survey year, including stables. Comparing maps from 1902, 1929, 1944, and 1955 shows the construction materials, approximate size, and lot placement for equine buildings located throughout the city and allows researchers to track how many stables were constructed and lost between those years, and how extant stables and carriage houses were repurposed over time. Of the approximately 842 stable buildings standing in the city in 1902, most were rectangular in plan, with only around 70 laid out with a square form. Rectangular buildings with a single bank of stalls ventilate better than square buildings and fit better on narrow Charleston lots. They were typically oriented behind and parallel to the main residence. The second, most common

residential lot arrangement places a rectangular stable perpendicular to the main residence on the rear lot line.[70]

The city of Charleston monitored equine buildings for fire safety before they became interested in sanitation and animal welfare concerns. An 1801 ordinance required new stables to be constructed of brick or stone and covered in slate or tile; it eventually became illegal to store more than 3,000 pounds of hay or fodder in one location.[71] With the creation of a paid city fire department in 1881, the city became laxer in allowing wood construction, particularly for detached outbuildings. There were 530 one-story wooden stables by 1902, which accounted for more than half of the stables in the city at that time. There were approximately 134 two-story wood stables, 124 two-story brick stables, and 39 one-story brick stables. One-story wooden stables were most common in the working-class upper wards, and the few brick examples in that part of the city belonged to large suburban estates. Brick stables and carriage houses were concentrated in Harleston and in lower Legare, King, Meeting, and South Bay Streets in the elite residential areas. The old French Quarter section of the city was densely developed and had fewer stables due to space constraints. The large livery barns near Market, Queen, and Cumberland Streets served the needs of French Quarter residents and businessmen working on Meeting and Broad Streets. There were also five wagon houses, five carriage repair shops, five dray houses, and one hearse house grouped near the Market.[72]

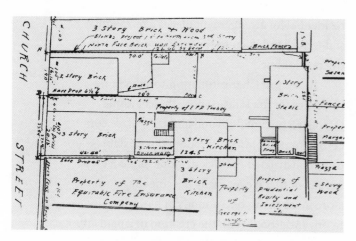

A plat showing a one-story brick stable owned by E. Towney in 1919, on a rear parcel partitioned from a Church Street lot in the midst of residences, accessed by a narrow passageway. Charleston County plat C, pg. 147.

Although the number of stable buildings in Charleston dropped by nearly seventy five percent between 1902 and 1929, that is, from 842 to 242 stables as auto garages became more common, 151 new stables were still constructed during that period. Most were erected in the growing upper peninsula neighborhoods of the East Side, Cannonborough-Elliottborough, the West Side, and near the Cooper River wharves for the lumber factories, fuel storage terminals, and small businesses that utilized horses and mules for deliveries. Of the new buildings, 108 were one-story wood, 27 were two-story wood, 6 were two-story brick, and 8 were two-story brick.[73]

With the rising national interest in public health and urban sanitation, municipalities passed laws to regulate stables and livestock facilities. Both New York City and Boston regulated stable size, and, in Charleston, it became illegal to keep a horse in the city without "a proper and suitable house or stable, kept constantly clean and free from dirt," on pain of a $5 fine and $2 for each additional day of neglect.[74] Charleston's board of health adopted "Stable Rules and Regulations" by which "many horse stables were transformed from fly breeding centers into sanitary places."[75] The department made a city-wide survey of stables in 1917, counting 527 total; "we passed rules and regulations for the Stables, requiring a water-tight floor either of concrete or boards, properly drained according to the number of horses kept, and a flyproof bin for the storing of manure, which was ordered emptied at least twice a week. It was necessary to make 131 cases against the stable owners in the police court, of this number four were fined, 3 forfeited bail and the balance complied. As a rule, the stables are in very good shape after this campaign."[76] The health department inspected and cleaned 117 stables in 1935, demonstrating that equine housing facilities were still in use throughout the city.[77] While the number of stables declined to only 109 by 1944, eighteen new stables were erected between 1929 and 1944.[78] After that point, surviving stables were converted to new uses, though the telltale carriage doors often remained to remind later occupants of the horses who had lived there.

Decline and Reminiscence

"There is little left to remind the citizens of Charleston of the horse drawn age. The hundreds of gaily painted high body delivery wagons bearing the names of retail and wholesale firms are long since gone, and fleets of huge express vans or light, speedy delivery trucks now cross the city. A few hitching posts and dismounting steps remain on the sidewalks, and in Mary Street there is a communal watering trough where horses going to the freight yards on East Bay used to pause and drink. And remaining are a few horses and mules that pull wobbly wagons about the streets dispensing coal, ice, fish, and vegetables, but they are a far cry from the dashing carts and buggies with matched teams of other years, and less than 10 are left," reporter Belvin Horres lamented in 1948.[1] His retrospective, however, demonstrates just how long traditional modes of transportation lingered

in Charleston, where economic struggles had staved off wholesale modernization and where equine traditions were never truly erased.

The city's urban population grew from 9,000 people in 1750 to 45,000 in 1865, and the equine population increased alongside that of humans.[2] Growth ceased with the American Civil War, which devastated the local economy. A massive fire in December 1861 along with one and a half years of Union shelling left the city devastated. Charleston fell in February 1865 and among the confiscated Confederate property were 200 horses, 161 mules, and numerous wagons.[3] Hurricanes in 1885 and 1893 decimated surrounding farmlands, and the earthquake of 1886 caused widescale damage to city buildings, businesses, and residences. The Lowcountry remained economically stunted into the twentieth century. Phosphate mining on former cotton and rice plantation lands for lime-rich "stinking stones" that could be processed as fertilizer, and timbering, and which took less labor than did traditional crop farming, were the only significant new industries in the postbellum decades.[4] Charleston experienced limited development or technological change until the population increases sparked first by the new Navy Base in North Charleston, which opened in 1901, and then by tourism.[5]

Most of the state's rail companies passed to indifferent non-local syndicates in the late nineteenth century, preventing any real initiative to modernize rail and port connections, which reinforced the fact horses and drays served as the most viable way to move goods for import and export through the city. Rail companies received permission to run track diagonally toward the Cooper River, and the East Shore Terminal Company built a belt-line rail, a short line railroad operation located within and/or around a city that connects with one or more larger or trunk line railroads, along the waterfront in the 1890s.[6] Local businessmen, however, decried the company's high shipping rates and opted for traditional drays.[7] The Charleston Cotton Mill, Imperial Fertilizer, Standard Fertilizer, Palmer Manufacturing at Atlantic Wharf, and Wieters Shipping all used horse wagons to bring goods from the wharves to customers into the twentieth century.[8]

Stuck in the past, Charleston's historic port area declined further as maritime development to the north of the harbor became more advantageous. The federal government approved a twenty-year dredging and jetty construction program to deepen the Cooper River from the Harbor northward to the proposed navy base site in North Charleston in 1878. The dredging created new wharves along the Neck; this meant that businesses located there had direct rail service, a more practicable arrangement.[9] The Standard Oil Company opened near the Cooper River marshes in 1903 and built a refining facility and company headquarters just north of Magnolia Cemetery in 1926. This marked another large technological change that further reduced reliance on equines in the shipping industry, namely, the emerging auto fuel industry.[10]

The introduction and rapid rise of automobiles impacted cities in profound and permanent ways such as altering urban planning practices, zoning, street layout, and paving choices. Auto delivery drivers replaced draymen, and car repair shops supplanted livery stables. In 1900, the United States had around 17,000,000 horses and 9,000 automobiles in 1900; the numbers had reversed to a total of 6,000,000 horses and 41,000,000 cars by 1949.[11] Charleston had 100 registered autos in 1907, 500 by 1912, and 4,500 by 1922.[12] As these statistics show, the city's equine population began to decline after 1910. The treasury office reported 969 registered horses and mules in 1913, and this number fell to 929 equines by 1915.[13] The city registered 67 mules and 94 horses, 70 "carriages, wagons, trucks, drays," and 6,869 motorized vehicles by 1931. The treasury offices collected just ninety dollars in cart and dray license fees in 1941.[14] The 1920 *City Directories* listed two "auto livery"

Broad Street in 1901 reflected changing modes of transportation at the turn of the century. New electric trolleys shared the street with horses and carriages and bicycles. *Charleston and the South Carolina Inter-state and West Indian Exposition.* Library of Congress.

businesses, the Charleston Transfer Company, previously an equine livery, and Thompson Transfer, which increased to four white-owned companies by 1930. There were eight taxi companies and only two surviving livery stables in 1940, namely, Crull's Red Stables on Cumberland Street and Livestock Sales at 60 Queen Street.[15]

Public transportation systems also transitioned from horses to mechanization. Converting streetcar lines from horsepower to electric was an expensive undertaking, requiring a new network for generating and transmitting power, but one by one, American streetcar franchises made the change. Montgomery, Alabama became the first public transit network in the South to switch to electricity in 1886, followed by Atlanta in 1889. In 1890 roughly 80 percent of street rail mileage in the United States used animal power.

Ninety-seven percent of American track used electricity by 1902.[16] The Charleston city railway purchased Enterprise Railway company assets in 1897, which gave the newly consolidated company control over all the city's fixed track while it planned the switch to electricity-powered streetcars. The *Street Railway Journal* reported, "for several years past, the city of Charleston has enjoyed the curious distinction of being the only city in the United States of 35,000 inhabitants or over which has not within its borders a single mile of electric railway . . . the companies appear to have been unwilling to venture into paths to them unknown."[17] Preparing to electrify, the Charleston Consolidated company constructed a "Trolley Barn" and generating station on upper Meeting Street and switched to electric in 1897.[18] One the eve of the transition to power, the equine-powered streetcars at that time employed around 300 men, many of whom would eventually lose their jobs. The *News and Courier* celebrated the move toward modernity: "nearly everybody in Charleston is glad that the two horse railroads have been sold. While they appreciate the years of good service given on both lines, they realize the necessity of a trolley system, and believe that it will be the greatest enterprise for Charleston that has been established in years."[19] Charlestonians who preferred a hayburner still had the option of hiring horse-drawn omnibuses that ran on peripheral routes not serviced by trolley until 1917, when the Charleston Transport Company purchased the first motorized buses in the city and began phasing out horses.[20] A diesel bus fleet, in turn, replaced electric streetcars in 1938, and the streetcar track was removed and paved roads replaced it.

City departments began incorporating engine-propelled vehicles into their rolling stock in the early twentieth century, gradually replacing their equine fleets. An anonymous writer lamented replacing fire horses with automobiles in 1907:

> With all the marvelous sagacity that the fire horse acquires in training, he can never be so responsive to control as the senseless

Firemen pose with an automated ladder truck and a horse-drawn truck pulled by two white Percherons in front of the John Street Station in the early 1930s. Gift of Mr. Robert Harrell. Historic Charleston Foundation.

machine. Humane persons always feel a sympathy for the fire horse. His work is so perilous . . . On the other hand, with the elimination of the horse, firefighting will lose much of its romance . . . great, glorious horses at full speed, and driver and crew clinging to [the engine], going to the fire . . . When the horses are gone, what will the departments do for traditions?[21]

Charleston fire chief Behrens reported in 1909 that motor-propelled fleets were proving more economical than horse-drawn equipment in departments across the country, and after attending a 1911 firefighting conference in Milwaukee he was convinced that "equines must give way to motor apparatus."[22] Charleston's first motorized engine, purchased in 1897, was cheaper to maintain than a horse, covered territory three times faster, and the department was saving money by employing fewer drivers.[23] As of 1921, Behrens requested annual funds for replacing three horses and their conveyances with motorized vehicles.[24]

"Old Dick," South Carolina Power Company's last horse, died in 1928, ending an era for the utility company. Old Dick had worked for South Carolina Power for at least twenty years, first pulling a service wagon and later, a package delivery vehicle. Driver John Anderson had worked with Old Dick for a decade and looked after him diligently in the horse's old age. There was a,

> mutual understanding between Dick and John. When Dick died his old keeper wept

bitter tears, such as can come only from the loss of a true friend. John is too old to learn the methods of driving a truck even he even wanted to, so he will now devote his time to the janitor work around the storeroom buildings of the company. Dick was the last of a group of faithful company horses before the advent of the motortruck. Some were retired years ago and spent their last days on Isle of Palms, but Dick and faithful John had worked together so long, none of the officers of the company had the heart to separate them. The devoted pair spent Dick's declining days together, and Dick basked in the tender care of the faithful Negro.[25]

As city and public transportation companies shifted from equine to auto power, so too did private hack companies, delivery drivers, and residents. Undertaker Alexander Connelley took over the family funeral business upon his father's death in 1913. He purchased the first limousines and motorized hearses in September 1916, "when it was unheard of for automobiles to be used in processions to the cemetery . . . the cemetery custodians were doubtful about letting the noisy vehicles through the gates. Before that, carriages drawn by horses were always used for funeral processions."[26] The transition from horse hacks to motor-powered taxis brought a demographic transition for the drivers. There were over 100 white auto chauffeurs carrying passengers, deliveries, and providing baggage service by 1917, when "only a few years ago there were only four or five white chauffeurs here. Now, instead of taking one of the carriages at the rail station, usually called a "night hawk," travelers use an automobile conveyance, and it has just about come to pass that the "night hawks" are seeing their "last days.""[27] Equine-affiliated trades also suffered as the number of horses in the city declined over time. Only two farriers operated in the city by 1948, and a small shop on Queen Street repaired saddle and harnesses, but no one was making and selling new tacks.[28]

The ice industry was the last large business to abandon equines. They introduced gas vehicles in the late 1910s, but it was not until the early 1930s that "motorized equipment began to take over to a major extent," though single-animal carts remained popular for short-distance deliveries in the crowded city center.[29] Southern Ice had sixteen single-animal carts in 1925, six in 1940, and only two by 1950.[30] Veteran ice man Kelly Hughes welcomed his auto truck, "his sentiment for the big horses who used to pull the ice wagon deep enough, but he likes his present electric-driven little truck much better. It maneuvers in King Street's congested traffic with great ease."[31] Southern Ice offered for sale their last two mules, their harnesses, and three single-shaft wagons in October 1951.[32] The *Charleston Evening Post* interviewed the former ice wagon drivers in a nostalgic article titled "End of an Era" which said,

> Not long ago an era ended in Charleston. It passed quickly and almost unnoticed as two mules were hauled away from the old Southern Ice Company stables on Hayne Street.

The last animal-drawn commercial delivery wagon has disappeared from this city's streets. Quartered in a corner of the old stable building, their stalls nearly hidden behind a row of shiny orange trucks, they were used on delivery routes in downtown sections near the stable and plant, giving satisfactory and economical service in that limited area. Perhaps on a simple dollars and cents basis they could have competed with trucks for short hauls indefinitely, but a number of other factors had to be considered. The problem of shoeing, for example, had become so acute, as experienced blacksmiths died or entered other trades, that it alone seemed to make complete mechanization desirable. A big brown mule named Mamie [had] the semi-historic role of being the last animal to haul ice deliveries through the streets of Charleston.[33]

Julius O. Belding, a veteran ice wagon driver with 43 years' experience, drove of one of the last two mules.

> Back in 1908 when he took the reins for his first route, practically all delivery wagons were double rigs, with a team of horses or mules, and trucks were nonexistent. He spoke of busy stables and roaring forges, of matched teams of Percherons, of the mule who knew her route better than the drivers and the horse who started with the green traffic light. Unless children happen by the market as some elderly farmer is unloading vegetables or go down by the battery where the tourist

Old and New: A horse pulls a wooden cart loaded with debris down an unpaved road heading to a shanty town next to the new Grace Bridge over the Cooper River in 1937. Charleston Museum.

bedecked in studded harness . . . as he reminisced, his feeling of real loss at the disappearance of animals from the routine of nearly half a century was revealed.[34]

Belding's favorite equine was "Prince, a big strapping bay, a good looker. He was a horse Mr. Belding drove for the entire decade ending in 1946. He had wisdom and he had strength, blended quite happily with a harmlessly mischievous spirit. He savvied traffic and learned quickly. He made many friends along the route from whom he extracted apples and sugar lumps—often refusing to leave a stop until he had been given his accustomed tribute."[35]

Belding and Prince were out on deliveries when the tornado of 1938 struck, ripping metal roofs from the warehouses along the waterfront and hurling them one hundred feet away and land with a crash alongside their delivery wagon. "Mr. Belding shuttered to think what most horses would have done. Prince's dark eyes rolled wildly, but he didn't move a muscle. By the time Belding jumped from the driver's seat, Prince was his [usual] calm and nipped with characteristic playfulness at the arm that reached up to untangle the harness."[36] Down on East Bay Street, a banker hiding behind a column of Citizens and Southern Bank as the tornado ripped through saw "signs and debris flying past and an ice wagon without a driver went careening by."[37] The wagon flying past with the debris had "blown from Society St. across the lot to Seaboard [rail] building. The driver saw the tornado coming and released the horse."[38]

carriages roll, they'll never get to pet a horse in Charleston anymore. It 'had been sort of nice to see youngsters tiptoeing to give a hesitant but admiring pat on the massive head above them.' It is hard to take the same pride in a piece of steel, no matter how bright the paint, that one did in a glossy bay coat,

The last livery stable in the city, Crull's Red Stables, closed in January 1948. Following severe tornado damage to his Cumberland Street stable in 1938, Crull began relocating to a new facility in St. Andrew's parish outside the city, where he was "in position to render better service to his customers."[39] He sold 12/16 Cumberland to Fred Martschink in 1940, who constructed a one-story Art Deco brick office on the site, now numbered 26 Cumberland.[40] Crull's Church Street stable was converted into an upholstering workshop before being demolished in 1946 and replaced with an office building.[41] He continued operating Red Stable at State and Cumberland until 1948. On the stable's closing, the *Charleston Evening Post* reported,

> so was written the end to what was once one of the most important industries in the city." [Gone were the cattle trains carrying] "handpicked Missouri jenny mules; or 'fine Kentucky thoroughbreds, broken to saddle or harness. And many a Charlestonian of the older generations will recall somewhat wistfully the days when the cobblestoned streets of the city rattled to iron-tired wheels and iron-shod hooves. Crull's was the last of a long line of stables that have been as much a part of the life of Charleston as the tall, masted ships that came from the seas to make this, at one time, the country's richest port. For more than 35 years, [Charles] Crull's stables had resisted the onslaught of the motorized world. Today there is little demand for horses either for work or pleasure and the business is gone.[42]

A large one-story, wood frame stable stood on the rear of the lot, at 9 Linguard Street, until 2019. It had been converted into a carpentry shop by 1951, then into an office, before its demolition for a hotel. Crull sold riding horses, mules, puppies, and livestock from his West Ashley barn into the 1950s, and he died in 1966.[43]

Equine Spaces: Retention

Cities across the nation experienced rapid modernization and accompanying auto-driven development, which hemorrhaged their historic fabric at the start of the twentieth century. In New York City, for example, "most [equine buildings] are gone, the victims of back-alley cleanup campaigns in the mid twentieth century or of later slum clearance and redevelopment programs, erasing from the built environment the memory of the horse powered city."[44] By comparison, Charleston shines as a community with a long-standing preservation ethos, and a place where the legacy of the working equines who built and maintained America's cities is still visible today. Charleston retains historic buildings and outbuildings, and its streetscapes preserve a pedestrian scale suited for both humans and equines; this reflects the pre-modern transportation era in which they were created.

Charleston Renaissance artists of the 1920s and 30s romanticized the city's courts, alleys, narrow lanes, and work yards in their paintings and sketches.[45] Artist Elizabeth O'Neill Verner's works featured decaying but beautiful historic buildings with carriages rolling down

cobblestone streets, and author Dubose Heyward described as Charleston as "an ancient and beautiful city that time had forgotten before it destroyed."[46] Verner and Alice Ravenel Huger Smith nostalgically depicted Black street vendors and horse drawn carts, which were still in use in Charleston but were disappearing in other cities as their governments embarked on slum clearance campaigns that removed stables as well. Verner regretted that she "did not begin etching until 1923. I would prefer having etched the Charleston of my childhood, with its horse drawn streetcars."[47]

Gas stations and surface parking lots had begun encroaching in Charleston by 1920 and were built on the sites of demolished historic buildings. The Preservation Society was founded that year by Susan Pringle Frost and like-minded wealthy residents who wanted to prevent further modern intrusions into the city's historic area. They used their political connections to help pass the first preservation legislation in the United States in 1931, thereby creating Charleston's historic district and establishing a board of architectural review whose purpose is "the preservation and protection of the old historic or architecturally worthy structures and quaint neighborhoods which impart a distinct aspect to the city and which serve as visible reminders of the historical and cultural heritage of the city,

Black vendors unload flowers from horse and cart to sell on Broad Street in a ca. 1930s Charleston Renaissance photograph. Charleston Museum.

the state, and the nation."[48] The nascent parallel tourism movement created further motivation to prevent redevelopment of Charleston's historic core even as the need for auto arteries on and off the peninsula increased with visitor numbers.

"Charleston is perhaps the only city in America that has slammed its front door in Progress's face and resisted the modern with fiery determination," a travel writer quipped in the early twentieth century.[49] As other cities experienced major reconfigurations through the highway acts and urban renewal policies of the post-World War II era, Charleston escaped a wholesale reworking of its transportation grid. Except for the US 17 Crosstown, no major arteries were carved across the existing city to facilitate auto traffic.[50] Preservation-centric choices hinder traffic flow and parking in twenty-first century Charleston, but leave the scale of an equine-dominated era of transportation intact.

The city's preservation ordinances and zoning code prevent demolishing historic buildings including carriage houses and stables and regulate new construction in the historic district. Extant outbuildings are often larger than what current zoning setbacks would permit, so residents readily repurpose outbuildings. Kitchen houses were often attached to the main residence with a hyphen, while carriage houses and stables were usually detached and, as a result, they have been more easily converted into separate residences, offices, and short-term rental units.[51] Adaptive use varies by neighborhood and zoning allowances; in Harleston, outbuildings become offices for College of Charleston's academic departments, and closer to commercial corridors, they might become small shops. Adaptive use predates preservation laws, however, as residents pragmatically reused well-constructed buildings after their initial function became obsolete. In two early examples from the 1880s, the city repurposed Jonathan Lucas's two-story wooden carriage house and stable building on Calhoun Street as part of the new city hospital facilities, while a stable and carriage house at the former Charleston orphan house became a laundry.[52] Many of Charleston's livery stables, warehouses, and carriage shops were converted into auto repair and sale facilities.

Smaller stables and carriage houses mixed in with the city's residential fabric were easy to repurpose. Fifty-five of the approximately 858 stable and affiliated buildings occupied by equines in 1902 were still in use as stables in 1944. As of 1955, at least 238 equine buildings were still extant. Of these buildings, 10 still functioned as stables behind private residences, 135 had been converted to garages and storage, and 93 had been adaptively reused, primarily as residences. Two-thirds of the remaining equine buildings were brick and one-third were wood; 13 one-story wood, 19 two-story wood, 10 one-story brick, 46 two-story brick, and 3 three-story brick buildings. The ten stables in use in 1955 were one-story wooden buildings, located mostly in the upper wards, such as those at Kennedy and Bee Streets, and one at 96 America Street; and behind large residences south of Broad Street, such as those at 3 Lamboll, 31 Legare, 39 Church, and 140 Tradd Streets.

40 Pinckney Street, constructed between 1838 and 1852, was a Kennedy farrier and blacksmith shop in the past and has been adaptively reused as the Andrew Pinckney Inn. The building retains wide carriage doors. Photo by Author.

Repurposed garages were found in every neighborhood of the city—73 were one-story wood; 2 were 1.5-story wood; 22 were two-story wood; 7 were one-story brick; and 31 were two-story brick.[53]

Eighteen stables became business spaces, located near the market area and on commercial corridors or near the waterfront on the east side of the peninsula. Other adaptive commercial uses included a grocery at the corner of Cumberland and State Streets; an antique shop at 62 Queen Street; an appliance store at 23 Pinckney Street; a restaurant at 82/84 North Market

Street; and as ice company offices located at the corner of Anson and Hayne Streets, at 18 Hayne Street, and at the three-story brick buildings at 20 Hayne and 25 Pinckney Streets, Other equine buildings became produce stores, welding shops, and auto service businesses.

The retention of outbuildings preserves the equine past and also provides important reminders of the formerly integrated buildings and neighborhoods as, for instance, carriage houses and stables were home to enslaved Blacks and, later, to freed Black tenants and paid servants. A writer in 1874 observed that, "the magnificent and mean jostle each other very closely in all quarters of the city; tumble down rookeries

are side by side with superb houses."[54] It was common for tradesmen, laborers, hack drivers, draymen, hostlers, and porters to rent small buildings on alleyways partitioned from large lots or portions of outbuildings behind larger residences. Now heavily gentrified and less diverse, we can visualize the racial and ethnic diversity and the equine-human proximity to one another in the city's past by studying the outbuildings turned into condos and apartments that are still found in every neighborhood of the city. Indeed, the very buildings that early preservationists, such as Susan Pringle Frost, viewed as "visible remnants of an inherited set of values— of continuity, gentility, and order—that she and others like her perceived to be threatened in post-World War I Charleston," can now be used as important teaching tools to remind tourists and locals alike of the city's complex and diverse past.[55]

Two early carriage houses successfully turned into dwellings are found at 61 Meeting Street and 11 St. Michael's Alley. They are atypical in that they were located next to, not behind,

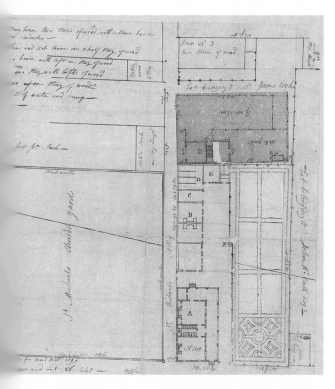

Surveyed in 1780, the McCrady plat 515 shows a single house at the corner of Meeting Street and St. Michael's Alley. The property features a side garden, kitchen house (B), carriage house (C), and a rear one-story stable building (D) with standing stalls. An overlay of a portion of the undated McCrady plat 519 shows the neighboring property's "carriage house and stable with a range of rooms on the second story. of brick" (letter D) and the stable yard. These stable and carriage houses buildings are extant. Charleston County Register of Deeds.

Both the brick carriage house, now 11 St. Michael's Alley, and the one-story brick stable shown on the plats above survive and have been converted into residences. 11 St. Michael's Alley retains a large carriage opening that has been retrofitted with a fanlight and large window. Photo by author.

the house they serviced, which simplified their conversion into separate residences. 11 St. Michael's Alley was built ca. 1780 and converted into dwellings by 1884. It retains an infilled carriage door, and its stable yard is now a garden and used for parking; the original accompanying residence is there no longer.[56] The stable at 61 Meeting Street serviced the neighboring Branford Horry House and opened out to the street. The windows on the first floor originally ventilated the stall bays, with carriage parking on the other side of the carriage door, which, in all probability, aligned with a rear door to access the

work yard. The second floor held a hayloft and living space for the enslaved coachmen; a study of the stable walls revealed the presence of haint blue lime wash paint, indicative of an African American residential space. The building was converted to a dwelling between 1888 and 1902, and fully renovated by Judge Waties Waring as a finer residence after 1913.[57]

Originally George W. Williams's palatial coach house, 19 Church Street was converted in 1943 by engineer Humphrey W. Chadbourne to serve as his residence. The large, brick, hipped roof building was updated with Georgian Revival windows and quoining, but tell-tale fenestration hints that horses once lived there.[58] One hundred eleven Tradd Street is a sizeable brick carriage house that runs lengthwise along the street. Though the orientation makes it appear to be a back building for the house on the corner of Tradd and Legare Streets, it was actually the equine building, constructed ca. 1803, for the palatial Sword Gate House one door down at 32 Legare Street. The carriage building is now a residential space and still part of the Sword Gate parcel and retains an arched carriage passageway that led vehicles and horses into the rear yard.[59]

Recently renovated 12 Lamboll Street is a study in transforming historic stables for modern use. The building encompasses three eras of construction at two properties: the kitchen and carriage house at 12 Lamboll Street are from approximately 1790, while a projecting addition designed to mimic a repurposed outbuilding was constructed in the late 1920s facing Lamboll Street. The ell shaped building shared a party wall with the carriage building of the antebellum O'Donnell House. An arched passageway through the brick wall creates an expansive residence, which retains its carriage bay openings and original interior framing; one family now owns both properties. [60] The carriage house and stable at 25 East Battery Street, constructed in the 1830s, are another exemplary rehabilitation of an equine space, and one of the few that retains its stall features. The Carolopolis Award-winning design by the Glenn Keyes architecture firm converted the carriage house into a guest house, with a kitchen and bathroom installed in the first stable bay at the back of the building. The rest of the stall bays were repaired, the mangers rebuilt, and the floor repaved with brick.[61]

The James Simmons house, constructed ca. 1760 and remodeled in the 1840s, at 37 Meeting Street has a prime example of a stable converted to a weatherized and heated/air conditioned outbuilding as the residents' needs changed. The two-story brick stable located along the northern property line retains its original exposed brick interior walls but has been converted into a home theater. The 0 Atlantic Street lot began as a stable and carriage house for the adjacent Porcher Simons House and is now a separate residence. The Elizabeth Williams house, built ca. 1790, at 35 Legare Street retains an antebellum dependency with arched carriage openings that has been repurposed as a pool house and guest house in an adaptive use that reflects the residential tastes of Charleston's elite in the twenty-first century[62] The brick stables behind

19 Church Street was constructed as the carriage house for the George Williams Mansion on Meeting Street. The building's placement opening onto Church Street facilitated its renovation into a Georgian Revival style residence in 1943. Historic American Buildings Survey.

20 Charlotte Street, the Joseph Aiken house, built ca. 1848, and those at 16 Charlotte Street, and the Robert Martin House, built ca. 1835, are both fitted with formal side-lit entry doors in the former carriage openings and have off-street car parking in the driveways horses and carriages used to access the rear buildings in the past. These are just a few of the dozens of examples of stables and carriage houses turned into residences in the city. Buildings remain a powerful tool for helping modern city residents connect with and visualize the city of the past, especially when they are viewed while riding in horse carriages, reminiscent of those used long ago.

Continued Legacies

Even before trucks and vans replaced the last horse-drawn delivery wagons, Charleston's first equine-powered carriage tour company opened for business. Joseph P. Riley, president of the chamber of commerce and father of future mayor Joseph P. Riley Jr., and Eugene Corrigan established Carriage Tours Inc. in 1949. Thousands of visitors of the past including Presidents Roosevelt and Taft, exposition attendees, northern visitors, and Race Week enthusiasts had toured the city by horse-drawn vehicles so sightseeing by carriage was an existing, if forgotten, concept. "The clop-clop of horses' hooves and the nostalgic site of Victorias with drivers in livery will become a reality on the streets of Charleston within the next three weeks," the *Charleston Evening Post* enthusiastically reported in October 1949.[1] Reintroducing carriages tapped into the growing historic

tourism industry, lending "an Old-World air to already charming Charleston."[2] Drivers would be "trained to point out the historic sites to the tourists. Regular routes for the carriage will be through the old sections of Charleston."[3]

Corrigan purchased four horses from Augusta, Georgia and hired Frank Rembert, a Black coachman with thirty five years of experience, and Andrew Johnson, "who at the turn of the century, drove similar vehicles through the streets of Charleston for private families and for hire."[4] The company secured permission from the city zoning board and the Hibernian Society, of which Riley was a member, to operate a loading stand at Hibernian Hall on Meeting Street. Their advertisements invited customers to "capture the romantic, leisurely mood of bygone days by seeing Charleston scenes from an unhurried, horse drawn carriage."[5] Chamber

A sightseeing coach in front on East Battery Street in 1901. "Thousands of tourists have enjoyed the sights from the elevated seats upon the top of the coach, the places of interest being pointed out by an attendant." *Charleston and the South Carolina Inter-state and West Indian Exposition.* Library of Congress.

of commerce clerk Blanche Cohen took an inaugural ride in a 120-year-old Victoria carriage purchased from the Pistasio Livery of New York City. She said of the experience, "it makes you feel terribly dignified. You wonder how people felt back in the days when it was the only way to travel."[6]

Harry A. Waagner (1890–1980) bought Carriage Tours Inc. in May 1950.[7] Born in Austria, Waagner attended the Spanish Riding School in Vienna and trained polo horses and riding horses in Austria before emigrating to the United States. Charleston's carriage industry grew to include other sole proprietors like Charlie Parker and Wendell Weeks, who expanded in the 1980s to form the Old Towne Carriage Company. Multi-guide companies proliferated in the city, such as Charleston Carriage established by

Dan Hydrick in 1972, who also founded the Carriage Operators of North America organization, and Old South Carriage formed by David J. Compton in 1983.[8] John Roberson established Palmetto Carriage Works in 1972, the longest operating carriage company in the city to the present day. Thomas Doyle Sr. purchased the Palmetto works in 1981 and the company still remains in his family. There were far fewer tourists in the 1980s and being a tour guide was easier because, "you could go wherever you wanted." Drivers used to ride in town during the evenings and trained their horses at Vendue Range when the waterfront park was still a spoilage lot. Male tour guides still outnumber women at least two-to-one, but there were even fewer female drivers in the 1970s.[9]

Sharing the road, a tour guide and his team of horses pass an auto at the turn of the Battery in 1950. Charleston Museum.

RIGHT: Harry Waagner driving his signature touring carriage on East Battery Street in the 1950s. Courtesy of Tom Doyle Sr.

Carriage horse Francis Marion takes a break to graze in the yard of the Patrick O'Donnell House in August 1976. "21 King was our regular water stop and offered limited grazing. Things were a little different forty-five years ago." Courtesy of Tom Doyle Sr.

There are currently four carriage companies in the city, which conduct approximately 40,000 carriage trips per year. The carriages can hold from two to sixteen passengers per ride. Charleston's carriage stables are located around the Market where livery, icehouse, and delivery stables once operated. Waagner's company, later run by the Classic Carriage company, which unfortunately closed as a result of COVID-19, was located at 10 Guignard Street. The building is now rented by the Old South Carriage Company. Palmetto Carriage Works operates from a former sign and carpentry shop at 8 Guignard Street. The Carolina Polo and Carriage company operates from 45 Pinckney Street from a ca. 1858 carriage house.[10] Charleston Carriage, formerly known as the Old Town Carriage company, runs its operations at 20 Anson Street, the site of the former Leonard and Magrath farrier company.

The Tours

Heritage tourism, or "traveling to experience the places, artifacts, and activities that authentically represent the stories and people of the past and present," is an established industry; millions of tourists prioritize visiting historic sites and cities in their travels each year.[11] Public history and heritage tourism professionals have long incorporated living history tools as a way of interpreting the city's vibrant past. Some examples of this are guides that wear costumes of the period, tours incorporating material culture and furnishings of the time, and historic building tours. Interpreters give guided tours, using traditional modes of transportation, as another way of engaging visitors.

Colonial Williamsburg was the first comprehensive living history site in the United States. Its interpreters sought to immerse visitors in the pre-Revolutionary era by restoring and reconstructing the small city back into the old colonial town. Williamsburg offers horse-drawn carriage rides, inviting visitors to "immerse yourself with the sights and sounds of our unique city, far removed from the bustle of modern streets."[12] Historic sites across the United States also utilize traditional transportation as a tourist draw, such as riding mules found at national parks of the

American West, heritage breed programs featuring visiting barns and carriage rides at historic rural sites, and carriage tours in urban historic districts. Whereas Colonial Williamsburg is privately owned site that bars automobiles from the town center, urban historic districts in cities are modern, functioning communities replete with cars, buses, and modern construction mixed in with historic buildings and streetscapes. City carriages now have safety features, such as hazard lights, but they still remain effective tools for connecting visitors with the past.[13]

The local carriage industry fits seamlessly with the city's longstanding practice of connecting tourists with the "old Charleston." Historian Stephanie Yuhl explains that in the early twentieth century, Charleston's "artists, writers, and preservationists enthusiastically celebrated the region's historical artifacts and physical beauty, emphasizing in the process the city's time-worn, nostalgic, and "exotic" aspects."[14] Yuhl and others have noted that the shaping of the city's past for tourists took on an elitist, nostalgic, and even whitewashed view of a colonial and pre-Civil War "golden age," "when the city bustled with commerce and culture and national political influence."[15] Taken against the backdrop of rapid industrialization and changing urban streetscapes in other larger American cities, however, Charlestonians' ambitions to preserve their city coupled with visitors desiring to experience the past with its seemingly agrarian simplicity, makes sense. Tourists from the north and beyond have visited the Lowcountry and even bought former rice plantations, using them as vacation retreats

for horseback riding and hunting. Horses naturally fit in with the region's tourism model as a living link to the past.

The city government has marketed, shaped, and regulated the tourism industry. The city began requiring new and veteran carriage drivers, walking, and bus tour guides alike to get a license for their operations, obtained by passing a written and oral Lowcountry history exam as of 1975. Licenses renewed every three years when guides completed the requisite city-sponsored continuing education classes. After decades without contest, three aspiring walking tour guides unable to pass the exam challenged the licensing requirement in court. A federal judge ruled the Charleston's tour guide licensing requirements as unconstitutional as a free speech violation in 2017. Though no longer mandated by the city, many walking guides and bus companies and all, but one, carriage business still require that their guides be licensed. The Charleston Tours Association's Palmetto Guild "represents certified tour guides who have demonstrated proficiency on an exam administered by the City of Charleston. Guild members are professionals who are committed to historical accuracy, continuing education, and providing an engaging experience for all visitors."[16]

Tourists consistently rate history as their top reason for visiting Charleston, a draw that the city's tourism management office and the Charleston Visitors Bureau along with myriad tour companies and agencies use in their marketing of the city as a desirable vacation spot. Visitors are diverse, however, and have varying expectations of the kind of history they want to experience. Carriage tour guides are similarly varied in their interpretive approach; some guides favor conveying information with a more traditional and conservative perspective, while others reflect the changing larger interpretive movement when they interpret history in a more inclusive, honest, and critical way.[17] Discussion of slavery and Black Charlestonians in general was often patronizing at best or completely absent from previous tourism narratives. Part of that traditional bias has likely stemmed from the limited amount and the way the content was presented in the city-sanctioned tour guide training manual (it was not until the 2010 version of the guide that a chapter on Black Charlestonians was added), and also perhaps because novice guides have been trained by those with more conservative views.[18]

Carriage and other tour companies are businesses that must balance education with entertainment, providing accurate history in a way that does not whitewash the complex history of southern cities, while engaging paying customers of varying ages, education levels, and areas of interest. Carriage drivers have a unique opportunity to share and interpret the city's diverse history with a wide range of visitors. In their work on the commemoration and memory of slavery, race and the Confederacy in Charleston, historians Blain Roberts and Ethan Kytle took several carriage tours in 2007 and 2008, finding that "moonlight and magnolias often accompanied denial and deflection".[19] They also made note of one company's uniforms, kitsch

pseudo-Confederate ensembles replete with white cotton shirt, red sash, and grey kepi caps, as particularly egregious; the company has since replaced them with khaki shorts and simple straw hats. Roberts and Kytle's tour survey was but a snapshot of an industry, but their assessment raised important interpretive questions.[20]

A preliminary survey of Trip Advisor carriage tour customer reviews from the past decade regarding mentions of slavery demonstrates that some visitors felt slavery was not adequately covered in the hour-long narrative.[21] Fewer customers complained of too much emphasis on slavery, one customer called their tour "a page straight out of the BLM playbook . . . the overarching theme of the ride was slavery."[22] Two critical reviews in May 2016 condemned a male guide's argument that the Civil War was about states' rights, not slavery, "the whole neo-Confederate nonsense that has no place in the 21st century."[23] An April 2019 rider found the tour to be a "whitewash history of Charleston"[24] and a June 2016 passenger was disappointed that "slavery and the Civil War, which shaped and contributed to the very essence of Charleston, would barely get a mention."[25]

Carriage tour narratives are changing due to larger changes in historical interpretation; the city's more detailed account of Black history in their guide manual and continuing education series reflects this. Before closing, Classic Carriage offered a "Slavery to Freedom" tour that focused on the city's Black history. Roberts and Kytle noted narrative improvements during a 2015 research visit—"we overheard several tour guides talking about the region's history of slavery. One even mentioned plantation overseers and slave drivers, topics that were virtually unspeakable a mere decade earlier."[26] Hundreds of later positive Trip Advisor reviews mentioned that slavery was discussed, along with other aspects of Charleston's history.

Responding to customer feedback asking for more Black history, Tommy Doyle Jr. implemented a tour guide continuing education course in late 2020 for Palmetto Carriage employees, bringing in experts such as Joe McGill of the Slave Dwelling Project; Shawn Halifax, director of McLeod Plantation, a Charleston county park that pioneered the practice of interpretation occurring at slave dwellings themselves rather than at the main mansion; and brought in other professional historians to lecture on Black history topics. When training tour guides for the company, the author emphasizes that slave dwellings and carriage houses are a tangible way to bring slavery into the narrative. The sheer quantity and diverse locations of outbuildings show modern-day visitors how widespread both equines and enslaved persons who built and operated the city were in the landscape of the past.

Regulating the Carriage Industry

Carriage tourism has grown in tandem with the city's overall tourism industry and has become one of the most-regulated aspects of tourism. Rules expanded over time to address the handling of equine waste on city streets, animal welfare and traffic issues along with carriage volume. Some carriage operators fought the changes, claiming they were counter to tradition or injurious to their businesses, while others have seen regulations as necessary for carriages and cars to safely coexist, and as necessary for creating the best atmosphere for residents, customers, and their equines.

As more carriages came, there was more manure left on city streets than there had been since equine delivery businesses ceased operations, and in December 1975, Charleston became the first city in the nation to adopt an equine diaper ordinance. Downtown resident Francis Brenner joked, "the fact that the odor of so much carriage traffic through the streets only makes the picture of life in the 18th century more real did not make residents happy."[27] *Carriage Journal* reported that "the operators are fighting on the grounds that such an ordinance is discriminatory and contrary to tradition."[28] John Roberson contacted St. Augustine's city manager and learned that instead of using diapers, they employed a "white wing" street sweeper during the day, followed by a mechanical sweeper each night.[29] Their city manager noted, "we do feel that our carriage fleet greatly enhances our tourist trade, since they have been on the scene so many years, they have become a tradition." Roberson sent a proposal to the city offering to conduct street cleaning during tour hours for $700 per animal per year.[30]

In a temporary victory for the carriage operators, Charleston municipal Judge Hugo Spitz declared the diaper ordinance, "invalid

Tour guide David Roach has fun with a mule for Palmetto Carriage's Mule Day competitions in the 1980s. She is wearing the requisite equine diaper to keep the streets clean. Author's collection.

and unreasonable, and constitutes unnecessary suffering, physical distress, and inflammation." Residents countered that a New Orleans company had been using diapers for three years with no reports of harm or discomfort. The diaper debacle garnered national attention when Johnny Carson discussed the regulations on his show. Tom Doyle Sr. attributes the "free advertising" with boosting carriage ridership for decades; "the press was everywhere. People got interested in us."[31] Mayor Joseph Riley Jr. took office in 1976 and reinstated the ordinance and Harry Waagner retired when the new diapering regulations took effect.[32] Carriage equines are still required to wear diapers when on tour and the diapers are emptied every hour. A sanitation truck, paid for by the carriage companies through annual fees, responds to diaper malfunctions and urine spills.

Drivers drop a marker on the street and an on-call sanitation worker sprays and disinfects the area.

The city council amended the carriage ordinance in March 1978 to prohibit driving carriages on cobblestone and brick streets, and barred them from several narrow streets to prevent traffic bottlenecks. John Roberson broke the rules to create a test case and was arrested for driving down a prohibited street. County Judge Theodore Stoney ruled in favor of Roberson, so the city's attorneys filed an appeal with the state supreme court. Roberson's lawyers argued that buses were just as likely to cause traffic congestion, that pushing carriages onto the main streets traversed by more cars would add to the congestion, and that the new regulations were injurious to his business. Tours had become monotonous with the street limitations, and, worse, "carriages now must travel past sometimes dangerous situations such as workmen using equipment that could startle an animal."[33] The court countered that "no one has the inherent right to carry his private business along the public streets. Such rights are exercised only under such terms and conditions imposed by the city authorities." [34] The street restrictions were upheld.

The city began regulating tour departure locations in the 1980s. Drivers previously left from self-selected points on White Point Garden and near the Battery, but thenceforth all tours would leave from the market area. Many operators believed that relocating would be catastrophic for business. "Roberson fought the change; it was a deal breaker for him. I had 'save the carriages' stickers made and hired attorney Gedney Howe to strong arm the city," said Tom Doyle Sr. Roberson even placed a funeral wreath at White Point Garden with a banner reading "end of an era."[35] The market relocation, however, proved to be a boon rather than deterrent when the city revitalized the city market in the 1980s as a tourist draw.[36]

In 1986, the city council divided the residential historic district into zones to reduce carriage congestion, similar to the designated draying and carting zones of the antebellum era, but for passengers instead of freight. East and South Battery and Rainbow Row, the most sought-after tourist areas, comprised zones 1 and 2. Companies competed in a monthly lottery for the twenty zone 1 and 2 tags, while the remaining carriages would operate in zone 3. *News and*

Courier editor Thomas Waring noted, "as a resident of the neighborhood, I am familiar with the good and bad things about carriages. The novelty of horses appeal to me as a community asset, so long as they do not make traffic too slow or dangerous." At that time, five companies ranging in size from twenty-five guides to a single driver operated thirty-seven carriages in the city.[37]

The city prohibited evening tours in residential areas and further reduced the number of carriage tags for the South of Broad zones in 1993, "to improve the quality of life for downtown residents who understand tourism's value to the city but who are often bothered by the horse urine and congestion from traffic." Tom Doyle Sr. struck back at the wealthy residents, saying, "for the people who have the highest quality of life, they do the most complaining." The ordinance set a cap of twenty carriages on tour at any given time. Medallions would be issued for each tour to reduce animosity over having a zone 3 tag for the entire month. City tourism staff at the city gate at the corner of North Market and Church Streets determined each carriage's route by operating a bingo machine with colored balls, six for zone 1, six for zone 2, and 8 for zone 3.[38] The city charges a head tax per passenger, paid by the carriage companies, to generate revenue and fund their regulatory staff. The routes have been adjusted periodically by ordinance. As of 2022, there are 28 medallions for the principal carriage routes, zones 1, 2, 3, and 5, broken into A and B sub-routes with different ingresses to further disperse carriage traffic. There are six additional medallions for zone 4, "used as a relief valve system . . . for use on city holidays, on the 30 busiest days of the year as determined by the industry, and on other such days as the director of livability and tourism deem necessary."[39] When all tags are in use, carriages queue to await a returning tag.

Even with street restrictions, the zones are large and there are myriad route iterations a driver can create within their designated zone. Charleston's zones comprise the largest carriage operating area in the nation with its many possible carriage routes. While New York City carriage tours are restricted to Central Park and tours in New Orleans only operate in the French Quarter and Faubourg Marigny neighborhood, Charleston's departure point at the market area is in the middle of the city, which has no large central business district to divide one historic borough from another. Carriage tours travel through South of Broad, Ansonborough, the French Quarter, Harleston Village, and even the Wraggborough area above Calhoun Street. The zone and route diversity not only spreads carriages out and reduces congestion, it also means that people see horses and mules in a much larger context than in other cities, further reinforcing modern Charleston's connection to equines.

New Orleans, which began operating historic carriage tours in 1941 and has an equally large carriage trade, has similar industry regulations which have informed Charleston's ordinances and vice versa. Royal Carriages of New Orleans is the largest company currently operating in the United States with a sixty-mule herd;

Palmetto Carriage is the second largest. In the 1980s, Royal owner Jimmy Lauga and Dr. James Beirmann, DVM, "worked with the City of New Orleans to establish the laws and regulations regarding the commercial carriage industry that are still in effect," including setting passenger limits, animal condition and harnessing standards, stall size and feed requirements, a minimum number of breaks and work hour limitations per day, and speed limits no faster than a slow trot. Mules, owing to the fact they tolerate heat better than other kinds of equines, are the only ones permitted on city streets before 5 p.m. in summer months, per city ordinance; all New Orleans companies now use mules exclusively, as a way of ensuring more uniform compliance with regulations.[40] The city proposed legislative changes in 2019, including the institution of a policy of ceasing tour operations when temperatures reach 95 degrees; this change has not been implemented to date. Most New Orleans companies run a 6-hour morning tour shift starting around 9:00 a.m., and a second shift of mules and drivers operate night tours from late afternoon until 11:00 p.m. during the summer.[41] The number of carriage licenses in both Charleston and New Orleans are fixed, although the number of tourists in general continues to increase.

Veteran carriage man Tony Youmans spent 20 years in the Charleston carriage industry and witnessed most of the regulatory changes. He began as a guide for Palmetto Carriage, became a manager, then took a management position at Old Towne Carriage. Youmans is now the director of the Old Exchange and Provost Dungeon, a city-operated historic site, and remembers his time working with equines and carriages fondly, crediting the industry with introducing him to heritage tourism. In the 1980s, "we were constantly growing and learning to do business better. Every company had their own marketing. Old South brought the flashy look, moonlight and magnolias, and the uniforms. But we all did our homework, were hungry to read and learn more. I'm so proud of the product we offered." Companies invested in satellite ticket stands and sold pre-booked specials, where tour guides picked up cruise ship passengers or conference attendees from hotels like the Omni Charleston Place. "The city learned too, what worked for residents and the operators. There was a point where you couldn't get all the companies in a room together, we all hated each other over the competition. The growth period was stressful. Bob Reed suggested the rotating tag idea, the lotto system, and it ended the warring. But we were all friends. I never knew someone gay, and there were so many in the industry. I grew as a person from the diversity, I got to know an incredible variety of talented individuals."[42] As manager at Old Town, Youmans set to work renovating the barn, saying,

> We'd go to pains to keep [the horses] happy and comfortable in their stalls, loads of bedding, good baths. It's the ultimate compliment that our animals would lay down at night. We started getting more equine professionals. Jenny Nance [an active guide who started in

the 1980s] was on the College of Charleston equestrian team, she brought loads of knowledge. The companies partnered to hire two UGA vets to do a report about how we could improve animal welfare and they came back with the main critique that some of them were too fat! Tom Doyle started working more with the Amish. We learned by doing. And operators from across the country come here to Charleston still to learn from us. We do it safely, responsibly, and professionally. When you look at the number or tours and animals and accident incidents, you won't find safer [transportation].[43]

The carriage business is not without controversy in this twenty-first century. Residents continue to complain about carriage traffic congestion and zone violations. Based on the recommendations of the thirty-member tourism management advisory committee, the city, in 2014, hired three tourism enforcement officers charged with regulating carriage, walking and bus tours, and managing tourism issues writ large.[44] The results of a study published in the *Journal of Tourism Research* found that out of 524 Charleston area residents surveyed on eight questions related to tourism management, of whom 12% live in the historic district, 66% in the nearby suburbs, and 22% lived further from the city, only 19.5% believed carriages should be banned from the city, a finding that surprised people.[45] Where the respondents lived did not impact their answers:

for example, horse carriages can be a legitimate aggravation to those living downtown, for their noise, odor, and traffic obstruction. As such, one would have expected to see downtown residents more strongly opposed to carriage tours than other residents. However, no such difference was noted. The debate between those wishing to maintain the nostalgic draw of carriages versus those wishing to discontinue the tours based on a concern for the animal's rights does not hinge on where one lives.[46]

Animal rights activists clash with the people who work with animals. The Charleston Carriage Horse Advocates campaign for ending the carriage industry while the Charleston Association for Responsible Equine Safety promotes the industry and its goal is "to educate the public about the love and care we provide our animals and dispel the myths that surround our industry."[47] Some carriage industry supporters argue that anti-carriage people are, for the most part, wealthy city residents who feign animal welfare concerns as a guise for their real goal of preventing tourism and traffic in their neighborhoods.[48] The Carriage Horse Advocates stance is that the carriage industry exploits animals, that Charleston is too hot for equines, that the city-mandated carriage weight limit is too heavy; some of its members equate equine work to slavery.[49] The Charleston Animal Society (CAS), the current nonprofit iteration of the local SPCA, "is not opposed to working animals and has not called for a ban of the carriage industry," but is

campaigning for an industry review to evaluate current ordinances and lower the temperature operating threshold.[50] It is worth noting the ASPCA's, which was founded to protect carriage animals, stance on the industry:

> The ASPCA is not opposed to the use of horses and other equines in pulling carts and carriages for hire, provided that all of the animals' physiological and behavioral needs are fully met, housing and stable conditions are humane, and their working hours and conditions are carefully regulated as to temperature, humidity, proximity to traffic, rest periods, etc. Working equines should receive regular veterinary and farrier care and be provided a humane retirement when no longer able to work.[51]

Mayor Bill De Blasio placed New York City at the forefront of the anti-carriage movement in 2014 when he vowed to disband the carriages in Central Park. Linda Almeida interviewed carriage drivers, stable owners, and historians about their experience in the industry. De Blasio's "pronouncement set off a storm of controversy with heated pushback from horse drivers and stable owners, many of them Irish, who protested their portrayal as abusers of animals. They defended their industry and its practices as ethical and a cultural staple of the city."[52] Historian Hilary Sweeney argues that horse and carriages have been a part of Central Park from its initial design, and though "suggestions that horses should not live in cities continue today . . . there is no evidence that horses cannot thrive in cities once they are cared for properly."[53] New York City's anti-carriage controversies have heightened tensions in cities across the nation that also rely on carriage tourism dollars. Charleston's carriage debate is similar in that differing classes of residents have a variety of opinions about the tension between preserving tradition and supporting animal rights.[54]

Charleston's summer tourism operating parameters have been a key issue for animal rights activists. Following two years of meetings and research, a special committee of city representatives, including equine veterinarian Dr. John Malark, carriage operators, and city-government appointed members, presented their recommendations for regulating the industry in 2006. One such recommendation called for the institution of an operating heat cap of 98 degrees or a combined heat and humidity reading of 180 degrees. Activists pushing for lower temperature limits claimed that the committee was biased because Dr. Marlark counted a carriage company as one of his clients; he owned the Edisto Equine Clinic, and was the only board-certified equine surgeon in the state. "I really felt like we were hitting a spot where everyone was pretty happy, and all of a sudden it was like a political movement just jumped up," said Malark. He continued by saying, "I hope they don't derail the whole process and cut down two years of work."[55] Following continued tourism management committee meetings and welfare activist requests, the city, in 2017, lowered the heat threshold to 95 degrees or to a heat index limit of 110.[56] Calls to further lower the threshold

continue. CAS requested an "independent study" to review heat and weight guidelines, both bones of contention. Charleston's carriage operating ordinance stipulates that carriage horses must weigh at least 950 pounds and are allowed to pull a maximum of three times their weight, including passengers and the weight of the wheeled vehicle.[57] Both the Palmetto and Old South carriage companies told the subcommittee of the city's Tourism Commission that "they would not allow their animals to be used an any study arranged by CAS because they didn't believe it would be unbiased and fair."[58]

In the last decade, studies have been published in the *Journal of Equine Veterinary Science* and other periodicals addressing carriage equine care and the impact of work, with favorable findings for the industry. A 2015 study measured the physiological and hematological state of ten small breed carriage horses in Vina del Mar, Chile to assess any negative work impacts by analyzing their heart and respiratory rates, rectal temperatures, bloodwork, and general dispositions. Heart and respiratory rates showed significant increases after work but recovered to basal values within ten minutes. No physiological issues were observed, nor any blood variations after exertion. The study authors concluded that, "the light crossbred tourism carriage horses studied seem to have adapted physiologically to their work activity, and the existence of a welfare problem cannot be determined with the variables assessed. Future studies should also include indicators of good mental and behavioral state to provide a more holistic view of their welfare state."[59]

The Rosser and Ardis study of Charleston carriage horse and mule welfare conducted in the years 2009–12 analyzed data from city veterinary reports for five carriage companies operating at the time, and from private management records, and from additional veterinary data provided voluntarily by one company. The authors explained, "welfare concerns regarding equids working as carriage animals have been recently highlighted by the press, although little data exists to describe working conditions, regulations, and veterinary attention. Despite the paucity of objective data, many articles and websites advocate a ban on carriage animals in different parts of the United States. Outlawing carriage companies will increase the numbers of unwanted horses as did the ban on USDA regulated horse slaughter." Their research was intended to assess veterinary care and overall herd health. They found that city equines worked an average of 4.6 hours per work day, led an average of 865 tours per year, and worked between 163 and 188 days per year. The authors assessed city veterinary records and determined that the animals for all companies were receiving adequate care and that the industry was well regulated. Hoof issues were the most common health concern. The findings from the survey company that had voluntarily provided their data showed that equines worked an average of 173 workdays, had 128.5 pasture days, and were given 62 barn days off. Their records showed that equines in their care were up to date with required city serviceability

examinations, vaccinations, and worming. Feed consisted of grain and pelleted fodder, hay, hoof and salt supplements, and bran mash to encourage water consumption and prevent impactions that can cause colic. The survey company had no work violations during the four survey years. The authors concluded that in their "opinion, these animals were thriving [for the survey company], and management had implemented good record keeping and regularly scheduled hoof maintenance."[60] Edisto Equine Veterinary Practice owner Dr. John Malark noted in 2009 that, "Charleston is the gold standard in the United States, maybe a lot of folks don't appreciate what a good job they do", as he rated Palmetto and Old South Carriage Company animal care as "phenomenal"; the statements were made in response to industry-wide criticisms after a city judge fined Carolina Polo and Carriage Company for animal care violations.[61]

Veterinary researchers from Western University, in 2015, studied eighteen New York City horses to evaluate the health and welfare of carriage equines, by measuring cortisol in saliva and examining fecal samples for evidence of stress. Thirteen randomly-selected horses on work rotation and stabled in the city, and five pastured horses on scheduled annual furlough were the control group; the researchers used the data obtained and analyzed as a reference point for the study. Chief researcher Joseph Bertone DVM explained,

> I wanted to identify the effect [city work] has on these horses. Ultimately, I'm concerned

about equine welfare. On the other hand, I'm also concerned over claims that could dismantle, or likely end, the lives of these grand horses. The same claims could see the loss of an iconic NYC institution, the loss of the important human-animal bond the drivers have with these spectacular animals. As well as have a profound negative economic impact on the people whose lives this would touch . . . it's important we collect the research and analyze the results objectively. In other words, let's deal with the facts."[62]

The researchers found no physical evidence of stress such as ulcers, and noted that the horses rested comfortably at night, indicating a safe, peaceful environment. "The data showed no statistical difference in the level of fecal cortisol in working and resting horses," leading the authors to conclude that "these working NYC carriages horses did not have physiologic responses indicative of negative welfare status."[63]

The debate in Charleston will likely continue simmering while city tourism authorities, anti-carriage advocates, residents, and pro-carriage proponents continue meeting periodically to review operating standards. Tom Doyle Sr. notes, "there's not many options for horses in today's world, but animals still have a place in society, they're very adaptable. I've watched it my whole life, don't tell me they can't work in the city." The most important trait for a city equine is disposition. Tommy Doyle Jr. explains, "it has zero to do with strength and all to do with having the right mind and being able to deal

Standardbred crosses Yogi and Booboo take a water break under fans and shade screens on a summer day. Courtesy of Palmetto Carriage Works.

with city stimuli. The environment is conducive for easy work, it's flat and load sizes are limited. I look for animals that already work under harness, and we take an animal that knows the trade and teach them a new environment."[64] Coming from a farm, "they don't know what a napkin is blowing across the street. They might startle at a car trunk opening. But it's cute to see them watch and learn something new. You bond with your animal, you train yourself to relax, they feel your energy. I talk in a calm voice, I'm there to reassure them. I'm always communicating with my horse," says Youmans.[65] He was appointed by Mayor Riley to the tourism management commission and spent seven years as its only carriage operator member; "it's so difficult to sit there with people who hate what you do. But my job was to explain the reality on the street, give an unbiased opinion about whether a driver could have or should have pulled over when they got a citation, and to find a balance between residents' and carriage business concerns. I'd challenge opposition folks to take a tour and come visit the barns."[66]

Current touring carriages include vis-à-vis models, wagonettes, and larger wagons with four bench seats facing forward to accommodate sixteen passengers. They are all double axled, four-wheeled vehicles with frames placed on leaf springs with roller bearing wheels and rubber tires; they also have a fifth wheel below the carriage frame for a tighter turning radii and better maneuverability. The sixteen-person wagons were created by Old South's carpenter Jerry Osmore. Tony Youmans calls it, "the Nimitz class, and the other companies started using the wagon size too. That's when the business really changed."[67] Today, the large carriage frames are made with composite materials to create a lighter frame than those on traditional wagons or omnibuses.[68]

Charleston carriage animals wear rubber or composite shoes attached to traditional metal horseshoes for absorbing shock and protecting them from heat on the pavement. The lighter carriage bodies and the commendable city mandates that animal must receive a minimum of fifteen-minute break between tours and that operations cease at 95 degrees have made carriage work less physically demanding on equines than it was when the tourism industry first began. City ordinances require that equines' temperatures be taken after every tour when outdoor temperatures rise to 85 degrees or higher, although most companies already take and record temperatures

year-round, and that equines could only work a maximum of eight hours in a 24-hour period. The rules also state that they cannot work more than six consecutive days and that they are put out to pasture for at least six weeks annually. The city's livability and tourism division regulates stable conditions, feed, animal size, carriage weight and working conditions. The carriage companies have farms on neighboring islands where horses and mules spend their time off. The Palmetto and Old South Carriage companies rest their equines for an average of nineteen weeks per year, which goes beyond the required minimums.[69]

Charleston annual visitor numbers increased by 70% between 1980 and 2015. In 2019 alone, 7.3 million visitors came to the region, which led to an economic impact of more than $8 billion.[70] Tom Doyle Sr. attributes part of the anti-carriage sentiment to the sheer volume of tourists, but "there's a place here people want to see, we can't get away from that now. Look at a big recession after the Civil War, all the way to the 1960s. I was here then, it was still a mess. We spend a billion for a seawall, but who are we protecting it for if we don't want visitors anymore?"[71] The industry continues to evolve with technological change and tourism trends. Doyle also cites incorporation of business management changes early as key to Palmetto Carriage's success, first with careful placement of ticket stands in the city, and now with the use of the Internet for pre-booking and advertising purposes.[72]

Tommy Doyle Jr. notes that the logistics of the job has become harder as the city grows, and as more strict regulations are implemented. "Some of the old sole proprietors had a hard time adjusting to all the new regulations. For Waagner it was the diapers, for Parker it was the zones, for Roberson it was not being allowed on certain streets. I haven't hit my tipping point. I was born into this industry, and most of it I still love. Talking to people, sharing the horse experience. I love letting people meet animals and bridging that gap between modern and historic Charleston."[73] Youmans notes, "we work in an industry that's so unique, but then it's not! It's a timeless tradition that we keep alive in an age of technology. You're transported back a hundred years. When you drive in Charleston, you can see things no one else gets to see. We see the city from horse height, it's a gift and a blessing."[74] When asked about the future of carriage tourism in Charleston, Tom Doyle Sr. says, "I really hope it continues and animals will always have a place in our lives. Carriages have long been the symbol of Charleston, and it's still the case today."[75]

Afterword

Writing this book was challenging as it was enjoyable, because many aspects of the equine city of the past were so ubiquitous that residents took horses and mules, their sounds and smells, and constant presence in the city for granted. Mentioning the sound of a draymen giving verbal commands to his mule, or the clatter of horse hooves on hard pavement in a letter or diary would be akin to a twenty-first century city dweller noting that they stopped for gas or

honked at a slow driver on the way to work. On the other hand, there are hundreds more extant equine buildings in the city, each with their own untold story. *Charleston Horse Power* is intended to be a first foray into an important subject. Future scholars might delve further into studying equine buildings, a chapter that can expanded into a comprehensive book of its own, with additional survey work and cataloging.

Carriage manufactory, technology, stylistic changes over time, along with biographies of drivers and the class and racial parameters in which they operated, deserves further attention. Charleston tourism is a complex topic, and a future researcher might want to parse out the nuances of how the city's interpretive story, for both carriages and the local tourism industry as a whole, has changed over time, and how the carriage tour industry in Charleston compares to businesses in other cities or countries. My goal in writing this book is to help residents and visitors understand that equines played a key role in building the city, bringing supplies into and out of the city, and conveying humans through it daily for hundreds of years. I hope readers will become cognizant of the equine past that resonates through the city today through extant equine buildings, through the tourist carriages that meander through the historic district, and understand why present-day Charlestonians view the equine impact as both a source of frustration and delight. Those of us who work with horses are fortunate to witness the timeless enjoyment they bring, and they have ability to share that joy with others.

APPENDIX A

SANBORN FIRE INSURANCE MAP
ANALYSIS OF STABLE BUILDINGS

Stables and associated buildings, extant in 1902

One-story wood	530 in the city; several outside city limits
One-and-a-half-story wood	18 in city; one outside
Two-story wood	134; one outside
Three-story wood	1
One-story brick	39
One-and-a-half-story brick	1
Two-story brick	124
Three-story brick	3

Stables and associated buildings constructed between 1902 and 1929

One-story wood	108
One-and-a-half-story wood	2
Two-story wood	27
Three-story wood	0
One-story brick	8
One-and-a-half-story brick	1
Two-story brick	6

Stables and associated buildings constructed between 1929 and 1944

One-story wood	15
One-and-a-half-story wood	1
Two-story wood	2

APPENDIX B

Number of animals and vehicles taxed in the city

YEAR	HORSES AND MULES	CARRIAGES, BUGGIES, ETC.	DRAYS, CARTS, WAGONS	YEAR	HORSES AND MULES	CARRIAGES, BUGGIES, ETC.	DRAYS, CARTS, WAGONS
1881	1,524	456	1,108	1903	1,160	298	617
1882	1,599	423	1,098	1904	1,240	280	660
1883	1,530	433	1,080	1905	1,628	257	689
1884	1,524	456	1,108	1906	1,168	283	647
1885	1,513	430	1,078	1907*			
1886	1,543	443	1,136	1908	1,131	299**	639
1887	1,584	473	1,096	1909	1,070	294	625
1888	1,510	433	1,091	1910	1,044	308	604
1889	1,477	455	1,036	1911	1,057	422	613
1890	1,528	457	1,078	1912	973	445	592
1891	1,478	470	1,026	1913	959	459	593
1892	1,523	436	1,062	1914	929	526	592
1893	1,545	463	1,046	1915	787	506	551
1894	1,364	415	914	1916	785	803	555
1895	1,335	387	860	1917	766	1,175	555
1896	1,307	387	771	1918	767	1,155	536
1897	1,077	338	765	1919	639	1,033	470
1898	1,135	316	741	1920	506	1,043	357
1899	1,222	333	735	1921	439	2,849	340
1900	1,212	302	726	1922	401	3,444	338
1901	1,218	314	696				
1902	1,178	306	659				

Note. Not itemized after 1923.

*Year not itemized. **Includes autos, carriages, and buggies.

City fire department equines

YEAR	NO. OF EQUINES	YEAR	NO. OF EQUINES
1882	25	1909	30
1884	28	1910	31
1885	28	1911	34
1886	28	1912	28
1888	29	1913	28
1892	29	1914	28
1893	28	1918	24
1894	27	1919	21
1895	29	1921	13
1896	28	1923	13
1897	27	1924	11
1898	30	1925	11
1899	30	1926	4
1900	*	1927	4
1901	30	1928	4
1902	32	1929	4
1903	30	1930	4
1904	29	1932–35	3
1905	28	1936	3
1906	28	1939	3
1907	28		
1908	29		

Note. * = no data return in Charleston Yearbook.

Public works/streets department equines

YEAR	HORSES	MULES
1903	*	17 for scavenger
1904	*	31
1905	*	*
1906	3	23
1907	3	27
1908	3	39
1909	4	44
1909	1	44
1910	3	47
1911	3	47
1912	3	45
1913	3	42
1915	3	36
1917	3	50
1919	*	49
1920	3	49
1921	3	48
1922	3	48
1932	*	45
1933		42 in January; 24 by December

Note. 1934 onward, not enumerated.

* = no data return in Charleston Yearbook.

APPENDIX C

LIVERY STABLE LISTINGS
FROM THE *CITY DIRECTORIES*

1861

LOCATION	BUILDING MATERIAL	OWNER	STABLE NAME
9 Legare	Brick	Samuel D. Holloway, fpc. [free person of color]	Holloway Livery Stables
14 Chalmers	Brick	Estate of John Chas. Blum	John M. Haley's Stables
24 Chalmers	Brick	Estate of William Calder	Planter's Hotel Stables
30 Chalmers	3 Brick buildings	James P. Earle	Purcell's Stables
144 Church	Brick	William Hockaday	Hockaday's Stables
7 Anson	*	William Hockaday	Hockaday's Stables
29 Pinckney	Brick	R. Douglas and Co.	Charleston Hotel Stables
9 Bedons	Wood	Moses Levy	Stables
70 Church	Wood	John Deighen	Deighen's Stables
13 Shepard	Wood	R. Douglas and Co.	R. Douglas and Co. Stables
10 St. Philip	Wood	William Schnierle	R. Mackhunny's Livery Stable

Note. This table presents 1861 Charleston Census data.

* = no building material data available.

1870

LOCATION	OWNER	OWNER RACE OF
Spring near King	J. M. Alexander	White
137 Market	F. Brailsford	Colored
504 King	John Christopher	White
29 Pinckney	Douglas and Jackson	White
24 Chalmers	J. Kessel	White
49 Society	P. Lee	White
51 Hasell	Richard McHunny	Colored
36 Bull	Riley, Stephney and Son	White
12 Chalmers	M. Wallace	White

1882 Stables

CARRIAGE

LOCATION	OWNER	OWNER RACE OF
30 Meeting	Eugene Brown	Colored
70 Queen	J. Brown	Colored
22–24 Chalmers	John Fraser	White
131 Coming	J. Jones	Colored
49 Society	P. Lee	White
129 Church	Jerry Rhodes	Colored
21 Bull	S. W. B. Riley	Colored
129 Church	J. Robertson	Colored
25 Duncan	W. H. Shrewsbury	Colored

LIVERY AND SALE

LOCATION	OWNER	OWNER RACE OF
29 Pinckney[1]	Charleston Hotel Stables	White
691 King	Gooding and Mull	White
85, 87, 89 Church	C. D. McCoy	White

1882 STABLES (CONT.)
SALE

LOCATION	OWNER	OWNER RACE OF
30 Chalmers	R. Graham and Co.	White
105 Meeting	H. Horres	White
9 Bedons Alley[2]	M. Levy	White
King	A. W. Meyer	White

1890

LOCATION	OWNER	OWNER RACE OF
164 Church	W. J. Black	*
87 Rutledge	Eugene Brown	Colored
62 Queen	Jason Brown	Colored
29 Pinckney	Charleston Hotel	White
22 Chalmers	John Fraser	Colored
King north of Shepard	Gooding and Co.	*
60 Queen	Robert Graham	White
620 King	Henry Haesloop	White
635 King	J. H. Hawthorn	White
143 Coming	John Jones	Colored
87 Society	G. B. Lee	White
4 St. Philip	James McAllister	White
117 Church	Charles McCoy	White
29 Vanderhorst	S. W. Robinson	White
76 Market	J. P. Sweeney	White
624 and 626 King	Alexander Williford	White

Note * = race unknown.

1901

LOCATION	OWNER	OWNER RACE OF
4 St. Philip	C. Bacon and Co.	White
62 Queen	Jason Brown	Colored
58, 60 Queen	Charleston Livestock	N/A
63 Market	Jonn F. Fraser	White
162, 164 Church	Harper Brothers	White
635 King	J. W. Hunt	White
155–157 Meeting	John McAllister	White
109 America	William Mazyck	Colored
30, 32 Chalmers	J. W. Meservey	White
138 Spring	Cecilia A. Minort	Colored
622 King	J. M. Mohlenhoff	White
47 Queen	J. B. Stoffel	White

1911

LOCATION	OWNER	OWNER RACE OF
375 King	Bacon and Co.	White
62 Queen	Jason Brown	Colored
15–26 Hayne	Charleston Transfer	White
52 Radcliffe	F. J. H. Haesloop	White
155, 159 Church	Harper Brothers	White
4 America	A. Lartigue	Colored
163, 169 Meeting	John McAllister	White
30 Chalmers	J. W. Meservey	White
21 Queen	Palace Sale Stables	White
28 Morris	J. D. Parker and Co.	Colored

1920

LOCATION	OWNER	OWNER RACE OF
62 Queen	Jason Brown	Colored
16 Cumberland	C. E. Crull	White
59½ State	F. A. Frisbie	White
*	Harper Brothers	White
2 Kracke	Eva D. Hoffman	Colored
53 State	S. L. Maddox	white
109 America	W. W. Mazyck	Colored
53, 55 Queen	Dr. W. Messervey	White
21 Queen	Palace Sale	White

Note * = No data available.

1920

LOCATION	OWNER	OWNER RACE OF
60 Queen	A.B. Bennett	White
14–16 Cumberland	Crull's Sales and Exchange Stables	White
53–55 Queen	JW Messervy	White
113 Church	JR Simmons	White

NOTES

Abbreviations

CC *Charleston Courier* (1803–52; succeeded by *Daily Courier*)

CEP *Charleston Evening Post* (succeeded by *Post and Courier*)

CG *City Gazette*

CGDA *City Gazette and Daily Advertiser*

CM *Charleston Mercury*

DC *Daily Courier* (1852–1873; succeeded by *News and Courier*)

DN *Charleston Daily News*

HCF Historic Charleston Foundation

NC *News and Courier* (1873–1991; succeeded by *Post and Courier*)

PC *Post and Courier*

SCG *South Carolina Gazette*

SCAGG *South Carolina American and General Gazette*

SCGCJ *South Carolina Gazette and Country Journal*

SCG *South Carolina Gazette*

SP *Southern Patriot*

Introduction

1. NC, 20 June 1961, pg. 9.
2. NC, 6 April 1924, pg. 38.
3. Tyrwhitt-Drake, "Carriages and Their History," 171.
4. Sweeney, "Pasture to Pavement," 140.
5. Tarr, *Horse in the City*, 117–18. Blacks and poor people of the "laboring classes" in general were criticized as being disruptive noise makers in nineteenth century cities.

6. Ibid, 37–38.
7. *Book of Old Time Trades and Tools*, 163–167, 241–246. Zierden, *Charleston: An Archaeology of Life in a Coastal City*, 186. Oxford English Dictionary, "livery," https://www.oed.com/ (accessed 25 October 2022).
8. Bonnetheau, *Ordinances (1807)*, 369. White people commonly referred to Black people as Negros or Colored during this time period. The term is reproduced here in its original form, and there are numerous other examples throughout the text when citing original sources. We understand and acknowledge that this term and its usage has evolved over time.
9. Tarr, *Horse in the City*, ix.
10. Plank roads were paved with wooden planks and were popular in the nineteenth century as a smooth and affordable road surface. See also Chapter 2.
11. SCG 7 February 1771, pg. 2; SCGCJ 27 October 1772, pg. 3.
12. *CEP*, 9 July 1900, pg. 4, references the first "horseless carriage" on the streets of Charleston.
13. Butler, *Lowcountry at High Tide*, 163; 1925 *Charleston Yearbook*, xlviii.

Chapter 1: Working Equine Traits and Breeds

1. Dietmeier, *Beyond the Butcher's Block*, 2–3.
2. Tarr, *Horse in the City*, 2, 6.
3. Miller, *Work Horse Handbook*, 125.
4. Christina Butler, unpublished interview with Tom Doyle Sr. 21 February 2022.

5. Miller, *Work Horse Handbook*, 17; Dietmeier, *Beyond the Butcher's Block*, 3, 218.

6. Mason, *Pocket Farrier*, 21.

7. Mayer, *Horse Educator*, 17.

8. Greene, *Horses at Work*, 183.

9. Tarr, *Horse in the City*, 7.

10. Tarr, 3–4, 6; Youatt, *The Horse*, 407. See 411–16 for equine efficiency calculations. Kirby, *Engineering in History*, 170–1.

11. Dietmeier, *Beyond the Butcher's Block*, 98, 136–37.

12. Oxen are typically referenced for sale as part of plantation accoutrement, for example, "a quantity of corn, pease [sic], and potatoes, also the plantation tools. Ox cart and exceeding good oxen" listed in the SCGGA, 20 December 1780, pg. 2, or "two prime young mules, 46 head of fine stock cattle, a pair of oxen, and all the provisions that may be on the plantation at the time of sale", CC 3 January 1850, pg. 1.

13. Miller, *Work Horse Handbook*, 21.

14. Youatt, *The Horse*, 411.

15. Miller, *Work Horse Handbook*, 79.

16. Ibid, 87.

17. Speed, *Horse in America*, 253, 258–59.

18. Tarr, *Horse in the City*, 54.

19. Sweeney, "Pasture to Pavement," 144.

20. Greene, *Horses at Work*, 183.

21. Christina Butler, unpublished interview with Valerie Perry, 12 October 2020; Christina Butler, unpublished interview with Tony Youmans, 15 March 2022.

22. Mason, *Pocket Farrier*, 2, 19–20.

23. Miller, *Work Horse Handbook*, 24–25, 30.

24. Tarr, *Horse in the City*, 16.

25. Estimate derived from the number of horse licenses issued in 1882 (1,599) and the population of the city in 1880 (49,984), per US Census data. CEP, 13 February 1978, pg. 19. 1900 US Census listed 55,807 residents.

26. Green, *Horses at Work*, 174.

27. Dietmeier, *Beyond the Butcher's Block*, 86, 218–19.

28. NC 20 May 1888, pg. 3.

29. Tarr, *Horse in the City*, 20.

30. Collections of the SCHS, Vol. 5, pg. 240–42, 286, 296–98.

31. McCord, *Statutes at Large*, Vol. 2, 164–65; A. S. Salley, ed., *Journal of the Commons House*, March 6, 1705/6-April 9, 1706, 11–12, 14.

32. Lawson, *New Voyage to Carolina*, 3. Charlestown was the colonial era spelling, prior to the town's incorporation as a city in 1783, at which time the spelling was changed to Charleston. Butler, *Lowcountry at High Tide*, 6.

33. SCG 6–13 May 1732, pg. 4, SCG 13–20 January 1732, pg. 4.

34. Chard, "First Spanish Horses," 98–99. Alva Nunez Cabeza de Vaca was allegedly the first to import horses to the United States. Landing them in Florida in 1527, they "were turned loose, and soon increased wonderfully . . . in 1678 horses existed in great numbers in Louisiana, Illinois, and Texas." Irving, *South Carolina Jockey Club*, 24. Ivers, *This Torrent of Indians*, 1, 4, 12. Dietmeier, *Beyond the Butcher's Block*, 140.

35. Catesby, *Natural History of Carolina, Florida, and the Bahama Islands*, Volume 2, xxxi.

36. Irving, *South Carolina Jockey Club*, 34; SCG 13–20 May 1751, pg. 2, ad for two "chair horses (Indian breed)". A "dark brown bay mare with a Chickasaw head" strayed from a pasture near Dorchester in 1757 (SCG 28 April 1757, pg. 8) and a "bright bay gelding with a Chickasaw head" strayed from pasture four years earlier (SCG 7 May 1753, pg. 2). Hand is a unit of measure for equines equal to four inches. Hands are measured from the ground to the top of the withers, or the highest part of the equine's back, below his or her shoulders.

37. CC 7 April 1853, pg. 3. SC Horseman's Council, "Marsh Tacky," https://www.schorsemenscouncil.org/ (accessed 21 June 2020).

38. Wallace, *Horse in America*, 140–41.

39. SCG 26 May 1767, pg. 5.

40. SCG, 1 May 1762, pg. 2; SCG, 9 June 1767, pg. 5

41. SCG 11 May 1765, pg. 1; SCAGG 13–20 March 1767, pg. 1.

42. SCG 27 June 1743, pg. 3.

43. SCG 3 September 1772; Two examples are found in CGDA 26 May 1804, pg. 1, "an elegant saddle and draft horse about five, for sale," and CGDA 12 March

1818, pg. 3, "a large strong sorrel chestnut riding and draft horse."

44. CG 25 April 1804, pg. 2.
45. CC 16 July 1818, pg. 2.
46. SCG 14 June 1742, pg. 4.
47. CG 12 June 1818, pg. 3. 1803 ad for an equine "used in town three years past, as a family horse, and can be warranted quiet and gentle." CC 17 February 1803, pg. 1. Ad for a "gentle family draft horse," CC 5 March 1834 pg. 2.
48. CC 5 January 1850, pg. 3; CC 11 April 1843, pg. 2.
49. CGDA 12 February 1824, pg. 3.
50. CC 4 June 1852, pg. 3.
51. CGDA 9 November 1812, pg. 2; CGDA 10 September 1806, pg. 2.
52. CC 11 May 1843, pg. 2.
53. CC 16 December 1837, pg. 3.
54. CC 29 August 1849, pg. 3; CC 3 September 1851, pg. 3; CC 19 April 1853, pg. 3.
55. SP 22 September 1832, pg. 3.
56. CC 28 March 1861, pg. 2.
57. CC, 8 February 1853, pg. 2.
58. Dietmeier, *Beyond the Butcher's Block*, 136–37.
59. Sweeney, "Pasture to Pavement," 133. See also Ellenberg, "African Americans, Mules, and the Southern Mindscape."
60. Hinson, *New Encyclopedia of Southern Culture*, Vol, 14, Folk Life, 332; Walker, *New Encyclopedia of Southern Culture*, Volume 11, *Agriculture and Industry*, 171. Historians note a metaphorical link between slavery and mules and the South's inability or unwillingness to adopt progressive farming techniques. Ellenberg, "African Americans, Mules, and the Southern Mindscape," 383. Ellenberg also observes that, "horses symbolized authority and wealth, mules connoted low status," 386.
61. Speed, *Horse in America*, 187.
62. Faulkner, *Flags*, 289–90.
63. Tarr, *Horse in the City*, 14; *Speed, Horse in America*, 195.
64. This assessment is echoed in *Speed, Horse in America*, 196; "the mule is less liable to become frightened and start suddenly; and if they do start, they usually

stop before damage is done, while the horse seldom stops until completely freed."

65. CN, 12 February 1875 pg. 2; CN 14 April 1906, pg. 3 lists several "timber mules" for sale at a local wood yard". NC, 16 December 1874, pg. 2, "rice mules for sale". Williford's stable at 23 Queen Street listed sixty horses, mares, and mules "from the west . . . fine driving horses and large mules suitable for lumber and turpentine." NC 3 April 1882, pg. 4.
66. 13th Census, *Statistics*, 621.
67. Hinson, *New Encyclopedia of Southern Culture*, Volume 14, Folk Life, 331; Ellenberg, "African Americans, Mules, and the Southern Mindscape," 384–85.
68. Dietmeier, *Beyond the Butcher's Block*, 118, 214; Wigge, "Mapping a Spanish Donkey's Long Journey," https://washingtonpapers.org/ (accessed 2 June 2021).
69. SCG 30 September–7 October 1732, pg. 2.
70. SCGCJ 20 May 1766, pg. 4.
71. SCG 25 August 1779.
72. SCGCJ 22 March 1783, pg. 2.
73. SCG 24 December 1771, pg. 4.
74. CG 22 February 1803, pg. 4.
75. CG "Egyptian Jackass." 6 March 1820, pg. 3.
76. CG 9 February 1798, pg. 3; CG 16 December 1807, pg. 2.
77. CG "Spanish Mules for Sale." 22 October 1803, pg. 3.
78. Twenty-two "prime mules broke to the draft . . . in this state for one year and fit for immediate service," CGDA 28 December 1804, pg. 2; CG 24 November 1818, pg. 1; CG 27 September 1819, pg. 2; CG 28 June 1820, pg. 3.
79. CC, 28 May 1856, pg. 3; CC, "Lot of mules from Kentucky." 17 September 1834, pg. 3; CC 24 February 1845, pg. 3. Henry Clay imported Catalan asses in 1832 for breeding, and a "Dr. Davis" imported a 16-hand Catalan jacks in 1836. Speed, The Horse in America, 190–91.
80. NC 26 September 1908, pg. 7.
81. Ibid; NC 15 February 1891, pg. 3.
82. Walton, "Mules," *South Carolina Encyclopedia*, https://www.scencyclopedia.org/ (accessed 28 December 2020); NC 29 May 1901, pg. 2.

83. Tom Doyle Sr. interview.
84. Christina Butler, unpublished interview with Tommy Doyle Jr., 9 March 2022.
85. Greene, *Horses at Work*, 72, 166. McNeur, *Taming Manhattan*, 101.
86. CM 15 March 1858, pg. 3; CC 23 August 1859, pg. 3.
87. Greene, *Horses at Work*, 174. SCG 17 February 1780, pg. 2 ad for "strong, able draught horse a full fifteen hands high."
88. NC, 14 April 1887, pg. 3 lists various types of working horses for sale; NC, 12 March 1902, pg. 3.
89. Bell, "Breeds of Draft Horses," 2.
90. Tarr, *Horse in the City*, 10–11.
91. The earliest references are to Percherons bred in the upstate in Pendleton. NC 10 October 1884, pg. 1; Bell, "Breeds of Draft Horses," 6–9.
92. Tarr, *Horse in the City*, 12–13.
93. Bell, "Breeds of Draft Horses," 3–5.
94. Miller, *Work Horse Handbook*, 14.
95. Tommy Doyle Jr. interview.
96. See www.spotteddraftregistry.com (accessed 18 December 2021).

Chapter 2: The Equine Streetscape

1. Butler, *Lowcountry at High Tide*, 6–7.
2. Schriber, *Tucked Away*, 70; Butler, "A moderate trot through the history of street speed," *Charleston Time Machine*, https://www.ccpl.org/charleston-time-machine/ (accessed 12 November 2020.)
3. McCord, *Statutes at Large*, Vol. 9, 49–57.
4. McCord and Cooper, *Statutes at Large*, 7: 97–100.
5. *Statutes at Large*, Vol. 7, 115.
6. Calhoun, *Charleston's Commercial Landscape*, 27–30.
7. SCAGG 20–27 April 1770, pg. 4.
8. Ford, "Diary of Timothy Ford," 141. Williamsburg also lacked paved or cobbled streets, and contemporaries noted that carriages and horses were quieter than in other cities. Smith, M. *Listening to Nineteenth Century America*, 350.
9. Butler, *Lowcountry at High Tide*, 81; CM, 9 August 1838, pg. 2.
10. NC, 12 August 1886, pg. 3.
11. 1908. *Charleston Yearbook*, 106; 1913 *Charleston Yearbook*, 88.
12. Peterson, "Impact of Sanitary Reform," 83–84.
13. *Journal of the Commissioners of Streets and Lamps*, 9 December 1817, pg. 369–70.
14. City Council, *Final Report on the Committee on Health and Drainage*, 23.
15. CC 5 August 1872, pg. 1.
16. 1880 *Charleston Yearbook*, 27.
17. 1880 *Charleston Yearbook*, 178.
18. Greene, *Horses at Work*, 48–49.
19. 1880 *Charleston Yearbook*, 26; 1883 *Charleston Yearbook*, 44.
20. CC, 17 May 1854, pg. 2; NC, 31 March 1891. pg. 8.
21. NC 10 November 1896, pg. 8.
22. Butler, *Lowcountry at High Tide*, 45, 78, 83–84. Frederick Law Olmsted's Central Park in New York is a famous, later example of antebellum park development, begun in 1858 with a series of coach drives. Drays and carts were not allowed in the park.
23. McInnis, *Politics of Taste*, 169; Buckingham, *Slave States of America*, 559–60.
24. CC, 20 July 1850, pg. 2.
25. Appleton, *Illustrated Handbook of American Travel*, 251.
26. Bachand, "Gendered Mobility and the Geography of Respectability," 74.
27. The City Beautiful movement was an American urban planning concept that was used successfully in parts of New York City and in the planning of the fairgrounds for the Chicago World's Fair of 1893. It was popular from the 1890s to the 1920s, ending when new construction and planning was curtailed by the Great Depression. https://www.britannica.com/ (accessed 24 October 2022). Murtagh, *Keeping Time*, 114.
28. CEP 31 October 1903, pg. 2.
29. Butler, "A Moderate Trot"; 1913 *Charleston Yearbook*, 114. Vitrified brick is fired at higher temperatures than standard building bricks, rendering them harder, stronger, and more impervious to water intrusion, all ideal traits for street paving.
30. DN, 10 September 1868, pg. 3.

31. CM, 21 September 1868, pg. 1.

32. DN 31 January 1870, pg. 3.

33. NC 31 July 1897, pg. 2. Wheelmen is a historic term for cyclists.

34. 1900 *Charleston Yearbook*, 147.

35. CEP 17 August 1911, pg. 2.

36. 1914 *Charleston Yearbook*, 111.

37. SCDAH, *Journal of His Majesty's Council for South Carolina*, No. 15, pg. 61 (13 November 1747).

38. Butler, "Speeds."; *Harris, Horse Gaits, Balance, and Movement*, 32, 35–37, 47–49.

39. Butler, "Speeds." Act amendments are found in Cooper, ed., *The Statutes at Large of South Carolina*, Vol. 4, 13–14.

40. Schirmer, *Schirmer Diary*, 71–72.

41. CM 9 August 1838, pg. 2.

42. Thompson, *Working on the Dock of the Bay*, 25.

43. Ibid, 56.

44. Ibid, 116.

45. NC 25 October 1887, pg. 2.

46. Revised Ordinances (1903), 244; Eckhard, Ordinances (1844), 132–33; 1894 *Charleston Yearbook*, 195.

47. 1899 *Charleston Yearbook*, 206.

48. CC 7 July 1856, pg. 4; 1905 *Charleston Yearbook*, 365.

49. 1912 Charleston Yearbook, 385.

50. CM, 10 May 1830, pg. 2.

51. CC, 28 February 1839, pg. 1.

52. Ordinances (1895), 185–86; Revised Ordinances (1903), Sec. 630.

53. 1897 *Charleston Yearbook*, 331.

54. CEP, 24 February 1905, pg. 5.

55. 1901 *Charleston Yearbook*, 260.

56. 1915 *Charleston Yearbook*, 509–10; 1924 *Charleston Yearbook*, 318–19.

57. 1925 *Charleston Yearbook*, 301.

58. Stoney, Crosland, and Pritchard case records, 100.48/14, Nelson v. Jones, 1937.

Chapter 3: Urban Equine Lifestyles

1. CEP, 19 July 1913, pg. 7.

2. Tarr, *Horse in the City*, 127; Dietmeier, *Beyond the Butcher's Block*, 3.

3. Miller, *Work Horse Handbook*, 55, 58. Corn lacks niacin and has inferior nutritional value to oats. Speed, *Horse in America*, 230–31.

4. Tarr, *Horse in the City*, 1; Dietmeier, *Beyond the Butcher's Block*, 230.

5. Merrens, "View of Coastal South Carolina in 1778," 192; SCAGG 17–24 December 1771. Corn blades have 64.2 percent digestible fiber content. *Cheboygan Democrat*, 7 April 1894, pg. 5.

6. White, *George Washington's Mount Vernon Stables*, 178.

7. See https://www.horsefeedblog.com/2011/12/grains-in-horse-feeds/ (accessed 21 November 2021); CC 10 March 1860, pg. 3; DC 8 March 1862, pg. 2.

8. Molony and Carter's store Meeting Street store was selling beet pulp by 1907. NC 16 December 1907, pg. 2.

9. "Differences between Timothy, Bermuda Grass & Alfalfa Hay," https://horseracingsense.com/ (accessed 19 December 2021).

10. SCG 14–21 September 1765, pg. 3.

11. SCGCJ 30 January 1770, pg. 4.

12. SCRG 19–22 December 1781, pg. 1.

13. *Columbian Herald*, 26 October 1786, pg. 1; 16 November 1786, pg. 3; CGDA 1 March 1803, pg. 4; Bounetheau, *Ordinances of the City of Charleston* (1815), 523–24.

14. Charleston City Railway records, SCHS, 23/265/14. 1879 Bulwinkle and Co. feed invoice letterhead. 23/265/15, 1880 invoice to William H, Jones; CC 21 November 1844, pg. 2.

15. 1884 *Sanborn Map*, sheet 15.

16. 1902 *Sanborn Map*, sheet 32.

17. "Records for the Assessor," box 3, 1896 licenses.

18. Charleston Museum, "Trade and Advertising," box 3.

19. For creating a common, see Rivers, *Sketch of the History of South Carolina*, 366–69; *Journal of the Grand Council, 1671–1680*, 29; January 1739/40, *Commons House Journal, 1739–1741*, p. 146; McCord, *Statutes at Large, Vol. 7*, 87–90.

20. Butler, "Genesis of Harleston Neighborhood,"

https://www.ccpl.org/charleston-time-machine/ (accessed 13 June 2020); SCG 26 February 1750.

21. Coclanis, "Sociology of Architecture," 611; SCG 11 May 1738, pg. 4; SCG 28 June 1742, pg. 2.

22. NC, 24 March 1875, pg. 4.

23. Butler, *Lowcountry at High Tide,* 36, 47, 52, 71.

24. 1880 *Charleston Yearbook,* 218; 1881 *Charleston Yearbook,* 179; NC 13 December 1924, pg. 6; *Southern Planter* (February 1884), pg. 71; NC 2 January 1929, pg. 14.

25. CC 2 July 1858, pg. 2.

26. NC 20 October 1875, pg. 7; NC 25 August 1888, pg. 8; NC 21 July 1889, pg. 8.

27. NC 26 March 1912, pg. 10.

28. 1881 *Charleston Yearbook,* 192; 1889 *Charleston Yearbook,* 123; 1939 *Charleston Yearbook,* foldout.

29. Tom Doyle Sr. interview.

30. PC, "The once ubiquitous boot scraper now mainly an adornment for historic homes." 19 January 2020, pg. 1.

31. CGDA, 9 December 1797, pg. 4. Garrison, *A Catalog of Carriage Steps,* 11–16, 22.

32. 1907 *Charleston Yearbook,* 63.

33. Greene, *Horses at Work,* 175.

34. Jordan, *Art of Making Harness,* 34, 90–93.

35. Fitz-Gerald, *Harness Maker's Illustrated Manual,* 56–57.

36. SCAGG 8 May 1769, pg. 1;1790 *City Directory,* pg, 10; 1816 *City Directory* pg. 1. Walsh, "Charleston Mechanics: A brief study, 1760–1776," 125–27, 132.

37. *Miscellaneous Records,* SCDAH, 31 March 1744, Vol. 2F, pg. 50.

38. SCAGG 3 April 1767, pg. 6.

39. Reitz, *Charleston: An Archeology of Life,* 176.

40. CM 10 August 1857, pg. 3.

41. 1959 *City Directory* pg. 49; Lander, "Charleston: Manufacturing Center of the old South," 345; Stavisky, "Industrialism in Antebellum Charleston," 320.

42. Charleston City Railway records, 1862–1895. 1205.01.02. 23/265/3, invoice, February 1873.

43. Charleston Museum, "Trade and Advertising," Box 4 and 7.

44. A. G. Cudworth & Co. records, 1880–1884. (152.06.12), cash books pg. 5–35, SCHS.

45. Miller, *Work Horse Handbook,* 19. Blinders were first mentioned in the Oxford English Dictionary in 1856. McShane, "Gelded Age Boston," 283.

46. CN 24 July 1942, pg. 10.

47. Sweeney, "Pasture to Pavement," 139.

48. SCG 9–16 March 1734, pg. 4. "Grease melted down" refers to horses with fever conditions, usually after overwork.

49. CC 30 April 1852, pg. 3.

50. 1881 *City Directory,* 560; 1883 *City Directory,* pg. 160.

51. Poston, *Buildings of Charleston,* 177.

52. 1860 US Census, "Schedule 2: Slave Inhabitants", Charleston County, pg. 6.; McInnes family papers, 258.01 folder 6, SCHS.

53. *Historical and Descriptive View,* pg. 94.

54. McInnes family papers, 258.00 folder 2, SCHS.

55. 1880 census lists John B. McInnes in a household with his father, horseshoer Peter McInnes. 1910 US Census; City death certificate O.T. 20; 1911 *City Directory*; McInnes family papers, 258.00 folder 1 and 2, SCHS. City death certificates were created by the City of Charleston's board of health and are held by the Charleston Archive at CCPL. The city's death records begin in 1819, predating the State of South Carolina death records, which do not begin until 1915.

56. 1883 *City Directory,* 446, 1911 *City Directory,* 335–336; South Carolina death record 3032; 1890, 1904 *City Directory,* pg. 492. CEP 6 March 1937, pg. 4.

57. McInnes family papers, 258.01 folder 6, SCHS. "Memorial Resolution."

58. Charleston City Railway Records, 23/265/12, 1876 invoices for kegs of fronts and hinds in horse and mule sizes 2,3, and 4; 23/265/8, January 1878 invoices; 23/265/14, Anvil Shoe and Nail Co. invoice of front and hind shoes. Their letter head indicated that they carried calked and plain Goodenough shoes.

59. *Transactions of the Highland and Agricultural Society,* 1872, 123–24.

60. Parson, *Industries and Wealth,* 57.

61. NC, 11 May 1875. pg. 3.

62. 1890 *City Directories,* 684, 703; 1904 *City Directory* pg. 3, 617, 249.

63. 1904 *City Directory,* 349; and 1924 *City Directory,* 659; State Death Certificate 7327.

64. "Rinderpest and the first veterinary School," https://cvm.msu.edu/ (accessed 3 July 2022).

65. Heber, *A Historical List of Horse Matches, 1765,* 152–56.

66. CG 13 September 1798, pg. 3; CC 5 February 1803, pg. 1.

67. SCG 19 March 1771, pg. 4.

68. McShane, "Gelded Age Boston," 288.

69. Myers, *Managing Horses on Small Properties,* 90.

70. Tarr, *Horse in the City,* 147, 158.

71. Cavender and Ball, "Home Cures for Ailing Horses," 313, 318, 328; Charleston City Railway records, 1862–1895. 1205.01.02 23/265/12, Aimar Drug Company invoice, 1876.

72. Greene, *Horses at Work,* 167; Tarr, *Horse in the City,* ix. See also McShane, "Gelded Age Boston," on the impact of the great fire of November 1872 in that city, which raged unchecked for thirty-five hours because most of the city's fire horses were unable to work due to the epizootic. McClure, "Epizootic of 1872," 6.

73. 1883 *Charleston Yearbook,* 85; 1884 *Charleston Yearbook,* 48. The health department reported Dr. Paquin's study of glanders equine to human transfer in 1891. 1891 *Charleston Yearbook,* 68.

74. Zierden, *Charleston: An Archeology of Life,* 176; Zierden and Reitz, "Animal Use and Urban Landscape," 357–58.

75. McNeur, *Taming Manhattan,* 210; Tarr, *Horse in the City,* 27. Dietmeier, *Beyond the Butcher's Block,* 140. The Charleston SPCA, in 1904, seized a horse, "blind in both eyes and so so emaciated in flesh that it could not get to its feet. The horse was declared unfit to work and the owner's consent was given to have it destroyed." NC 5 November 1904, pg. 8.

76. Tarr, *Horse in the City,* 29. SCG, 25 November 1756, pg. 3: "Edw. Weyman, upholster . . . gives the best price for hogs bristles, horses mane and tails, and cows tails."

77. Lambert, *Travels,* 132.

78. CC 1 February 1847, pg. 3; CC 18 September 1857, pg. 1; CC 10 December 1857, pg. 1.

79. Zierden, *Charleston: An Archeology of Life,* 176; 1884 *Charleston Yearbook,* 218.

80. NC 28 March 1890, pg. 8.

81. 1900 *Charleston Yearbook,* 318; 1915 *Charleston Yearbook,* 118.

82. McShane, "Gelded Age Boston," 282; Parker, *Animal minds, Animal Souls, Animal Rights,* 16. Gaukroger, *Descartes' System of Natural Philosophy,* 213–14.

83. *American Husbandry,* 80.

84. Ellenberg, "African Americans, Mules, and the Southern Mindscape," 387.

85. Curth, *Care of Brute Beasts,* 30.

86. The phrase was first used by Thomas Hobbes in *Leviathon,* a 1651 philosophical treatise.

87. SCG, 27 March–3 April 1742.

88. Beers, *For the Prevention of Cruelty,* 27.

89. *Communications to the Board of Agriculture,* 16–17.

90. SP 11 August 1842, pg. 3.

91. CGDA 18 June 1810, pg. 4; Bounetheau, *Ordinances (1815),* 510.

92. Favre, "The Development of the anti-cruelty laws during the 1800's." Detroit College of Law Review https://www.animallaw.info (accessed 29 August 2021.) Lord Erskine presented an unsuccessful anti-cruelty bill to the British Parliament in 1809. Richard Martin's attempts led to an 1822 act that set a precedent from which states and municipalities later borrowed language. See the "History of the RSPCA." https://www.rspca.org.uk/ (accessed 5 September 2021.) Connecticut passed a statute with similar wording to the Charleston ordinance in 1838 *Poulson's American Daily Advertiser,* 23 December 1812, pg. 2; *Connecticut Courant,* 21 July 1838, pg. 1. Richmond, Virginia passed an ordinance in 1827 making it illegal to beat a working equine cruelly, and set weight limits for carriages, wagons, and drays. *Ordinances of the Corporation of Richmond,* 54.

93. Robichaud, *Animal City,* 129–30; ASPCA, "History of the ASPCA," https://www.aspca.org/about-us/ (accessed 29 May 2020).

94. The S.P.C.A. ran animal care ads advising "better treatment of animals. Spare the whip," such as NC 2 April 1914, pg. 10.

95. Tarr, *Horse in the City,* 9, 51–53.

96. Rarey, *Modern Art of Taming Horses;* DC 4 August 1859, pg. 1; 6 August, pg. 1; 9 August pg. 1; 11 August pg. 1; 13 August, pg. 2.

97. Magner, *Art of Taming and Educating the Horse,* preface, 61–63.

98. Mayer, *Horse Educator,* 4, 7.

99. NC, 21 February 1888 pg. 2; NC 29 May 1899, pg. 8, letter from Ball to Police Chief Boyle thanking his officers for their aid in preventing and punishing animal cruelty. https://www.animallaw.info/intro/ (accessed 9 March 2022). A CPD officer was arrested by the SPCA for unnecessarily whipping his horse in 1893. 1893 *Charleston Yearbook,* 152.

100. Robichaud, *Animal City,* 141, 144; Sweeney, "Pasture to Pavement," 141–142. Charleston SPCA officers euthanized suffering horses, such as one with sores who was "poor as a snake" who was shot at St. Philip and Shepard Street (NC 18 August 1898, pg. 5) and a lame horse who could not get up that was euthanized at 8 Short Street at the owner's request (CEP 8 April 1899, pg. 4). Driver A. White's badly abused horse was confiscated and euthanized (NC 24 June 1902, pg. 8). In 1911, SPCA officers killed seventeen horses and mules for broken limbs, and successfully prosecuted 14 cruelty cases. NC 9 March 1911.

101. NC, 16 June 1891, pg. 8.; Greene, *Mr. Skylark,* 70.

102. NC, 8 May 1888, pg. 8.

103. NC, 24 March 1894, pg. 8 listed arrests for a lame and thin mule pulling an ice cart, exhausted cotton dray mules, and a lame horse carting on King Street.

104. NC 24 July 1910, pg. 12.

105. CEP, 18 October 1895, pg. 2.

106. NC 30 November 1892, pg. 8.

107. CEP 28 October 1903, pg. 5.

108. NC, 23 September 1893, pg. 8.

109. NC 16 November 1910, pg. 8.

110. NC 14 November 1876, pg. 2.

111. CEP, 6 December 1910, pg. 9. A spavin is a bony growth in the lower hock joint caused by osteoarthritis.

112. NC, 31 July 1914; NC, 5 November 1914, pg. 8.

113. NC, 7 October 1908, pg. 3; 1900 US Census, Charleston, Ward 2, sheet 5.

114. NC 27 July 1916, pg. 6.

115. NC, 14 June 1906, pg. 10.

116. NC, 15 January 1911, pg. 6; NC, 20 January 1911, pg. 4.

117. CEP, 5 August 1918 pg. 7; CEP 20 September 1911, pg. 8; 1911 *Charleston Yearbook,* 124.

118. CEP, 5 August 1898, pg. 8.

119. NC, 14 April 1909, pg. 9.

120. CEP, 24 June 1925, pg. 13.

Chapter 4: Equine Occupations

1. Bennett, "Charleston in 1774," 179–80.

2. Tarr, *Horse in the City,* 88.

3. SCDAH, Inventory Book Y (1769–1771), pp. 369–71

4. Lambert, *Travels,* 155–56.

5. SCG 25 April 1771, pg. 6; SCG 20–27 October 1758, pg. 3; CGDA 14 May 1796, pg. 2.

6. CH 10 December 1793, pg. 3; CGDA 25 January 1794, 3; CGDA 19 November 1798, pg. 3; CGDA 22 November 1798, pg. 3; CGDDA 21 August 1800, pg. 3; CGDA 2 October 1801, pg. 3.

7. CGDA 8 December 1812, pg. 3; CC 7 November 1814, pg. 3.

8. Soltow, "Socioeconomic Classes in South Carolina and Massachusetts," 18, 29.

9. Moffatt, "A Frenchman Visits Charleston," 140.

10. Gallant, "Recollections of a Charleston Childhood," 65.

11. Fraser, *Reminiscences of Charleston,* 64–65.

12. Buckingham, *Slave States of America,* 559–60.

13. McInnis, *Politics of Taste,* 170.

14. Bachand, "Gendered Mobility and the Geography of Respectability," 57, 59.

15. CM, 27 October 1859, pg. 1.

16. Tarr, *Horse in the City,* 92.

17. Irving, *South Carolina Jockey Club,* 33–34; Speed, *Horse in America,* 40–41.

18. Walsh, "Charleston Mechanics," 134; PC, "Before

the Kentucky Derby was Created," 13 November 2019, pg. 1.

19. McInnis, *Politics of Taste*, 24–25; Edgar, *South Carolina*, 171; Preservation Society, "Halsey Map," Washington Race Course; Mooney, *Race Horse Men*, 37. Williams, *Rice to Ruin*, 72.

20. Lambert, *Travels*, 151–53. Vlach, "Plantation Tradition," 40.

21. CC 3 March 1837, pg. 2.

22. Mooney, *Race Horse Men*, 27–28, 37–38, 40.

23. Sparks, "Antebellum Racing," 27; Dietmeier, *Beyond the Butcher's Block*, 237; Mooney, *Racehorse Men*, 42, 50.

24. Sparks, 27; Mooney, *Race Horse Men*, 119.

25. Mooney, *Race Horse Men*, 50–51.

26. Mooney, *Race Horse Men*, 40, 43, 45, 48.

27. Roberts and Kytle, "Looking the Thing in the Face," 647, 654.

28. Halsey Map, "Race Track, Gentlemen's Driving Association," http://www.halseymap.com/Flash/window.asp?HMID=33 (accessed 28 October 2022).

29. NC 4 November 1887, pg. 1.

30. NC 29 October 1890, pg. 1–2.

31. NC 25 February 1897, pg. 8.

32. Chibbaro, *The Charleston Exposition*, 33, 78, 81–82, 122.

33. Bruce, *World's Fairs in a Southern Accent*, 104; https://www.scencyclopedia.org/sce/entries/ (accessed 24 July 2022); Doyle, *New Men*, 182–84.

34. CEP 19 November 1902, pg. 2.

35. Walker, *New Guide to Modern Charleston*, 44. 1915 plat by Dingle; "Race Track, Gentleman's Driving Association." www.halseymap.com (accessed 18 April 2021) http://halseymap.com/ (accessed 1 October 2022); NC 5 February 1897, pg. 8; NC 30 December 1883, pg. 4; NC 2 January 1884, pg. 4; NC 10 November 1896, pg. 8.

36. Yuhl, *Golden Haze of Memory*, 141.

37. See https://steeplechaseofcharleston.com/the-south-carolina-jockey-club/ (accessed 4 August 2022).

38. Dietmeier, *Beyond the Butcher's Block*, 93, 163.

39. Dietmeier, *Beyond the Butcher's Block*, 265.

40. A Reynolds-built rockaway was listed in the 27 March 1852 *Charleston Courier* on page 3. Charleston city railway records, 1862–1895. 1205.01.02 23/265/4, Nathan and Son invoice, July 1873.

41. CGDA, 3 March 1815, pg. 4 is one of many ads for "elegant barouche with plated harness" for sale; CGDA, 28 January 1819, pg. 2; CC 14 October 1835, pg. 3 "a Charleston built barouche and good family draft horse accustomed to this city;" CC 30 January 1852, pg. 2.

42. Carriage Association of America, "What is a Buggy?" https://www.carriageassociationofamerica.com/ (accessed 23 June 2020).

43. "Carriages," *The Decorator and Furnisher*, 164.

44. Laurens, "Letters from Laurens, Continued (1923)," 53–68.

45. Laurens, "Letters from Laurens, Continued (1924)," 77–87.

46. Letter of Nathaniel Heyward II, 29 November 1816. Heyward and Ferguson Papers, College of Charleston Special Collections.

47. Philadelphia trained coachmakers were highly desired in southern cities especially in the Federal era, "as American training began to supplant the once heralded qualifications of London, Dublin, and Edinburgh experience." Powell, "Coach making," 104.

48. CGDA 18 August 1796, pg. 2; Lander, "Charleston: Manufacturing Center of the Old South," 339; CGDA, 14 November 1795, pg. 3; CGDA 14 May 1798, pg. 2.

49. CC 13 November 1813, pg. 2. Baily, "Baily's Magazine of Sports and Pastimes," 257.

50. CH, 19 August 1796, pg. 3; CGDA 27 June 1797, pg. 4; CGDA 3 June 1799, pg. 4; CGDA 23 July 1806, pg. 3.

51. CGDA 17 September 1799, pg. 2; *Charleston Times*, 18 July 1801.

52. Charleston County ROD book K3, pg. 237, mortgage dated 26 August 1803; CG 6 July 1804, pg. 3.

53. CGDA 29 March 1796, pg. 2.

54. CGDA 13 September 1819, pg. 3.

55. SCG 8 October 1772, pg. 3.

56. SCG 26 April 1773, pg. 1; SCG 8 October 1771, "a very neat London made phaeton", pg. 3; Straus, *Carriages and Coaches,* 222.

57. SCGCJ, 18 March 1766, pg. 1.

58. SCGCJ, 11 November 1766, pg. 1.

59. CGDA 21 March 1807, pg. 3.

60. *Charleston Times,* 25 February 1811, pg. 3; Charleston deed book N3, pg. 203, 1 April 1811, mortgage from Reynolds to Ash.

61. 1850 US Census lists 87-year-old Reynolds in a household with his son, a coachmaker; 1859 *Charleston City Directory,* pg. 62.

62. Lander, "Charleston: Manufacturing Center of the Old South," 339.

63. CC 6 August 1859, pg. 2; CM 8 August 1859, pg. 3; Lloyd, E. W. Carriage warehouse ledger, 1859–1861, SCHS 34/0658. pg. 3, 12, 51, 172, 202.

64. Ads for NYC companies appear in the 1866 *Charleston City Directory,* pg. 10.

65. Tyrwhitt-Drake, "Carriages and Their History," 169; CC, 2 January 1878, pg. 3.

66. NC, 27 February 1900, pg. 8.

67. 1890 *City Directory,* pg. 19, 412; Poston, *Buildings of Charleston,* 346, 402; 181 Church Property file, HCF; Charleston Museum, "Advertising and Trade Collection", box 3, Franke Co; CD Franke catalog cover, SCHS, 684.7.

68. Speed, *Horse in America,* 232.

69. SCGCJ 6 June 1769, pg. 3.

70. McInnis, *Politics of Taste,* 28–29; Dietmeier, *Beyond the Butcher's Block,* 236–37.

71. Hundley, *Social Relations in Our Southern States,* 351–52.

72. *Statutes At Large, Vol.* 7, 352, 382, 396.

73. CC 23 August 1823, pg. 2.

74. Haney, *Slavery in the City,* 97.

75. CG 20 August 1802, pg. 3.

76. CC 28 June 1832, pg. 3.

77. McInnis, *Politics of Taste,* 261.

78. Gaillard, "Recollections," 120–21.

79. 1880 Census, City of Charleston, pg. 45, 57, 74, 77.

80. CEP 20 January 1927, pg. 4.

Chapter 5: Commercial Transit and Livery

1. Butler, "Omnibus Revolution," https://www.ccpl.org/charleston-time-machine/ (accessed 2 June 2020).

2. Ibid.

3. SCG 6–13 October 1766, pg. 3.

4. CGDA 30 September 1797, pg. 1.

5. Greene, *Horses at Work,* 54–57.

6. Butler, "The First Century of Ferry Service Across the Cooper River," https://www.ccpl.org/charleston-time-machine/ (accessed 29 May 2020); SCG 5–12 January 1765, pg. 4. See Greene, *Horses at Work,* 177 for a discussion of horse machinery.

7. Alverez, *Travel on Southern Antebellum Railroads,* 27–28. Poole, "Best Friend of Charleston." https://www.scencyclopedia.org/sce/entries/ (accessed 10 March 2022). Doyle, *New Men,* 173–74.

8. Tarr, *Horse in the City,* 83.

9. McShane, "Gelded Age Boston," 280.

10. Tarr, *Horse in the City,* 66.

11. SP, 9 October 1833, pg. 1.

12. Horsey, *Ordinances (1854),* 35–37.

13. CC 30 September 1837, pg. 2; CC 17 March 1852, pg. 2.

14. CC 21 March 1855, pg. 2.

15. CM 24 June 1858, pg. 2; CM 9 July 1858, pg. 2; SCDAH, Petition S165015, item 17, 1860.

16. Tarr, *Horse in the City,* 6.

17. Butler, "Rise of Streetcars and Trolleys," https://www.ccpl.org/charleston-time-machine/ (accessed 2 June 2020.); Tarr, *Horse in the City,* 60, 65.

18. CC, 20 October 1865, pg. 1; CC 24 November 1865, pg. 2.

19. Charleston City Railway records, 1862–1895. 1205.01.02. 23/264/1. Estimate dated 20 June 1866.

20. Ibid, 1205.01.02 23/265/9. John Stephenson Co. invoices, September and November 1874.

21. *Historical Map of Charleston,* 1670–1883, Charleston, March 1884.

22. *New York Times,* 2 April 1867, pg. 2.

23. Charleston city railway records, 1862–1895. 22/264/2, 6 April and 22 April 1867 letters.

24. Tarr, *Horse in the City,* 81; Hine, "1867 Charleston Streetcar Sit-ins," 110–14.

25. Doyle, *New Men,* 231.

26. "Enterprise Rail," https://www.scencyclopedia.org/ (accessed 7 July 2022).

27. CC, 3 December 1866, pg. 2; Butler, "Rise of the Streetcars and Trolleys," https://www.ccpl.org /charleston-time-machine/ (accessed 2 June 2020); Enterprise Railroad Company records, 1871–1872. 308.03.01.03. SCHS.

28. NC, 31 August 1892, pg. 5.

29. 1895 *Charleston Yearbook,* 20.

30. Butler, "Decline of the Streetcars," https://www.ccpl .org/charleston-time-machine/ (accessed 2 June 2020); Butler, "Omnibus Revolution," https://www .ccpl.org/charleston-time-machine/ (accessed 2 June 2020).

31. Greene, *Horses at Work,* 176; Tarr, *Horse in the City,* 6. For example, the police department veterinary surgeon "condemned" four horses, who were exchanged for younger ones in 1908. 1908 *Charleston Yearbook,* 118. For depreciation, also see Miller, *Work Horse Handbook,* 191–92.

32. Tarr, *Horse in the City,* 6.

33. Charleston city railway records, 1862–1895. 1205.01.02, 22/265/3, Mills House Stables invoices. Sigwald (1827–1889) was born in Germany and worked as superintendent for the city railway, then for the CPD at the time of his death. 1880 Census; City Death certificate 2057; 1889 *City Directory,* pg. 148, 600; NC 2 July 1875, pg. 4.

34. Charleston City Railway records, 1862–1895. 1205.01.02 23/264/4, "Annual statement of receipts, 1870–71."

35. Charleston City Railway records, 1862–1895. 1205.01.02, 23/265/3, January–June 1873 receipts and invoices, Franke and C., January, February.

36. Charleston City Railway records, 1862–1895. 1205.01.02, 23/265/4. July–December 1873 invoices. "Records for the Assessor," box 3, 1896 licenses.

37. Tarr, *Horse in the City,* 112.

38. SCG 18 30 October 1749, pg. 2.

39. Fraser, *Reminiscences of Charleston,* 117.

40. SCGDJ 2 December 1766, pg. 2; SCAGG 28 November 1766, pg. 1.

41. SCGCJ 3–10 May 1768, pg. 2.

42. SCG 10 May 1770, pg. 3; SCGCJ 5 November 1771, pg. 3. Charleston did not have street numbers until the 1780s, so businesses often used signage related to their line of business as in lieu of an address or to create an easily identifiable geographic locator. For more on street numbering, see "Street numbers of peninsular Charleston," https://www.ccpl.org/.

43. SCGCJ 26 May 1767, pg. 5.

44. CG 2 March 1816, pg. 3.

45. CC 20 June 1853, pg. 3.

46. CC 29 November 1825, pg. 3.

47. 1816 *City Directory,* pg. 144; CC 26 February 1841, pg. 3. C.D. McCoy ran a stable there in the 1860s.

48. NC 16 December 1888, pg. 3; NC 21 July 1918, pg. 11; CEP 27 Feb 1917, pg. 10; CEP 6 July 1917, pg. 10.

49. Charleston Museum, "Trade and Advertising," Box 3.

50. Walker, *New Guide to Modern Charleston,* 32.

51. Charleston Museum, "Trade and Advertising," Box 4.; "Records for the Assessor," box 3, 1896 licenses.

52. CEP 6 November 1899, pg. 5; NC 7 November 1899, pg. 8.

53. "Records for the Assessor," box 3, 1896 licenses; NC 2 December 1941, pg. 66.

54. Poston, *Buildings of Charleston,* 461.

55. Funeral carriage exhibit display label, Charleston Museum.

56. 1861 *Charleston Census.* By 1880 Holloway had relocated to Spring Street. US 1880 Census, pg. 527B.

57. Charleston Museum, "Trade and Advertising," box 4.

58. Powers, *Black Charlestonians,* 167–68. 1870 *City Directory,* pg. 192. Deed book N15, pg. 485, Ling to Riley.

59. Campbell, *The American People,* 327.

60. NC 24 September 1875, pg. 2.

61. NC 3 October 1885, pg. 1.

62. Fant, *Sojourns in Charleston,* 97; Hoffius, *Upheaval in Charleston,* 76; City of Charleston Death certificate 917, NC 14 November 1885, pg. 4.

63. 1870 *City Directory,* pg. 273; 1893 *City Directory,* pg. 740.

64. Sale and feed stables were almost exclusively operated by white proprietors. 1900 *City Directory,* pg. 893; 1900 US Census, pg. 22. "Records for the

Assessor," box 3, 1896 licenses. See Appendix C for *City Directory* stable entries by year.

65. US 1880 Census, pg. 7B.

66. US 1880 Census, pg. 63A.

67. US 1880 Census, pg. 1A.

68. 1889 *City Directory,* pg. 76.

69. A driver named Henry Williams mentioned doing a "rushing business" on a fall 1909 evening, with so many passengers that he was not sure who had left their gold spectacles in his coach when he found them later that evening. NC 10 September 1909, pg. 8.

70. NC 8 February 1906, pg. 10.

71. NC 30 June 1895, pg. 5.

72. NC 3 March 1909, pg. 5.

73. NC 30 June 1895, pg. 5.

74. CEP 11 January 1899, pg. 2; 1904 *City Directory,* pg. 429.

75. NC 12 March 1907, pg. 10.

76. Gallagher, *The Spotsylvania Campaign,* 63.

77. CM 19 February 1856, pg. 2.

78. NC 30 August 1911, pg. 8.

79. 1880 Census, Chalmers Street and Warren Street, Charleston.

80. NC 22 June 1903, pg. 3.

81. NC 4 March 1902, pg. 11.

82. NC, 9 March 1911, pg. 10; NC, 25 December 1910, pg. 15.

83. NC, 31 January 1913, pg. 12.

84. CEP 6 March 1916, pg. 2.

85. CEP 3 February 1916, pg. 6.

86. "Records for the Assessor," box 3, 1925–1926 licenses.

Chapter 6: Carting, Draying, Machine Work, and Deliveries

1. Marrs, "Rice milling," https://www.scencyclopedia.org/ (accessed 12 September 2021); CC 4 April 1839, pg. 3; CC 26 May 1821, pg. 3.

2. Dietmeier, *Beyond the Butcher's Block,* 165; SCAGG, 6–13 May 1774, pg. 6.

3. Mofatt, "Frenchman Visits Charleston," 145.

4. CC 4 May 1846, pg. 3.

5. Alverez, *Travel on Southern Antebellum Railroads,* 41.

6. CC 22 September 1852, pg. 3.

7. "Records for the Assessor," box 3, 1896 licenses.

8. Thompson, *Working on the Dock of the Bay,* 15–16.

9. 1884 *Sanborn Map* sheet 5 shows a horse powered corn mill at 54 George Street, with a rear yard stable for the horses.

10. Tarr, *Horse in the City,* 38, 118.

11. Photograph in Historic Charleston Foundation's collection, for example, shows a mule pulling a two wheeled dump cart in 1912 (HCF 2016.013.8) in 1925 (HCF 2021.017.21).

12. SCG 21 July 1767, pg. 5; SCG 27 February 1770, pg. 6; SCG 15 March 1770, pg. 4.

13. Cooper, *Statutes at Large Vol. 9,* 697–705.

14. Thompson, *Working at the Dock of the Bay,* 46–48, 116, 154; Eckhardt, *Ordinances* (1844), 33–37.

15. Sweeney, "Pasture to Pavement," 138.

16. Youatt, *The Horse,* 408. McShane, "Gelded Age Boston," 276; Greene, *Horses at Work,* 78–80.

17. Butler, *Lowcountry at High Tide,* 79–80; Pease and Pease, *Web of Progress,* 60–62. See Greene, *Horses at Work* for horses in the nation's early transportation infrastructure.

18. *Sanborn Fire Insurance Maps* from 1884, 1888, and 1902 show few stables near the waterfront. For example, sheets 10–17 of the 1884 *Sanborn Map* show only six stables on the east side of East Bay Street between Market and Longitude Lane where the wharves and docks were located. See also Chapter 8 for stable locations.

19. *Sanborn Fire Insurance Map,* sheet 17; Property file, 28 Anson Street, HCF.

20. CEP 14 May 1897, pg. 5; *Ordinances* (1903), pg. 239–42; 1909 *Charleston Yearbook,* 362.

21. Thompson, *Working on the Dock of the Bay,* 42–45.

22. "Records for the Assessor," box 3, 1896 licenses.

23. "Cannonsborough Rice Mills, account book, entries from 1857–1859. SCHS.

24. 1904 *City Directory* listings; "Records for the Assessor," box 3, 1896 licenses.

25. 1878 *City Directory,* 345. An 1880 sale contract to an EB Whiting allowed a sixty-day trial for a gray mare. Deed D18, pg. 140. NC 16 December 1888, pg. 2.

26. 1869 *City Directory,* pg. 66; 1884 *City Directory,* pg.

62; Butler, "Charleston's First Ice Age," https://www
.ccpl.org/charleston-time-machine/ (accessed 7
February 2021).

27. NC 7 April 1874, pg. 3.

28. 1888 *Sanborn Fire Insurance Map,* sheet 11.

29. NC 15 February 1940, pg. 14.

30. CEP, 23 November 1951, pg. 1C.

31. Deed C22, pg. 513. Charleston Ice had licenses for
four team vehicles. "Records for the Assessor," box 3,
1896 licenses, pg. 617.

32. NC 22 May 1898, pg. 8; NC 5 July 1917, pg. 2.

33. NC 18 August 1917, pg. 6; Butler, "Charleston's Second Ice Age," https://www.ccpl.org/charleston
-time-machine/ (accessed 29 July 2022.)

34. "Records for the Assessor," box 3, 1896 licenses, pg.
615–17.

35. 1881 *Charleston Yearbook,* 76–77.

36. Simons-Mayrant Company records, 1283.00. folder
2, invoices. "Records for the Assessor," box 3, 1926
licenses. Selling and transporting iron by the bail
was common for scrap and unrefined metal.

37. "Records -for the Assessor," box 3, 1896 licenses.
1902 *Sanborn Map,* sheet 62, shows a long wood
stable next to Chisolm Rice Mill and Anderson
Lumber Company on Chisolm Street near the
Ashley River.

38. Henry Middleton, "colored drayman" for Fincken
and Jordan, was struck in his wagon by a streetcar on
the Gadsden Loop, allowing us to map the distances
that delivery drivers operated in Charleston. NC 1
August 1912, pg. 10.

39. "Mitchell & Smith records, 152.06.10. SCHS, Box 25,
"Charleston Teapot, 1909–1914."

40. CEP 9 July 1920; CEP 20 August 1908; NC 13 July
1907; 16 November 1910. "Records for the Assessor,"
box 3, 1896 licenses.

41. CEP, "Era Ends," 23 November 1951, pg. 1A.

42. Tarr, *Horse in the City,* 43–46.

43. Grimes, *Between the Tracks,* 48, 50; CC 29 October
1838, pg. 2; Thompson, *Working on the Dock of the
Bay,* 31, 55.

44. Green, *Slave Badges,* 136.

45. Thompson, *Working at the Dock of the Bay,* 99.

46. Edgerton and Paquette, *Denmark Vesey Affair,* 236,
249, 182.

47. Edgerton and Paquette, *Denmark Vesey Affair,* 83,
212, 293, 446; Thompson, *Working on the Dock,*
38–39; *London New Times* 20 August 1822, pg. 1.

48. Edgerton and Paquette, *Denmark Vesey Affair,* 63, 83,
197, 212, 216–17, 221, 228, 236, 242, 247, 249–51, 352,
391, 531.

49. The South Carolina Negro Seaman Act passed in
1822 was the first in a series of similar laws passed
throughout the eastern coastal United States following the Denmark Vesey conspiracy. The legislation
was intended to "forestall potentially dangerous
contact between nonresident free Blacks and slaves"
by restricting the movement of Black sailors in port.
South Carolina Encyclopedia, "Negro Seaman Acts",
https://www.scencyclopedia.org/sce/entries/
(Accessed 3 November 2022).

50. Thompson, *Working on the Dock of the Bay,* 18, 31,
64–66; Rubio, "Though He Had a White Face,"
52–53; Johnson, "Vesey and His Co-Conspirators,"
915–76.

51. SP 10 October 1844, pg. 2.

52. CC 26 January 1849, pg. 3.

53. CC 29 December 1856, pg. 2.

54. Thompson, *Working at the Dock of the Bay,* 96.

55. CM 27 July 1857, pg. 3.

56. Thompson, *Working on the Dock of the Bay,* 142–44,
155–58.

57. Sweeney, "Pasture to Pavement," 136; Taylor, "Civil
War Experiences of a New Orleans Undertaker," 264;
Thompson, *Working at the Dock of the Bay,* 105, 108.

58. Thompson, *Working on the Dock of the Bay,* 114.

59. Ibid, 114.

60. Ibid, 115, 224. See Thompson, chapter 4, "Laborers
from abroad have come to take their places", for
more on ethnic labor disputes on the Charleston
waterfront.

61. Strickland, "How the Germans Became White
Southerners," 54–56; Sholes *City Directory* 1882,
listings for Claussen and Wagener employees.

62. 1890 *City Directory* pg. 261, 503, 558, 567; Charleston
Museum, "Trade and Advertising," Box 7.

63. "Records for the Assessor," box 3, 1896 licenses.
64. 1882 *Shole's City Directory.* A keyword search for occupations including driver and draymen was conducted in the digitized volume, https://books .google.com/ (accessed 12 January 2021).
65. 1900 *Census, Statistics on Occupations,* pg. 514; NC 10 July 1907, pg. 24.
66. NC 15 November 1889, pg. 8.
67. CEP, 27 January 1925, pg. 13; State Death Certificate 2835; Deed book A16, pg. 103.
68. See https://wmbird150.com/?p=24 (accessed 22 August 2021).
69. See https://wmbird150.com (accessed 22 August 2021); "Our first motor truck," uncatalogued scrapbook page, Bird Co. archives.

Chapter 7: Public Services and the City of Charleston Fleets

1. 1880 *Charleston Yearbook,* 204, 208; 1882 *Charleston Yearbook,* 95; 1885 *Charleston Yearbook,* 149; 1899 *Charleston Yearbook,* 239; 1905 *Charleston Yearbook,* 22; 1907 Charleston Yearbook, 257; 1913 *Charleston Yearbook,* 263. The Hampton Park stable was leased to the US Quartermaster's Department during World War I for their horses. 1904 Charleston Yearbook, 205; 1915 *Charleston Yearbook,* 457. The Pleasure Grounds department is the previous name of the city's present-day park and recreation department.
2. Horsey, *Ordinances 1854–1859,* pg. 73, 95. CC, 8 December 1866, Petition of inspector LeCoste to board his horse at the Guard House Stable at the city's expense, pg. 4; CEP 25 January 1900, pg. 4.
3. NC 26 May 1909, pg. 12.
4. 1903 *Charleston Yearbook,* 130; Charleston City death certificate 211; NC 18 February 1903, pg. 8.
5. *Statutes At Large, Vol. 7,* pg. 11, 20, 59; CC 20 May 1808, pg. 3.
6. *Strength of the People,* 19 August 1809, pg. 1.
7. CG 1 February 1826, pg. 2.
8. CC 15 February 1826, pg. 2.
9. Norris, "Fire Steed," 48–49.
10. Ferrara, "Moses Henry Nathan," 275–79.
11. Moffatt, *Fire Houses of Charleston,* 1; Box 31, folder 14, "Records of the City of Charleston Fire Department, 1848–1979," includes contracts for two city-financed, volunteer company fire houses, March 1875.
12. Charleston Archive, "Finding Aid, Records of the City of Charleston Fire Department."
13. 1884 *City Directory,* City government, pg. 26–27.
14. Records of the City of Charleston Fire Department, 1848–1979, Box 6, "Bills for materials and supplies, 1881," pg. 1–30.
15. See https://digital.tcl.sc.edu/digital/collection /scook/id/186/ (accessed 5 August 2022) for an example of a horse-drawn fire engine.
16. CEP 6 July 1907, pg. 4; NC 11 October 1936, pg. 27.
17. CEP 9 December 1909, pg. 7.
18. NC 11 October 1936, pg. 27.
19. CEP 6 July 1907, pg. 4; NC 11 October 1936, pg. 27.
20. Records of the City of Charleston Fire Department, 1848–1979," Box 31, folder 50, "Stable utensils, 1923"; Box 4, "Ledger book for 1883–1890, 1891–1898"; Box 5, "Summary of Expenditures, ledger books for 1899–1991, 1912–1923."
21. Ibid, Box 6, "Bills for materials and supplies, 1881," pg. 1–30.
22. Ibid, Box 19, Engine House 8, pg. 147, 20 December 1911 entry.
23. 1881 *Charleston Yearbook,* 180; 1901 *Charleston Yearbook,* 136–38.
24. 1913 *Charleston Yearbook,* 193; CEP 3 July 1913, pg. 8; City death certificate 950. Hogan died of heart failure in 1913 and was interred at St. Lawrence Catholic Cemetery.
25. 1910 *Charleston Yearbook,* 105.
26. NC 11 October 1936, pg. 27. L. J. Hogan, no relation to Michael Hogan, was born in Iowa in 1886 and died in 1964. 1930 Census; South Carolina Death Certificate 64-011846.
27. 1898 *Charleston Yearbook,* 123–25; 1900 *Charleston Yearbook,* 136–38; 1907 *Charleston Yearbook,* 152–54; 1910 *Charleston Yearbook,* 189–90; 1914 *Charleston Yearbook,* 211–14.
28. NC 29 January 1910, pg. 5.
29. NC 3 May 1936, pg. 18.
30. CEP 26 August 1911, pg. 15.

31. CEP 29 June 1914, pg. 8.

32. NC 27 August 1915, pg. 8.

33. CEP 21 March 1916, pg. 9.

34. 1906 *Yearbook*, 135.

35. 1908 *Yearbook*, 166; 1913 *Yearbook*, 193.

36. NC 6 July 1907, pg. 4.

37. Ibid.

38. Moffatt, *Fire Houses of Charleston*, 37, 51, 43, 101, fold out charts. 1888 and 1902 *Sanborn Map*, sheets 9 and 41.

39. Moffatt, *Fire Houses of Charleston*, 14–15; Fraser, *Charleston! Charleston!* 317.

40. 1897 *Charleston Yearbook*, 125.

41. The 1884 *Sanborn Map*, sheet 12, shows the common arrangement for fire company stables, with a small wooden stable building directly behind the engine house on Chalmers Street. 1902 *Sanborn Map*, sheet 41 shows the Meeting Street facility.

42. Moffatt, *Firehouses of Charleston*, 16–17. Site visit to Meeting Street, Huger Street, and Cannon Street houses conducted by author, 10 July 2022.

43. 1885 *Charleston Yearbook*, 130; 1926 *Charleston Yearbook*, 138; Moffatt, *Fire Houses of Charleston*, 16; Board of Fire Master minutes, 5 October 1910, pg. 389–90. See also Appendix B of this book for number of horses in fire department service by year.

44. CEP 7 September 1926, pg. 2.

45. NC 3 October 1927, pg. 10.

46. NC 3 October 1927, pg. 10.

47. 1932 *Charleston Yearbook*, 202.

48. NC 11 October 1936, pg. 27.

49. 1939 *Charleston Yearbook*, 103; 1940 *Charleston Yearbook*, 120; 1942 *Charleston Yearbook*, 63, 121.

50. Butler, *Lowcountry at High Tide*, 20–22.

51. For the scavengers, streets departments, and carting refuse for fill, see Butler, *Lowcountry at High Tide*, 22, 35, 47, 51.

52. CGCDA 23 July 1813, pg. 1; CG 30 August 1813, pg. 4.

53. Butler, *Lowcountry at High Tide*, 36. For more on the title and organization of the Commissioners of Streets and Lamps see, https://www.ccpl.org/ (accessed 3 November 2022).

54. City of Charleston records management, "Engineering Records, 1867–1979," Box 12, folder 49, garbage collection. Letter from Hill to City Engineer, 14 February 1914; purchase invoice, 18 August 1915.

55. Ibid, "Engineering Records, 1867–1979," Box 12, folder 49, Marx catalog.

56. 1882 *Charleston Yearbook*, 38; 1906 *Charleston Yearbook*, 86.

57. 1912 *Charleston Yearbook*, 107; 1915 *Charleston Yearbook*, 152; 1922 *Charleston Yearbook*, 25.

58. CN, 30 April 1892, pg. 5; NC 15 October 1887, pg. 5.

59. 1909 *Charleston Yearbook*, 93–96.

60. CEP, 3 August 1917, pg. 9; Butler, "A Trashy history of Charleston's dumps and incinerators," https://www.ccpl.org/charleston-time-machine/ (accessed 22 September 2020.)

61. 1921 *Charleston Yearbook*, 120; 1922 *Charleston Yearbook*, 134.

62. 1909 *Charleston Yearbook*, 96.

63. Examples of acclimation, work conditions, and renting supplemental equines are found in 1906 *Charleston Yearbook*, 54, 57; 1907 *Charleston Yearbook*, 87; 1918 *Charleston Yearbook*, 123; CEP 17 February 1930, pg. 14.

64. 1904 *Charleston Yearbook*, 87.

65. 1905 *Charleston Yearbook*, 66.

66. 1907 *Charleston Yearbook*, 74–75.

67. 1911 *City Directory*, 287; 1910 *Charleston Yearbook*, 106; 1912 *Charleston Yearbook*, 47–48. *The Pocket Farrier* advised "checking for wind while starting and stopping; if his wind be injured he will blow unnaturally making a loud wheezing sound with great difficulty breathing." 16.

68. 1918 *Charleston Yearbook*, 124.

69. 1919 *Charleston Yearbook*, 130.

70. 1921 *City Directory*, pg. 400.

71. Please see Appendix B of this book for a table of the number of city-owned working animals from 1881 forward.

72. NC, 22 December 1932, pg. 2.

73. NC, 22 January 1933, pg. 14.

74. NC 15 April 1934, pg. 14.

75. NC 3 July 1936, pg. 16.

76. NC, 13 April 1933, pg. 10.

77. NC 26 January 1938, pg. 12; NC 3 March 1938, pg. 16.

78. *Collections of the SCHS, Vol. 5,* pg. 427–28. *Council Journal,* 3 September 1673, pg. 63.

79. Butler, "The Medieval Roots of the Charleston Night Watch," https://www.ccpl.org/charleston-time -machine/ (accessed 1 December 2020).

80. *Statutes At Large, Vol. 2,* 254.

81. Ibid, 121; *Governor Archdale's Laws,* 1–8.

82. Ivers, *This Torrent of Indians,* 60; Merrens, *The Colonial South Carolina Scene,* 32.

83. Lawson, *A New Voyage to Carolina,* 3; SCG 3–12 May 1739, pg. 3; SCG, 24–31 January1735/6, pg. 3 references a review of the Troop of Horse.

84. Charleston Archive, "Finding Aid: Records of the Charleston Police Department, 1855–1991;" Butler, "The Watch House: South Carolina's First Police Station," https://www.ccpl.org/charleston-time -machine/ (accessed 16 December 2020); McCord, *Statutes At Large, Vol. 8,* 545–49.

85. Powers, *Black Charlestonians,* 32–33.

86. McCord, *Statutes At Large, Vol. 8,* 560; SP 30 July 1841, pg. 3.

87. CM 18 October 1861, pg. 2. The city council referenced an "ordinance in relation to a horse guard [that] had not been repealed," but the text could not be located. CC, 20 October 1846, pg. 2.

88. CC, 7 October 1846, pg. 2; Walker, *Ordinances 1844 to 1854,* pg. 30–31 (November 1846).

89. CC, 9 December 1846, pg. 2. The contract was awarded to Preston West (CC 6 January 1847, pg. 2).

90. Walker, *Ordinances 1844 to 1854,* 95–98 (October 1850).

91. NC 15 January 1856, pg. 1.

92. Horsey, *Ordinances (1859),* 22–23, 66–67.

93. CC 14 November 1856, pg. 1.

94. 1893 *Charleston Yearbook,* 154.

95. 1897 *Charleston Yearbook,* 134.

96. Charleston Archive, "Finding Aid: Records of the Charleston Police Department, 1855–1991."

97. 1913 *Charleston Yearbook,* 93.

98. 1888 *Charleston Yearbook,* 104.

99. 1893 *Charleston Yearbook,* 149; 1898 *Charleston Yearbook,* 127.

100. 1885 *Charleston Yearbook,* 144. The CPD brought 16 mules and 22 horses in 1886. 1886 *Charleston Yearbook,* 123. They secured 14 horses, one horse and wagon, ten horse and buggy in 1890, and seven mules wandered around, unattended. 1890 *Charleston Yearbook,* 110. The department reported 69 goats, 17 mules, 24 horses, 23 cows, and one alligator at large in 1913. 1913 *Charleston Yearbook,* 69. The CPD collected a record number of 53 horses and 13 mules at large in 1922. 1922 *Charleston Yearbook,* 328.

101. Tarr, *Horse in the City,* 40–41; NC 10 February 1931, pg. 3.

102. NC 26 September 1909, pg. 15.

103. NC 6 February 1984, pg. 15.

104. NC 22 June 1914, pg. 3.

105. 1917 *Charleston Yearbook,* 276–77, 393.

106. NC 14 January 1920, pg. 6.

107. NC 26 June 1940, pg. 3.

108. NC, 12 July 1941, pg. 4.

109. 1944 *Sanborn Map,* pg. 1,6, 13, and 20.

110. NC 22 January 1948, pg. 10.

111. NC 16 March 1937, pg. 1–2.

112. NC 29 March 1978, pg. 41; NC 8 March 1985, pg. 18.

113. PC, 6 July 2000, pg. 7.

114. PC, 20 October 2008, pg. 1.

115. PC, "Charleston PD shutters mounted patrol unit," 21 February 2011, pg. 1A.

116. *New York Times,* "Police Departments downsize, from 4 legs to 2," 14 February 2011. https://www .nytimes.com/ (accessed 15 March 2020).

117. PC, "Charleston mounted police to patrol downtown once more." 19 October 2021, pg. 1B; Counton 2. "Mounted Patrol Units Return to Charleston," 30 March 2022. https://www.counton2.com/news/.

Chapter 8: The Buildings
Where Equines Lived and Worked

1. Lounsbury, Illustrated Glossary of Early Southern Architecture, 61, 68, 345; Greene, Horses at Work, 173.

2. Horlbeck Brothers records, 1824–1860. 0179.01 folder 1, estimate books (1842–1849). Tuck pointing

is ornamental mortar work that is struck to create a decorative profile or narrower, finer mortar joint. Flat pointing is simpler mortar work in which the surplus material is struck off roughly flush with the brick face.

3. Speed, Horse in America, 220–26.

4. Bernard Herman describes row house layout in more detail in "Slave and Servant Housing in Charleston, 1770–1820," 90–91.

5. Deed book S29, pg. 110, January 1920.

6. 1902 Sanborn Map. Research notes for historical marker for 91 East Bay Street. Preservation Society Archives.

7. Ichnography of Charlestown, 1739; Halsey Map of Charleston, 1949; Charleston County plat T7, pg. 109; McCrady plat 317.

8. Zierden, Big House, Back Lot, 537.

9. Ross, Charleston Urban Outbuildings, 99. McInnis also notes this arrangement (pg. 173), which is corroborated by plats and the Sanborn Map.

10. Poston, Buildings of Charleston, 183; McCrady plat 515. A similar single house and stable is depicted in a plat of 112 Queen Street in deed N6-69, surveyed in 1797.

11. 33 Hasell property file, HCF.

12. 51 East Bay property file, HCF.

13. Sanborn Maps from 1884, 1888, and 1902 confirm this arrangement throughout the city, as do plats of an East Bay and Union Street residence, 1806 (deed book T7, pg. 219) and a King Street residence, with a square plan wooden stable along back line, 1807 (T7, pg. 309.).

14. Zierden and Reitz, Charleston Through the Eighteenth Century, 99–101; 1902 Sanborn Map; site visits.

15. "Col. William Alston." https://www.gibbesmuseum.org/miniatures/ (accessed 21 January 2021).

16. Zierden, "Landscapes and Social Relationships of Charleston Townhouses," 534, 538; Poston, Buildings of Charleston, 243–44; NC, 2 June 1975, pg. 11; 1840 City Directory, pg. 23.

17. Legare Street property records, 1784–1841, SCHS, 33-121-01.

18. Zierden, Initial Archeological Testing at Nathaniel Russell House, 120.

19. Herman, "Slave and Servant Housing in Charleston," 96.

20. Ibid, 96.

21. Deed books: Eveleigh house, Z7, pg. 137; Blake tenements, K9, pg. 189; B8, pg. 396; Daniel Huger house, N7, pg. 363; Crawford house, T7, pg. 309; Douxsaint house, X9, pg. 270; Price house, N7, pg. 275. White, George Washington's Mount Vernon Stable, 145–46.

22. Smith, "Architectural Design and Building Construction," 16.

23. Charleston County Plat Book F6, pg. 281.

24. Though not widely used in current scholarship, the term "urban plantation" was popularized by architectural historian John Michael Vlach in his 1999 article "The Plantation Tradition in an Urban Setting". It is an effective concept in understanding the types of buildings and spatial arrangement of large residential complexes in the city with an enslaved staff.

25. Shaw, "Adaptive Use Potential," 23–27; Haney, Slavery in the City, 34; McInnis, Politics of Taste, 169, 197–201. Vlach, "Plantation Tradition in an Urban Setting," 58.

26. National Register, William Aiken House, 456 King Street.

27. Erin McNicholl, *Gothic Revival Outbuildings of Antebellum Charleston*, 54; Butler, Carolopolis nomination for 12 Lamboll Street, Preservation Society.

28. Poston, Buildings of Charleston, 212, 254; Doyle, New Men, 128.

29. Charleston Plat D, pg. 190; Library of Congress photographs; Poston, Buildings of Charleston, 579.

30. 25 East Battery property file, HCF; 2005.006.4a-p photographs, HCF; Charleston County plat book O-36, HCF; Hudgins, Vernacular Architecture of Charleston, 154.

31. White, George Washington's Stable, 115, 120, 128, 138; Communications to the Board of Agriculture 22; Pain, Practical Builder, plate 81 shows a plan for large standing stalls with vertical stall partitions that are

higher at the manger end like that of the stalls at 31 Legare Street.

32. McCrady plat 410; 1890 *City Directory*, pg. 707.

33. McCrady plat 3830.

34. SCRG 8 September 1781, pg. 3.

35. SCG 20–27 October 1758, pg. 3; SCAGG 26 May 1775, pg. 4.

36. CC 8 May 1852, pg. 3. 1877 City Directory, pg. 514, listed several Chalmers Street facilities: J. Fraser's carriage stable (24 Chalmers); J. McPherson (34 Chalmers); and Graham and Co. sale stable (30 Chalmers). There were numerous longstanding stables on this street, which changed proprietors over time. McCrady plat 631. City of Charleston Census of 1861; CC 16 May 1863, pg. 2.

37. CC, 30 January 1852, pg. 2; City of Charleston Census of 1861, 65; Deed book X12, pg. 569; City Death Certificate 865; Deed book X12, pg. 569, Reynolds to Spriggs and Hockaday; deed book R14, pg. 288.

38. "Seignious family papers, 1838–1904." 1013.01.01. SCHS. Lease, 1847.

39. CGDA 20 November 1802, pg. 2; CGDA 20 May 1803, pg. 2.

40. DC 26 July 1850, pg. 3; DC 3 February 1852, pg. 2.

41. McCrady plat 3707. Charleston County Register of Deeds.

42. 1884, 1888, 1902 Sanborn Maps.

43. 1882 City Directory, pg. 202–3, 1884 City Directory, pg. 127, 1890 City Directory, pg. 707, 1901 City Directory, pg. 933, 1920 City Directory, pg. 844.

44. Federal Writers' Project. 1936. WPA Federal Writers' Project Papers. USC South Caroliniana Lib., Columbia, SC. https://digital.library.sc.edu/collections/ (accessed 30 October 2022).

45. NC 28 December 1926, pg. 2.

46. National Register, Diana Brown Building; WPA Federal Writers' Project Papers. USC South Caroliniana Library. http://library.sc.edu/digital/collections/wpafwp.html (accessed 15 November 2020); CEP, May 13, 1903, pg. 5; "Records of the City Assessor," Box 3.

47. Deed books H18, pg. 8.

48. Deed book P17, pg. 157; Deed book U17, pg. 112.

49. 1872 *City Directory*, 273; 1879 *City Directory*, pg. 102.

50. 1918 *City Directory*, pg. 738, 1931 *City Directory*, pg. 254, 1934 *City Directory*, pg. 241. 1938 *City Directory*, pg. 308.

51. CEP 19 March 1924, pg. 59.

52. CEP 19 March 1924, pg. 59; CEP, 20 February 1935, pg. 1.

53. NC 26 September 1908, pg. 7.

54. CEP 2 October 1900, pg. 4; Deed book B19-411, Graham to C Ed Salinas for assorted carriages and harness, 20 April 1899.

55. 1888 Sanborn Map.

56. Sanborn Maps for the years 1884, 1888, 1902, 1944, 1951.

57. CEP 30 January 1948, pg. 12; 1890 *City Directory*, pg. 347.

58. 1929 *City Directory*, pg. 1001.

59. 1997 *Charleston Yearbook*, 181. 1880 *Charleston Yearbook*, 221, states that "men's quarter's [dormitory] is over the stable house."

60. 1892 *Charleston Yearbook*, 15, 156.

61. 1893 *Charleston Yearbook*, 15.

62. 1894 *Charleston Yearbook*, 183.

63. 1898 *Charleston Yearbook*, 133.

64. NC 10 September 1902, pg. 3.

65. Records of the Charleston Police Department, 1855–1991, Box 2, "Contracts, Bonds and Building Specifications."

66. 1889 *Charleston Yearbook*, 39; 1904 *Charleston Yearbook*, 86.

67. 1909 *Charleston Yearbook*, 68.

68. 1915 *Charleston Yearbook*, 146.

69. 1937 *Charleston Yearbook*, 64.

70. Analysis drawn from survey of extant Sanborn Maps for the city of Charleston. See Appendix A.

71. Young, *Ordinances* (1802), 223.

72. See Appendix A, *Sanborn Map Analysis*.

73. See Appendix A, *Sanborn Map Analysis*.

74. Tarr, *Horse in the City*, 109–10, 123–25; 1906 *Charleston Yearbook*, 331.

75. 1918 *Charleston Yearbook*, 159.

76. 1918 *Charleston Yearbook*, 159, 190–91.

77. 1935 *Charleston Yearbook*, 101.

78. See Appendix A, *Sanborn Map Analysis.*

Chapter 9: Decline and Reminiscence

1. CEP, 30 January 1948, pg. 12.

2. Coclanis, *Shadow of a Dream,* 64, 114–15.

3. US War Department, *War of the Rebellion,* 1021.

4. For more on phosphate mining, see McKinley, *Stinking Stones and Rocks of Gold: Phosphate, Fertilizer, and Industrialization in Postbellum South Carolina.*

5. For more on postbellum economy, see Doyle, *New Men, New Cities, New South,* 179–81, 79–81.

6. See https://www.csx.com/index.cfm/about-us/company-overview/railroad-dictionary/?i=B (accessed 30 October 2022).

7. Doyle, *New Men,* 75, 173–74.

8. "Records of the Assessor," box 3, 1896 licenses.

9. For more on harbor navigation and the jetty program, see Butler, "Navigating the Bar of Charleston Harbor: Gateway to the Atlantic. https://www.ccpl.org/charleston-time-machine/_(accessed 19 June 2022).

10. NC 17 December 1903, pg. 8; 1600 Meeting Street National Register nomination form. In 1910, Atlantic Coastline Railroad also received permission from the city council to run a rail spur to the Cooper River near Brigade Street, marking the shift of rail shipping northward with direct wharf connections.

11. CEP 30 December 1949, pg. 19.

12. Butler, "Decline of Charleston's Streetcars" https://www.ccpl.org/charleston-time-machine/decline-charlestons-streetcarso (accessed 21 June 2020.)

13. 1913 *Charleston Yearbook,* 67; 1915 *Charleston Yearbook,* 61.

14. CEP 5 December 1931, pg. 1; 1941 *Charleston Yearbook,* 23.

15. 1920, 1930, 1940 taxi and livery business listings.

16. Martin, "Mules to MARTA," 23; Greene, *Horses and Work,* 188.

17. *Street Railway Journal,* "Electric Railways in Charleston," 517; NC, 31 January 1897, pg. 8.

18. Known locally as the Trolley Barn, the building is extant and has been renovated as the American College of the Building Arts campus. The Trolley Barn

was listed to the National Register in 2017. https://schpr.sc.gov/index.php/Detail/properties/40956 (accessed 30 October 2022).

19. NC, 31 January 1897, pg. 8.

20. CEP 15 July 1895, pg. 5; Butler, "Decline of Charleston's Streetcars," https://www.ccpl.org/charleston-time-machine/ (accessed 2 June 2020); *NC* 14 July 1917, pg. 8.

21. NC 6 July 1907, pg. 4.

22. 1909 *Charleston Yearbook,* 158; 1911 *Charleston Yearbook,* 200.

23. 1912 *Charleston Yearbook,* 167; NC 25 September 1911, pg. 3. The New York City fire department also decided in 1913 to phase out their 1500 horse fleet. NC 18 December 1912, pg. 5; CEP 13 March 1913, pg. 5; 1914 *Charleston Yearbook,* 244.

24. 1921 *Charleston Yearbook,* 313.

25. NC 23 December 1928, pg. 25.

26. CEP 6 January 1947, pg. 11.

27. CEP 16 October 1917, pg. 4.

28. CEP, 30 January 1948, pg. 12.

29. CEP 23 November 1951, pg. 33.

30. "Records of the Assessor," box 3, 1925 licenses.

31. NC 11 February 1946, pg. 1B.

32. NC 16 October 1951, pg. 13.

33. CEP 23 November 1951, pg. 33.

34. CEP 23 November 1951, pg. 33.

35. CEP 23 November 1951, pg. 33.

36. CEP 23 November 1951, pg. 33.

37. NC 2 October 1938, pg. 5.

38. HCF image collection 2019.016.1.

39. NC 29 January 1939, pg. 13.

40. CEP 20 November 1940; Poston, *Buildings of Charleston,* 347.

41. 1944 *Sanborn Map,* sheet 59; CEP 16 August 1946, pg. 16.

42. CEP 30 January 1948, pg. 12; 1945 *City Directory,* pg. 261 lists Red Stable as the last sale barn in the city. It was listed on State Street in the 1942 *City Directory,* pg. 394.

43. NC 30 November 1966, pg. 13.

44. Tarr, *Horse in the City,* 126.

45. Schriber, *Tucked Away,* 2, 17, 22. Proponents of urban revitalization and new urbanism also see the value in narrow historic streetscapes.

46. Greene, *Renaissance in Charleston,* 135.

47. Yuhl, *Golden Haze of Memory,* 63.

48. Devoe, "Tale of Two Cities," 118; Charleston Municode section 54–230.

49. Yuhl, *Golden Gaze of Memory,* 141–43.

50. For more on the Crosstown and auto-oriented planning models, see Roach, *The Crosstown.*

51. Ross, *Charleston's Urban Outbuildings,* 71. For outbuildings in Ansonborough and Harleston, see Shaw, 49–59.

52. 1886 *Charleston Yearbook,* 135; 1887 *Charleston Yearbook,* 142.

53. See Appendix A, *Sanborn Map Analysis.*

54. Powers, *Black Charlestonians,* 246.

55. Yuhl, *Golden Haze,* 9. For more on the preservation movement and loss of diversity, see also Roberts and Kytle, "Looking the Thing in the Face."

56. McCrady plat 519; Poston, *Buildings of Charleston,* 194; property file, 11 St. Michaels, HCF; *Sanborn Map,* 1884.

57. 61 Meeting Street property file, HCF; 1902 *Sanborn Map.*

58. Property file, 19 Church Street, HCF.

59. Charleston County plat A9, pg. 76.

60. Butler, Carolopolis nomination form, 12 Lamboll Street, Preservation Society.

61. Carolopolis award file, 25 East Battery, Preservation Society. The award is given or exemplary preservation, rehabilitation, restoration, and new construction projects. Owners Reba and Harry Huge received the award in 2006.

62. A dependency is a detached building "which serves a subordinate service function such as a kitchen or stable and ordinarily located at the rear of Charleston lots." Poston, *Buildings of Charleston,* 652.

Chapter 10: Continued Legacies

1. CEP 26 October 1949, pg. 1.

2. CEP 9 December 1949, pg. 17.

3. NC, 11 December 1949, pg. 56.

4. CEP, 11 November 1949, pg. 20.

5. NC 17 November 1949, pg. 13; NC, 6 December 1949, pg. 9; NC 10 December 1949, pg. 3.

6. NC, 11 December 1949, pg. 56.

7. NC, 13 May 1950, pg. 9.

8. See https://obits.postandcourier.com/us/obituaries /charleston/ (accessed 6 March 2022.) Charlie Parker Collection. City Council Proceedings, 19 July 1983, pg. 20 lists the companies in operation.

9. Tom Doyle Sr. interview.

10. Property fil, 45 Pinckney Street, HCF.

11. American Council on Historic Preservation, "Heritage Tourism," https://www.achp.gov/heritage _tourism (accessed 13 August 2022).

12. See https://www.colonialwilliamsburg.org/explore /carriage-wagon-rides/ (accessed 13 August 2022).

13. Kidd, "'Immersive Heritage Encounters"; Schell, "On Interpretation and Historic Sites," 6; https:// apnews.com/article/ (accessed 13 August 2022.)

14. Yuhl, *Golden Gaze of Memory,* 141–43.

15. Yuhl, xxv, 135, 154, 177.

16. See https://tourcharleston.org/palmetto-guild/ (accessed 6 March 2022); PC 7 August 2018, pg. 1A; Charlie Parker Collection, letter from city, 18 June 1975.

17. See Roberts and Kytle, *Denmark Vesey's Garden,* chapter 10 for information on early and changing cultural focuses within the Charleston tourism industry.

18. Roberts and Kytle, "Is it OK to Talk About Slavery?" 138, 141–44.

19. Kytle and Roberts, *Denmark Vesey's Garden,* 312.

20. Ibid, 311–12.

21. Based on a cursory search of Trip Advisor reviews for carriage companies, referencing keyword "slavery," dated 2012–2022 (tripadvisor.com accessed 1 and 2 August 2022).

22. 21 March 2021 review of Charleston Carriage Works, https://www.tripadvisor.com/ (accessed 30 October 2022).

23. See https://www.tripadvisor.com/Attraction _Review-g54171-d1136044-Reviews-Old_South _Carriage_Company-Charleston_South_Carolina .html (accessed 30 October 2022).

24. See https://www.tripadvisor.com/Attraction
    _Review-g54171-d626818-Reviews-Palmetto
    _Carriage_Works-Charleston_South_Carolina
    .html (accessed 30 October 2022).

25. See https://www.tripadvisor.com/Attraction
    _Review-g54171-d626818-Reviews-Palmetto
    _Carriage_Works-Charleston_South_Carolina
    .html (accessed 30 October 2022).

26. Kytle and Roberts, *Denmark Vesey's Garden,* 338.

27. Brenner, *Old Codgers Charleston Address Book,* Guig-
    nard Street entry.

28. "Charleston Horse Diaper Story," *Carriage Journal,*
    181.

29. "White wing" is a historic term used in NYC in the
    late nineteenth century for white uniformed street
    sanitation crewmen. Melosi, *Sanitary City,* 121.

30. Charlie Parker Collection, 16 September 1974 and
    1 November 1977 letters.

31. Tom Doyle Sr. interview.

32. CEP 28 February 1978, pg. 10; CEP 13 February 1978,
    pg. 19.

33. NC 5 September 1980, pg. 9; NC 6 September 1980,
    pg. 9.

34. *City of Charleston v. John Roberson,* 275 S.C. 285, 269
    (1980), https://cite.case.law/sc/275/285/. (Ac-
    cessed 8 July 2022).

35. Charlie Parker Collection, December 1984 photo-
    graph.

36. Tom Doyle Sr. interview.

37. NC 12 May 1985, pg. 2F.

38. PC 20 March 1993, 1B; PC, 18 September 1999, pg.
    1A.

39. *Tourism Management Plan (2015),* 119–24; Charles-
    ton Municode.

40. See https://www.neworleanscarriages.com/about
    -us/news/french-quarter-carriage-mules (accessed
    16 July 2022); New Orleans Municode Sections
    162–496, 542, 543, 549. https://library.municode.
    com/la/new_orleans/codes/ (accessed 17 July
    2022); Christina Butler, unpublished interview with
    Ben Speight, Royal mule trainer and manager and
    president of CONA, 14 July 2022.

41. Times Picayune. "Here's what's in the new

42. Youmans interview.

43. Ibid.

44. PC, "Keeping an eye on tourism," 26 September
    2014, pg. 4.

45. Litvin et al. "Not in My Backyard," *Journal of Travel
    Research,* 678–81. https://doi.org/10.1177/00472875
    19853039 (accessed 30 October 2022).

46. Litvin et al. "Not in My Backyard," *Journal of Travel
    Research,* 678–81. https://doi.org/10.1177/00472875
    19853039 (accessed 30 October 2022).

47. See https://www.charlestoncares.com/our-mission
    (accessed 24 September 2022.)

48. PC, "Tourism sparks a carriage-load of opinions",
    18 July 2005, F6; PC, "Let date drive horse deci-
    sions", 31 July 2016, pg. 1F; A comment on Charles-
    ton CARES 22 March 2018 post about the CSA/
    Charleston Carriage Horse Advocate anti-carriage
    billboard on I-26 leading into the city (still in place
    as of October 2022), reads "bunch of nasty rich
    people that don't want carriages on 'their' street,"
    https://www.facebook.com/CarriageCARES
    /posts/ (accessed 4 November 2022).

49. See https://www.charlestoncarriagehorseadvocates
    .com/heat (accessed 10 July 2022); https://www
    .charlestoncarriagehorseadvocates.com/load (ac-
    cessed 30 October 2022); https://www.live5news
    .com/story/29600265/ (accessed 30 October 2022).
    One such example of a Carriage Horse Advocate
    follower equating working equines with slaverey
    occurred on 11 August 2022, "it's modern day slavery
    in a town infamous for this mistreatment." https://
    www.facebook.com/ccha.join/posts/ (Accessed 4
    November 2022).

50. See https://charlestonanimalsociety.org
    /humane-carriage-tours/ (accessed 24 July 2022).

51. ASPCA, "The History of the ASPCA," https://www
    .aspca.org/. Accessed 29 May 2020. Vertical file,
    "tourism – carriages," SCR, CCPL.

52. Almeida, "Horse Powered," 179, 180–82, 186–88.

53. Sweeney, "Pasture to Pavement," 144. Hutchinson,

"Should They Go the Way of the Horse and Buggy," 176. NYC has had carriage tourism in Central Park since the 1930s.

54. See http://carriageon.com/publicvoices/ (accessed 4 November 2022). *New York Times,* "Viral Video of horse collapse Reignites Debate: Do Carriages Belong?", 21 September 2022. https://www.nytimes.com/2022/09/21/ (accessed 30 October 2022).

55. PC, "Turning up the heat." 28 July 2006, pg. A1.

56. ABC News 4, "Charleston passes new horse carriage heat rules." 28 March 2017. https://abcnews4.com/news/local/ (accessed 19 July 2022); https://obits.postandcourier.com/us/obituaries/charleston/ (accessed 19 July 2022).

57. See https://library.municode.com/sc/charleston/codes/ (accessed 30 October 2022). For opposite viewpoints on the appropriateness of carriage load weight, see also https://www.charlestoncares.com/dispelling-the-myths/2018/2/21/weight and https://www.charlestoncarriagehorseadvocates.com/load.

58. PC, "There's no off season in the debate over Charleston's carriage horses." 26 December 2017, pg. 3.

59. Vergara and Tadich, "Effect of Work performed by tourism carriage horses on physiological and blood parameters," 213–17.

60. Rosser and Ardis, "Retrospective Review of Carriage Horse and Mule Welfare," 816–19.

61. PC, "Reining in carriage criticism," 23 August 2009, pf. B1.

62. "New Study Finds No Evidence of Stress," *Veterinary Practice News*, April 2015. https://www.veterinarypracticenews.com/ (accessed 24 July 2022).

63. "Reassuring research about carriage horses." Equus, Vol. 475, April 2016.

64. Doyle interview; Tommy Doyle Jr. interview.

65. Youmans interview.

66. Youmans interview.

67. Youmans interview.

68. PC 6 April 2014, pg. 3.

69. See City of Charleston Municode article V., divisions 1 and 2, section 29–201 through 29–222 for full guidelines regulating "animal-drawn vehicles for the purposes of touring," and animal care. Tom Doyle, Sr. interview. Youmans interview. https://palmettocarriage.com/animal-welfare-faq/ (accessed 27 February 2022); Tommy Doyle Jr. interview.

70. PC, 5 April 2019, "Why are so many hotels rising in Charleston?", pg. 1A.

71. Tom Doyle Sr. interview; City of Charleston, Tourism Management Plan 2015, 3.

72. Tom Doyle Sr. interview.

73. Tommy Doyle Jr. interview.

74. Youmans interview.

75. Tom Doyle Sr. interview.

Appendix C

1. This site was owned by R. Douglas Company and operating by 1861.

2. Moses Levy's stable was operating at this address as early as 1861. 1861 Charleston Census, pg. 39.

BIBLIOGRAPHY

Abbreviations

CCPL Charleston County Public Library
HCF Historic Charleston Foundation
SCG South Carolina General Assembly
SCHS South Carolina Historical Society
SCR South Carolina Room, CCPL
SCDAH South Carolina Department of Archives and History
SCHM *South Carolina Historical Magazine*

Manuscripts and Archive Collections

Blake Family Papers, 1794.1915. 1007.00. SCHS.

Charleston City Council. Charleston County Auditor's Ward Books, 1852–1902.

———. "Charlie Parker Collection," CCPL.

———. "City Council Proceedings. 1832–59." Compilation of proceeding abstracts from period newspapers. SCR.

———. Journal of Charleston City Council. Charleston. 1883–1979. Original bound volumes and microfilm of published volumes, CCPL.

———. "Records of the Assessor of the City of Charleston," Box 3, Dray and Cart Licenses, CCPL.

———. "Records of the Charleston Police Department, 1855–1991, City of Charleston Records," CCPL.

———. "Records of the City of Charleston Fire Department, 1848–1979, City of Charleston Records," CCPL.

———. "Records of the Commissioners of Streets and Lamps, 1806–1818", City of Charleston Records, CCPL.

Charleston City Railway Company records, 1862–1895. 1205.01.02. SCHS.

Charleston Museum. "Trade and Advertising." Box 3, 4, 7.

Charleston Register of Deeds. Charleston County Deed Books.

City of Charleston Board of Health. "Return of Deaths within the City of Charleston, 1819–1926, City of Charleston Board of Health Records." Charleston Archive, CCPL.

Enterprise Railroad Company records, 1871–1872. 308.03. SCHS. "Cannonsborough Rice Mills account book, 1855–1858." 34/0068 2. SCHS.

Franke, C. D. "Illustrated catalogue, C. D. Franke and Co Inc." 684.7 SCHS.

Heyward and Ferguson Family Papers, 1806–1923. College of Charleston Special Collections.

Horlbeck Brothers records, (Charleston, SC). 1824–1860. (179.00) SCHS.

Legare Street property records, 1784–1841. 33–121–01. SCHS.

Lloyd, E. W. "Carriage warehouse ledger, 1859–1861," 34/0658. SCHS.

McCrady, "John. John McCrady Plat Collection, South Carolina, 1670–1919." Filmed by South Carolina State Archives.

McInnis Family Papers, 1835–1996. (258.00) SCHS.

Mitchell & Smith. A. G. Cudworth & Co. records, 1880–1884. (152.06.12) SCHS.

———. Charleston Teapot records, 1909–1914. (0152.06.10) SCHS.

Preservation Society of Charleston. "Carolopolis Award folders": 12 Lamboll Street; 25 East Battery Street.

Property Files. 27 King; 51 East Bay; 2 King; 181 Church; 11 St. Michael's; 25 East Battery; 64 South Battery; 60 Queen; 112 Queen; 61 Meeting; and 33 Hasell Streets. Margaretta Childs Archive, HCF.

"Rutledge and Young case records, 1841–1887." 0308.01. SCHS.

Sanborn Fire Insurance Maps. Charleston, SC. 1884–1955. Microfilm. CCPL.

Seignious, Charles Washington. "CW Seignious Family Papers, 1838–1904." 1013.01.01. SCHS.

Simons-Mayrant Company records, 1900–1907. 1283.00. SCHS.

South Carolina General Assembly. "Grand Jury Presentments, 1783–1877." Series S165010. SCDAH.

———. "Journals of the Commons House of Assembly, 1692–1775." Manuscript. SCDAH.

———. "Miscellaneous Communications to the General Assembly, 1777–1877." Series S165029. SCDAH.

———. "Petitions to the General Assembly, 1776–1883." Series S165015. SCDAH. South Carolina Power Company Collection, 1848–1940. 1205.00 SCHS.

South Carolina Power Company. "Records of the Surveyors of the City of Charleston, 1817–1916."

———. South Carolina Power Company collection, 1848–1940. (1205.00) SCHS. City of Charleston Records Management Division. "City of Charleston Engineering Records, 1867–1979."

Toale, Patrick. "Patrick P. Toale legal papers, 1870–1878." 0431.02. SCHS.

William M. Bird and Co. Uncatalogued usiness records and scrapbook.

Secondary Materials

Almeida, Linda Dowling. "Horse-Powered: The Irish and the New York City Carriage Trade." *American Journal of Irish Studies* 11 (2014): 179–91.

Almeroth-Williams, Thomas. *City of Beasts: How Horses Shaped Georgian London.* Manchester, England: Manchester University Press, 2019.

Alverez, Eugene. *Travel on Southern Antebellum Railroads.* Tuscaloosa: University of Alabama Press, 2007.

American Society for the Prevention of Cruely to Animals. "History of the ASPCA," https://www.aspca.org/about-us/ (accessed 29 May 2020).

American Husbandry containing an account of the soil, climate, production and agriculture of the British colonies in North-America and the West-Indies . . . compared with Great Britain and Ireland, Vol. I. London: J. Bew, 1775.

Anderson, Virginia DeJohn. *Creatures of An Empire: how domestic animals transformed early America.* Oxford, England: Oxford University Press, 2006.

Armstrong, Ellis L., ed., Michael C. Robinson, and Suellen M. Hoy. *History of Public Works in the United States, 1776–1976.* Chicago: American Public Works Association, 1976.

Austin, Gloria A., and Mary Chris Foxworthy. *The Fire Horse: A Historic Look at Horses in Firefighting.* Weirsdale, FL: Equine Heritage Institute, 2018.

Bachand, Marise. "Gendered Mobility and the Geography of Respectability in Charleston and New Orleans, 1790–1861." *Journal of Souther History,* Vol. 81, no. 1 (February 2015), 41–78.

Bastian, Carole Uehlinger. *Mr. Gadsden's Neighborhood: An Historic Data Recovery Study of Portions of the Residential Wharf-front Neighborhood of Gadsdenboro (1850–1880).* Charleston: Barr & Associates, 2009.

Beers, Diane L. *For the Prevention of Cruelty: the history and legacy of animal rights activism in the United States.* Athens, OH: Ohio University Press, 2006.

Bell, G. Arthur. "Breeds of Draft Horses." *USDA Farmer's Bulletin* 619 (November 16, 1914), 2–19.

Bennett, John. "Charleston in 1774 as described by an English traveler." *SCHM* 47, no. 3 (July 1946): 179–80.

Berkebile, Don H. *Carriage Terminology: An Historical Dictionary.* Washington, DC: Smithsonian Institution Press, 1978.

Brenner, Betty, and J. Francis Brenner. *Old Codger's Charleston Address Book, 1990–1999.* Charleston: Old Codgers Inc., 2000.

Buckingham, James Silk. *Slave States of America, Volume 1.* New York: Fisher and Son, 1842.

Burton, E. Milby. *Streets of Charleston.* Charleston: Charleston Museum, undated.

Butler, Christina. *Lowcountry at High Tide.* Columbia: University of South Carolina Press, 2020.

Butler, Nicholas. "A Moderate Trot Through the History of Street Speed." 1 May 2020. CCPL.

———. "The Omnibus Revolution." 24 August 2017. https://www.ccpl.org/charleston-time-machine/ (accessed 29 September 2022).

———. "The Rise of Streetcars and Trolleys in Charleston." 24 May 2019. https://www.ccpl.org/charleston-time-machine/ (accessed 29 September 2022).

———. "A Moderate Trot Through the History of Street Speed." 1 May 2020. https://www.ccpl.org/charleston-time-machine/.

Calhoun, Jeanne, and Martha Zierden. *Charleston's Commercial Landscape, 1803–1860.* Charleston: Charleston Museum, 1984.

Campbell, George. *White and black, the outcome of a visit to the United States.* London: London, Chatto & Windus, 1879.

"Carriage On: All About the Famous New York City Carriages." http://carriageon.com (accessed 4 November 2022).

"Carriages." *The Decorator and Furnisher,* 5, no. 5 (February 1885): 164.

Carver, James. *Veterinary science, important to the physician, the student, and the gentleman of Philadelphia . . .* Philadelphia, PA: T. S. Manning, 1817.

Catesby, Mark. *The Natural History of Carolina, Florida, and the Bahama Islands, Volume 2.* London: n.p., 1743.

Cavender, Anthony P. and Donald B. Ball. "Home Cures for Ailing Horses: A case study of nineteenth century vernacular veterinary medicine in Tennessee." *Agricultural History* 90, no. 3 (Summer 2016): 311–37.

Chard, Thornton. "Did the First Spanish Horses Landed in Florida and Carolina Leave Progeny?" *American Anthropologist* 42, no. 1 (January 1940): 90–106.

Charleston Archive. Finding aid, "Records of City of Charleston Police Department, 1855–1991," CCPL. https://www.ccpl.org/.

———. Finding aid, "Records of City of Charleston Fire Department, 1848–1979," CCPL. https://www.ccpl.org/.

Charleston City Council. *The Code of the city of Charleston, South Carolina- General Ordinances of the City, code enacted as a whole May 12, 1964.* Charleston: Walker, Evans, and Cogswell, 1964. Section 34–6.

———. *Ordinances of the City of Charleston, South Carolina, Passed Since the First of September, 1807, and to the 12th of November, 1815.* Charleston: G.M. Bounetheau and Lewis Bryer, 1815.

———. *Digest of the ordinances of the City Council of Charleston, from the year 1783 to July 1818.* Charleston: Archibald E. Miller, 1818.

———. *The ordinances of the City of Charleston, revised and codified [microform]: and the acts of the General Assembly relating thereto.* [1783–1875, organized alphabetically by title.] Charleston: News and Courier Job Presses, 1875.

———. *General Ordinances of the City of Charleston, South Carolina.* Charleston: Lucas and Richardson, 1895.

———. *Revised Ordinances of the City of Charleston, To 1903.* Charleston: Walker, Evans, and Cogswell, 1903.

———. *Census of the city of Charleston, South Carolina, for the Year 1861. Illustrated by Statistical Tables. Prepared Under Authority of City Council by Frederick A. Ford.* Charleston: Steam Power Presses of Evans and Cogswell, 1861.

"Charleston Horse Diaper Story." *Carriage Journal* 13, no. 4 (Spring 1976): 181.

The Charleston Mercury. Charleston, SC: H. L. Pinckney (1825–1868), editor.

Charleston News and Courier. Charleston, SC, 1803–present. (Renamed *Charleston Post and Courier* in 1996).

Charleston Yearbook. Charleston, SC: Charleston Lithographing, 1880–1949.

———. *The Code of the City of Charleston, 1952; General Ordinances of the City. Code Enacted as a Whole September 16, 1952.* Charlottesville, VA: Michie City Publications, 1952.

———. *An Historical and Descriptive Review of the City of Charleston and her Manufacturing and Mercantile Industries, including many sketches of Leading Public and Private Citizens.* Volume I. New York: Empire Publishing Company, 1884.

———. *Final Report of the Committee of Health and Drainage on the Construction*, Cost, Etc. of the Sewers Recently Built in the Upper Wards. Charleston, SC: Walker, Evans, 1857.

———. *Digest of the ordinances of the City Council of Charleston, from the year 1783 to October 1844 to which are annexed the acts of the legislature which relate exclusively to the city of Charleston prepared under resolution of the City Council.* Charleston: Walker and Burke, 1844.

———. *Revised ordinances of the city of Charleston, South Carolina.* [ca. 1783–1929]. Charleston: Walker, Evans, and Cogswell, 1930.

———. *Tourism Management Plan, Updated 2015.* https://www.charleston-sc.gov/DocumentCenter/ (accessed 26 February 2022).

City of Philadelphia. "An ordinance, for the suppression of nuisances, for the regulation of the drivers of carriages and horses in and through the streets and alleys . . ." Philadelphia, PA: D. Humphreys, 1794.

Clutton-Brock, Juliet. *Horse Power: A History of the Horse and Donkey in Human Societies.* Cambridge, MA: Harvard University Press, 1992.

Coclanis, Peter A. *Economy and society in the early modern South: Charleston and the evolution of the South Carolina low country.* Ann Arbor, MI: UMI Press, 1993.

———. *The Shadow of a Dream: Economic Life and Death in the South Carolina Low Country, 1670–1920.* Oxford, England: Oxford University Press, 1989.

———. "The Sociology of Architecture in Colonial Charleston: Pattern and Process in an Eighteenth-Century Southern City." *Journal of Social History* 18, no. 4 (Summer, 1985): 604–23.

Communications to the Board of Agriculture. London: W. Bulmer, 1796.

Connecticut Courant, 21 July 1838.

Cooper, Thomas. *The Statutes at Large of South Carolina / edited, under authority of the legislature, by Thomas Cooper [and] David J. McCord, Vol. 2.* Columbia: A. S. Johnston, 1837.

"Curious Carriages." *Baily's Magazine of Sports & Pastimes* LXXX, no. 524. (October 1903): 253–57. London: Vinton and Company.

Curth, Louise Hill. *The Care of Brute Beasts: A Social and Cultural Study of Veterinary Medicine in Early Modern England.* Boston: Brill, 2010.

Darvill, Richard. *A Treatise on the Care, Treatment, and Training of the English Racehorse: In a Series of Rough Notes,* volume 2 of 2. (London: James Ridgway, 1840).

Day, William. *The Racehorse in Training: Seventh Edition.* London: Chapman and Hall, 1892.

Defenbaugh, Kayleigh Anne. *Living and Working on the Peninsula: A study of spatial home and work location relationships as related to occupations and Charleston's historic landscape at the turn of the twentieth century.* Master's thesis, Clemson University, 2020.

De Grey, Thomas. *The Compleat Horseman and Expert Ferrier.* London: Thomas Harper and Lawrence Chapman, 1639.

Devoe, Gareth A. "A Tale of Two Cities' Preservation Laws." *Real Property, Trust and Estate Law Journal* 50, no. 1 (Spring 2015): 113–34.

Dietmeier, Jenna Kay Carlson. *Beyond the Butcher's Block: The animal Landscapes of Eighteenth Century Chesapeake and Lowcountry Plantations.* PhD diss., College of William and Mary, 2017.

Dillon, James, and Cecil McKithan. "William Aiken House, 456 King Street." National Register of Historic Places Nomination Form. Washington, DC: US Department of the Interior, National Park Service, May 1981.

Ditzel, Paul C. *Fire Engines, Firefighters: The Men, Equipment, and Machines, from Colonial Days to the Present.* New York: Crown Publishing, 1976.

Doyle, Don. *New Men, New Cities, New South: Atlanta, Nashville, Charleston, and Mobile, 1860–1910.* Chapel Hill: University of North Carolina Press, 1990.

Drayton, John. *A View of Carolina, as Respects Her Natural and Civil Concerns.* Charleston: W. P. Young, 1802. Reprint. Spartanburg, SC: The Reprint Company, 1972.

Duggan, Edward P. "Machines, Markets, and Labor: The Carriage and Wagon Industry in Late-Nineteenth Century Cincinnati." *Business History Review* 51, no. 3 (Autumn 1977): 308–25.

Durand, E. Dana. *Thirteenth census of the United States: 1910. Bulletin. Population: United States. Population of cities.* Washington, DC: Government Printing Office, 1913.

Eckhard, George B. *Digest of the Ordinances of the City Council of Charleston, from the Year 1783 to October 1844.* Charleston: Walker and Burke, 1844.

Edgar, Walter, ed. *South Carolina Encyclopedia.* Columbia: University of South Carolina Press, 2006.

Edgar, Walter. *South Carolina: A History.* Columbia: University of South Carolina Press, 1998.

"Electric Railways in Charleston." *Street Railway Journal* 13, no. 9 (September 1897): 517–23.

Egerton, Douglas R. and Robert L. Paquette. *The Denmark Vesey Affair: A Documentary History.* Gainesville: University Press of Florida, 2017.

Ellenberg, George. "African Americans, Mules, and the Southern Mindscape, 1850–1950." *Agricultural History* 72 (Spring 1998): 381–98.

———. "Debating Farm Power: Draft Animals, Tractors, and the United States Department of Agriculture." *Agricultural History* 74 (Summer 2000): 545–68.

———. *Mule South to Tractor South: Mules, Machines, and the Transformation of the Cotton South.* Tuscaloosa: University of Alabama Press, 2007.

Fairfax, Harrison. *The John's Island Stud (South Carolina), 1750–1788.* London: Old Dominion Press, 1931.

Fant, Jennie Holton. *Accounts of Charleston and Lowcountry, South Carolina, 1666–1861.* Columbia: University of South Carolina Press, 2016.

———. *Sojourns in Charleston, South Carolina 1865–1947.* Columbia: University of South Carolina Press, 2019.

Faulkner, William. *Flags in the Dust: The complete text of Faulkner's third novel, which appeared in a shorter version as Sartoris.* New York: Knopf Doubleday Publishing Group, 2012.

Favre, David, and Vivien Tsang. "The Development of Anti-cruelty Laws During the 1800s." *Detroit College of Law Review* 1993, no. 1 (Spring 1993): 1–31.

Federal Writers' Project. "Negro Interest in Charleston [Diana Brown]." 1936. WPA Federal Writers' Project Papers. USC South Caroliniana Lib., Columbia, SC. https://digital.library.sc.edu/collections/ (accessed 30 October 2022).

Felton, William. *A Treatise on Carriages: Comprehending Coaches, Chariots, Phaetons, Curricles, Whiskies, Etc.* London: William Felton, 1794.

Felzer, Lissa, and Christina Rae Butler. "Standard Oil Company Headquarters, 1600 Meeting Street." National Register of Historic Places Nomination Form. Washington, DC: US Department of the Interior, National Park Service, August 2014.

Ferrara, Marie. "Moses Henry Nathan and the Great Charleston Fire of 1861." *SCHM* 104, no. 4 (October 2003): 258–80.

Fetters, Thomas. *Palmetto Traction: Palmetto Railways of South Carolina.* Forty Fort, PA: H. E. Cox, 1978.

Fitz-Gerald, William N. *The Harness Makers' Illustrated Manual.* New York: Forgotten Books, 1880.

Ford, Timothy. "Diary of Timothy Ford." *SCHM* 13, no. 3 (July 1912): 132–47.

Fraser, Charles. *Reminiscences of Charleston.* Charleston: John Russell, 1854.

Fraser, Walter. *Charleston! Charleston! The History of the Southern City.* Columbia: University of South Carolina Press, 1989.

Gaillard, Samuel Gourdin. "Recollections of Samuel Gaillard." *SCHM* 57, no. 3 (July 1956): 119–33.

Gallant, Mary. "Recollections of a Charleston Childhood, 1822–1836." *SCHM* 98, no. 1 (January 1997): 56–74.

Garland, James. *The Private Stable: Its Establishment, Management, and Appointments.* Boston: Little, Brown, 1903.

Garrard, Tyrwhitt-Drake. "Carriages and Their History." *Journal of the Royal Society of Arts* 11, no. 4865 (January 1952): 167–80.

Garrison, Craig W. "A Catalog of Carriage Steps in the Historic District of Charleston: paving the way to understand the historic streetscape of Charleston." Independent study, College of Charleston. Approved by James L. Ward, RLA. Spring 2013.

Gaukroger, Stephen. *Descartes' System of Natural Philosophy.* Cambridge: Cambridge University Press, 2002.

Goodbody, Jody. "Carriage Touring in the 'Holy City.'" *Carriage Journal* 23, no. 2 (Fall 1985): 97–100.

Greene, Ann Norton. *Horses at Work: Harnessing Power in Industrial America.* Cambridge, MA: Harvard University Press, 2008.

Greene, Harlan. *Mr. Skylark: John Bennett and the Charleston Renaissance.* Athens: University of Georgia Press, 2001.

Greene, Harlan, and Harry S. Hutchinson Jr. *Slave Badges and the Hire Out System in Charleston, South Carolina, 1783–1865.* Jefferson, NC: McFarland Press, 2004.

Grimes, Kimberly. *Between the Tracks: The Heritage of Charleston's East Side Community.* Charleston: Charleston Museum, 1987.

Hagy, James William. *Directories for the City of Charleston, South Carolina: For the Years 1830–31, 1835–36, 1837–38 1840–41.* Baltimore: Genealogical Publishing Company, 1997.

Haney, Gina. *Slavery in the City: Understanding antebellum Charleston's backlots through light, sound, and action.* Charlottesville: University of Virginia Press, 2017.

Harris, Susan E. *Horse Gaits, Balance, and Movement.* Nashville, TN: Turner Publishing Company, 2016.

Harvey, Bruce G. "An Old City in the New South: Urban Progressivism and Charleston's West Indian Exposition, 1901–1902." Master's thesis, University of South Carolina, 1988.

Heber, Reginald. *A historical list of horse-matches run; and of plates and prizes run for in Great Britain and Ireland, in the year 1765/ By Reginald Heber. Vol. XV.* Farmington Hills, MI: Gale ECCO, 2010.

Henderson, Edward Prioleau. *Autobiography of Arab.* Columbia: R. L. Bryan, 1901.

Herman, Bernard L. "Slave and Servant Housing in Charleston, 1770–1820." *Historical Archeology* 33, no. 3 (1999): 88–101.

Hine, William C. "The 1867 Charleston Streetcar Sit-ins: A Case of Successful Black Protest." *SCHM* 77, no. 2 (April 1976): 110–14.

Hinson, Glenn, and William Ferris. *The New Encyclopedia of Southern Culture: Volume 14: Folk Life.* Columbia: University of South Carolina Press, 2009.

"History of the RSPCA." https://www.rspca.org.uk/ (accessed 5 September 2021).

Hoffius, Stephen, and Susan Millar Williams. *Upheaval in Charleston: Earthquake and Murder on the Eve of Jim Crow.* Athens: University of Georgia Press, 2012.

Horsey, John. *Ordinances of the City of Charleston from the 14th September, 1854, to the 1st December, 1859.* Charleston: Walker and Evans, 1859.

Hudgins, Carter; Historic Charleston Foundation (Charleston); Colonial Williamsburg Foundation; Department of Architectural Research, Mary Washington College; Center for Historic Preservation; and the University of Delaware. Center for Historic Architecture and Engineering. *Vernacular Architecture of Charleston and the Lowcountry.* Charleston: Historic Charleston Foundation, 1994.

Hundley, David R. *Social Relations in Our Southern States.* New York: Henry B. Price Publishers, 1860.

Hunter, George. *The Ichnography of Charles-Town, at High Water.* London: B. Roberts and W.H. Toms, 1739.

Hutchison, Katherine. "Should They Go the Way of the Horse and Buggy- How the New York City Horse-Drawn Carriage Industry Has Survived Thirty Years of Operation." *Animal Law* 17, no. 1 (2010): 171–96.

Irving, John Beaufain. *South Carolina Jockey Club.* Charleston: Russell & Jones, 1857.

Ivers, Larry E. *This Torrent of Indians: War on the Southern Frontier, 1715–1728.* Columbia: University of South Carolina Press, 2016.

Jaher, Frederick Cople. *The Urban Establishment: Upper Strata in Boston, New York, Chicago, Charleston, and Los Angeles.* Urbana: University of Illinois Press, 1982.

Jenkins, Wilbert L. *Seizing the Day: African Americans in Post-Civil War Charleston.* Bloomington: University of Indiana Press, 1998.

Johnson, Michael P., and James L. Roark. *Black Masters: A Free Family of Color in the Old South.* New York: W. W. Norton, 1984.

Johnson, Michael P. "Denmark Vesey and His Co-Conspirators." *William and Mary Quarterly,* Vol. 58, no. 4 (October 2001), 915–76.

Jordan, John Charles. *The Art of Making Harness Successfully.* Tuskegee, AL: Tuskegee Institute, 1913.

Jurga, Fran. "Thirst for Knowledge: 100 years ago, horses suffered when veterinarians and city officials disagreed." *Equus Magazine.* https://equusmagazine.com/ (accessed 27 November 2021).

Kaufman, Charles. *Moseman's Illustrated Guide for Purchasers of Horse Furnishing Goods: Novelties and*

Stable Appointments Imported and Domestic. London: Bracken Books, 1985.

Kauffman, Kyle Dean. *The Use of Draft Animals in America: Economic Factors in the Choice of an Early Motive Power.* PhD diss., University of Illinois at Urbana-Champaign. 1993.

———. "Why Was the Mule Used in Southern Agriculture? Empirical Evidence of Principal-Agent Solutions." *Explorations in Economic History* 30, no. 3 (1993): 336–51.

King, Hilary. "Charleston Trolley Barn." National Register of Historic Places Nomination Form. Washington, DC: US Department of the Interior, National Park Service, September 2016.

Kirby, Richard Shelton, Sidney Washington, Arthur Burr Darling, and Frederick Gridley Kilgour. *Engineering in History.* New York: Dover Publications, 1990.

Lamb, Robert Byron. *The Mule in Southern Agriculture. University Publications in Geography, Vol. 15.* Berkeley: University of California Press, 1963.

Lambert, John. *Travels through Lower Canada and the United States of North America in the years 1806, 1807, and 1808.* London: Richard Phillips, 1810.

Lander, Ernest M. Jr. "Charleston: Manufacturing Center of the Old South." *Journal of Southern History* 26, no. 3 (August 1960): 330–51.

Larsen, Lawrence H. *The Urban South: A History.* Lexington: University of Kentucky Press, 1990.

Laurens, Henry. "Letters from Laurens to William Ball of Philadelphia." *SCHM* 24, no. 2 (July 1923): 53–68.

———. "Letters from Laurens to William Ball of Philadelphia." *SCHM* 25, no. 2 (April 1924): 77–87.

Lawson, John. *A New Voyage to Carolina; containing the exact description and natural history of that Country: Together with the Present State Thereof. And a Journal of a Thousand Miles, Travel'd Thro' Several Nations of Indians. Giving a Particular Account of Their Customs, Manners, &c.* London, 1709.

Litvin, Stephen M., Wayne W. Smith and William R. McEwen. "Not in My Backyard: Personal Politics and Resident Attitudes toward Tourism." *Journal of Travel Research,* Vol. 59, no. 4 (June 2019), 674–85.

"London Street Accidents." *The British Medical Journal* 2, no. 662 (September 6, 1873): 291.

Lounsbury, Carl R. ed. *An Illustrated Glossary of Early Southern Architecture and Landscape.* Oxford, England: Oxford University Press, 1994.

Lynghaug, Fran. *The Official Horse Breeds Standards Guide: The Complete Guide to the Standards of All North American Equine Breed Associations.* Minneapolis: Voyageur Press, 2009.

Magner, Dennis. *The Art of Taming and Educating the Horse.* Battle Creek, MI: Review and Herald Publishing House, 1886.

Manning, Aubrey. *Animals and Society: Changing Perspectives.* New York: Routledge, 1994.

Marrs, Aaron. "Rice Milling." *South Carolina Encyclopedia.* https://www.scencyclopedia.org/ (accessed 12 September 2021).

Martin, Jean. "Mules to MARTA." *The Atlanta Historical Bulletin* 19, no. 2 (1955): 1–50.

Mason, Richard. *The gentleman's new pocket farrier: comprising a general description of the noble and useful animal the horse. To which is added A Prize Essay on Mules . . . Also, an addenda, containing Annals of the turf, American stud book, rules for training, racing, &c.* Philadelphia, Grigg & Elliot, 1841.

Mayer, N. R. E. *The Horse Educator by N. R. E. Mayer, of Charleston.* Macon, GA: J. W. Burke, 1873.

McClure, James P. "The epizootic of 1872: Horses and disease in a nation in motion." *New York History* 79, no. 1 (1998): 4–22.

McCord, David J. *Statutes at Large of South Carolina, printed under the authority of the legislature by David J. McCord. Vols. 6–10.* Columbia: A. S. Johnston, 1839–41.

McCord, David J., and Thomas Cooper. *The Statutes at Large of South Carolina / edited, under authority of the legislature, by Thomas Cooper [and] David J. McCord, Volumes 1–5.* Columbia: A. S. Johnston, 1836–39.

McInnis, Maurie Dee. *The Politics of Taste in Antebellum Charleston.* Chapel Hill: University of North Carolina Press, 2005.

McKinley, Shepherd W. *Stinking Stones and Rocks of Gold: Phosphate, Fertilizer, and Industrialization in Postbellum South Carolina.* Gainesville: University Press of Florida, 2014.

McNeur, Catherine. *Taming Manhattan: Environmental Battles in the Antebellum City.* Cambridge, MA: Harvard University Press, 2014.

McShane, Clay. "Gelded Age Boston." *The New England Quarterly* 74, no. 2 (June 2001): 274–302.

Mc Shane, Clay, and Joel Tarr. "The Decline of the Urban Horse." *Journal of Transport History* 24 (September 2003): 177–99.

Melosi, Martin V. *Coping with Abundance: Energy and Environment in Industrial America.* New York: Knopf, 1985.

———. *Effluent America: Cities, Industry, Energy, and the Environment.* Pittsburgh, PA: University of Pittsburgh Press, 2001.

———. *Garbage in the Cities: Refuse, Reform, and the Environment.* Pittsburgh, PA: University of Pittsburgh Press, 2005.

———. *The Sanitary City: Urban Infrastructure in America from Colonial Times to the Present.* Baltimore: Johns Hopkins University Press, 2000.

Menzies, Frederick N. *Transactions of the highland and agricultural society of Scotland. Vol 4.* Edinburgh: William Blackwood and Sons, 1872.

Merrens, H. Roy. "A View of Coastal South Carolina in 1778: The Journal of Ebenezer Hazard." *SCHM* 73, no. 4 (October 1972): 177–93.

Miller, Lynn R. *Work Horse Handbook.* Sisters, OR: Small Farmer's Journal Inc., 1981.

Moffatt, Lucius Gaston and Joseph Medard Carriere. "A Frenchman Visits Charleston, 1817." *SCHM* 49, no. 3 (July 1948): 131–54.

Moffatt, Rebecca Marie. *The Fire Houses of Charleston.* Master's thesis, Clemson University, 2011.

Mohl, Ray. *The Making of Urban America.* Lanham, MD: Rowman and Littlefield, 2011.

Mooney, Katherine C. *Race Horse Men: How Slavery and Freedom Were Made at the Racetrack.* Cambridge, MA: Harvard University Press, 2014.

Moore, John Hammond. *The South Carolina Highway Department, 1917–1987.* Columbia: University of South Carolina Press, 1987.

Mossman, Ellen Louise. "Charming Charleston: Elite Construction of an Idealized History in Twentieth-Century Tourism" (2007). Undergraduate Humanities Forum 2006–7: Travel. 6.

Muldrow, Ralph. "Diana Brown Antique Shop." National Register of Historic Places Nomination Form. Washington, DC: US Department of the Interior, National Park Service, March 2020.

Murtagh, William J. *Keeping Time: The History and Theory of Preservation in America.* Hoboken, New Jersey: Wiley and Sons, 2006.

Myers, Jane. *Managing Horses on Small Properties.* Australia: Landlinks Press, 2005.

New York City Court of General Sessions. People of the State of New York against Harry Wallace, 25 February 1914.

Norris, David A. "The Century of the "Fire Steed": David Norris looks at horse-drawn fire vehicles in the 19th century." *History Magazine* 31, no. 1 (2011): 48–51.

OED Online. September 2022. Oxford University Press. http://www.oed.com/viewdictionaryentry/Entry/11125 (accessed October 25, 2022).

Olmert, Michael. *Kitchens, Smokehouses, and Privies: Outbuildings and the Architecture of Daily Life in the Eighteenth Century Mid-Atlantic.* Ithaca, NY: Cornell University Press, 2009.

Olsen, Sandra L., Laszio Bartosiewicz, and Alice Choyke. *Horses and Humans: The Evolution of Human-Equine Relationships* (Oxford, England: BAR International Series 1560, 2006, with C. McShane), 365–75.

O'Neal, Diana M. *Thomas P. Stoney and the Modernization of Charleston, 1923–1927.* Master's thesis, College of Charleston/The Citadel, 1998.

Ordinances of the Corporation of Richmond.

"Papers of the Second Council of Safety and the Revolutionary Party in SC, November 1775–March 1776." *SCHM* 4, no. 1 (January 1903): 3–25.

Parker, James V. *Animal Minds, Animal Souls, Animal Rights.* Lanham, MD: University Press of America, 2010.

Parsons and Co. *Industries and Wealth of the Principal Point of Rhode Island . . .* New York: A. F. Parsons, 1892.

Pease, William H., and Jane H. Pease. *The Web of Progress: Private Values and Public Styles in Boston and*

Charleston, 1818–1843. Athens: University of Georgia Press, 1991.

Peterson, Jon. A. "The Impact of Sanitary Reform upon American Urban Planning, 1840–1890". *Journal of Social History* 13, no. 1 (Autumn 1979), 83–103.

Pierce, Christopher A. *A Brief Summary of Humane Societies and Enforcement Powers.* 2011. https://www.animallaw.info/intro/ (accessed 9 March 2022.)

Pomeroy, Samuel Wyllys. "A Dissertation on the Mule." *American Farmer* 7, no. 22 (1825): 169–73.

Poston, Jonathan. *Buildings of Charleston: A Guide to the City's Architecture.* Columbia: University of South Carolina Press, 1997.

Poulson, Zachariah. *Poulson's American Daily Advertiser,* 23 December 1812. Philadelphia: Zachariah Poulson.

Powell, Richard E., Jr. "Coach making in Philadelphia, Part II." *Carriage Journal* 35, no. 3 (Winter 1997): 99–108.

Powers, Bernard E. *Black Charlestonians: A Social History, 1822–1885.* Fayetteville: University of Arkansas Press, 1994.

Preservation Consultants. *City of North Charleston Historical and Architectural Survey.* Charleston: Preservation Consultants, 1995.

Ramsay, David. *Ramsay's History of South Carolina, From Its First Settlement in 1670 to the Year 1808.* Charleston, SC: Walker, Evans, and Cogswell, 1858.

Rarey, J. S. *A New Illustrated Edition of J. S. Rarey's Art of Taming Horses With the Substance of the Lectures at the Round House, and Additional Chapters on Horsemanship and Hunting, for the Young and Timid.* London: G. Routledge, Warne, and Routledge, 1859.

Roach, Melissa. *The Crosstown: Physical Effects of the Expansion of Highway 17 Across the Charleston Peninsula.* Master's thesis, Clemson University, 2014.

Robillard, T. H. "Stables and Care of Horses." *American Railroad Journal* 58 (1884): 3.

Robichaud, Andrew A. *Animal City: The Domestication of America.* Cambridge, MA: Harvard University Press, 2019.

Robinson, G., and J. Robinson. *The Sportsman's Dictionary; or the Gentleman's Companion: for Town and Country.* Dublin, EI: Peter Hoey, 1780.

Robinson, John Martin. *Georgian Model Farms: A Study of Decorative and Model Farm Buildings in the Age of Improvement, 1700–1846.* Oxford, England: Oxford University Press, 1984.

Ross, Kerr. *Charleston's Urban Outbuildings Within the Historic Walled City, 1884–1955.* Master's thesis, Clemson University, May 2019.

Rosser, Julie M. and Ann Ardis, "Retrospective Review of Carriage Horse and Mule Welfare in Charleston, South Carolina (2009–2012)." *Journal of Equine Veterinary Science* 34, no. 6 (June 2014) 816–19.

Routledge and Sons. *The Book of Boys' Trades and the Tools Used in Them. By One of the Authors of "England's Workshops."* London: George Routledge and Sons, 1866.

Russell, Lord John. *The Horse; with a treatise on draft and a copious index.* London: Baldwin and Craddock, Paternoster Row, 1831.

Ryder, Tom. "American Riding Chairs." *Carriage Journal* 45, no. 3 (May 2007): 144.

"Saddlery." *The Stable: A Monthly Magazine Published for the Livery Stable, the Private Stable, and the Harness* 1 (February 1886): 49.

Salley, Alexander S. *Journal of the Commons House of Assembly of South Carolina, March 6, 1705/6 to April 9, 1706.* Columbia: State Company for the Historical Commission of South Carolina, 1937.

Sandler, Martin W. *Galloping Across the USA: Horses in American Life.* New York: Oxford University Press, 2003.

Schirmer, Jacob Frederic. "The Schirmer Diary (Continued)." *South Carolina Historical Magazine,* Vol. 77, no. 1 (Jan. 1976), 49–51.

Schoff, James S. ed. *Life in the South 1778–1779: The Letters of Benjamin West.* Ann Arbor, MI: Williams L. Clements Library, 1963.

Schriber, Haley Marie. *Tucked Away: An Analysis of Charleston's Courts and Alleys & the Search for Graceful Density.* Master's thesis, Clemson University, 2016.

Severens, Kenneth. *Charleston Architecture and Civic Destiny.* Knoxville: University of Tennessee Press, 1988.

Shaw, Elizabeth. *Adaptive Use Potential of Kitchen and Carriage Houses Toward Smart Growth Goals in*

Charleston, South Carolina. Master's thesis, Clemson University, 2013.

Smith, Alice Ravenel Huger. *The Dwelling Houses of Charleston.* London: J. P. Lippincott, 1917.

Smith, Mark M. *Listening to Nineteenth Century America.* Chapel Hill: University of North Carolina Press, 2001.

Smith, Shelley, E. "Architectural Design and Building Construction in the Provincial Setting: The Case of the Colonial South Carolina Plantation House." *SCHM* 116, no. 1 (January 2015): 4–28.

Soltow, Lee. "Socioeconomic Classes in SC and MA in the 1790s and the observations of John Drayton." *SCHM* 81, no. 4 (October 1980): 283–305.

South Carolina Gazette. Charleston, SC: 1732–1775.

South Carolina General Assembly. *Acts and Joint resolutions of the General Assembly of South Carolina, in the Year 1942.* Clinton, SC: Jacobs Press, 1943.

———. *Acts and Joint resolutions of the General Assembly of the state of South Carolina passed at the regular session of 1920.* Columbia: Gonzales and Bryan, State Printers, 1920.

———. *The Statutes at Large of South Carolina, Vol. 11, containing the acts from 1838 exclusive, arranged chronologically.* Columbia: Republican Printing Company, 1871.

———. *The Journal of the Commons House of Assembly: Sept. 12, 1739 to Mar. 26, 1741.* Columbia, South Carolina: Historical Commission of South Carolina, 1951.

———. *Journal of the Grand Council of South Carolina, August 25, 1671 to June 24, 1680.* Edited by A.S. Salley, Jr. Columbia: The State Company, 1907.

South Carolina Historical Society. *Collections of the South Carolina Historical Society, Volume 5.* Richmond: William Ellis Jones, 1897.

Southern Patriot. Charleston, SC: J. N. Cardozo. 1818–1846.

Sparks, Randy J. "Gentleman's Sport: Horse Racing in Antebellum Charleston." *SCHM* 93, no. 1 (Jan 1992): 15–30.

Speed, John Gilmer. *The Horse in America: A Practical Treatise . . .* New York: McClure, Phillips, 1905.

Stavisky, Leonard Price. "Industrialism in Antebellum Charleston." *Journal of Negro History* 36, no. 3 (July 1951): 302–22.

Steen Ivan. "Charleston in the 1850s: As Described by British Travelers." *SCHM* 71, no. 1 (Jan 1970): 36–45.

Stine, Linda F., Martha Zierden, Leslie M. Drucker, and Christopher Judge, eds., *Carolina's Historical Landscapes: Archaeological Perspectives.* Knoxville: University of Tennessee Press, 1997.

Straus, Ralph. *Carriages and Coaches.* Philadelphia: J. B. Lippincott, 1912.

Strickland. "How the Germans became white southerners: German immigrants and African Americans in Charleston, 1860–1880." *Journal of American Ethnic History* 28, no. 1 (Fall 2008): 52–69.

Stroyer, Jacob. *Sketches of My Life in the South, Part I.* New York: Salem Press, 1879.

Sweeney, Hilary J. "Pasture to Pavement: Working Class Irish and Urban Workhorses in Nineteenth Century New York City." *American Journal of Irish Studies* 11 (2014): 125–52.

T., Gina. "Grains in Horse Feed." https://www.horsefeed blog.com/2011/ (accessed 21 November 2021).

Tarr, Joel. 2005. "Urban Horses and Changing City-Hinterland Relationships." In *Resources of the City: Contributions to an Environmental History of Modern Europe*, edited by Dieter Schott, Bill Lucking, and Geneviève Massard-Guilbaud, 48–62. London: Ashgate.

Tarr, Joel, and Clay McShane. 1997. "The Centrality of the Horse in the Nineteenth-Century American City," In *The Making of Urban America,* edited by Raymond A. Mohl, 107–32. Lanham, MD: Rowman & Littlefield.

———. 2007. *The Horse in the City: Living Machines in the 19th Century.* Baltimore: Johns Hopkins University Press.

Taylor, Michael. "The Civil War Experiences of a New Orleans Undertaker." *Louisiana History: Journal of the Louisiana Historical Association* 55, no. 3 (Summer 2014): 261–81.

Thompson, Michael D. *Working on the Dock of the Bay: Labor and Enterprise in an antebellum Southern Port.* Columbia: University of South Carolina Press, 2015.

————. *Working on the Dock of the Bay: Life and Labor along Charleston's Waterfront, 1783–1861.* PhD diss., Emory University. 2009.

Tull, Jethro. *Horse-Hoeing Husbandry.* London: A. Millar, 1751.

Upton, Dell. *Another City: Urban life and urban spaces in the new American republic.* New Haven, CT: Yale University Press, 2008.

US Census records, South Carolina.

US Census Bureau. *1900 Census, Statistics on Occupation. Principle Cities, Tables 42 and 43.* https://www.census.gov/ (accessed 20 June, 2020).

US Census (Slave Schedule), 1860." Database with images. NARA microfilm publication M653. Washington, D.C.: National Archives and Records Administration. *FamilySearch.* https://FamilySearch.org (accessed 18 July 2022).

US War Department. *The War of the Rebellion: A Compilation of the Official Records of the Union and Confederate Armies, Series 1, Vol. 47, Part 1.* Washington, DC: US Government Printing Office, 1895.

Vergara, Fernando, and Tamara A. Tadich. "Effect of the Work Performed by Tourism Carriage Horses on Physiological and Blood Parameters." *Journal of Equine Veterinary Science* 35, no. 3 (March 2015), 213–18.

Villers, David H. "The Smythe Horses Affair and the Association." *SCHM* 70, no. 3 (July 1969): 137–48.

Vlach, John Michael. "The Plantation Tradition in an Urban Setting: The Case of the Aiken-Rhett House in Charleston, South Carolina." *Southern Cultures* 5, no. 4 (1999): 52–69.

Walker, Evans, and Cogswell. *A New Guide to Modern Charleston.* Charleston, SC: WECCO, 1912.

Walker, H. Pinckney, comp. *Ordinances of the city of Charleston, from the 19th of August 1844, to the 14th of September 1854; and the Acts of the General Assembly Relating to the City of Charleston, and City Council of Charleston, during the Same Interval.* Charleston, SC: A. E. Miller, 1854.

Walker, Melissa, and James C. Cobb. *The New Encyclopedia of Southern Culture. Volume 11: Agriculture and Industry.* Chapel Hill: University of North Carolina Press, 2008.

Wallace, John Hawkins. *The Horse of America: In His Derivation, History, and Development.* New York: Wallace, 1897.

Walsh, Richard. "Charleston Mechanics: A Brief Study, 1760–1776." *SCHM* 60, no. 3 (July 1959): 123–44.

Weir, Robert M. *Colonial South Carolina: A History.* Columbia: University of South Carolina Press, 1983.

White, Meghan Paige. *George Washington's Mount Vernon Stable in Context: A Comparative Analysis of Early American Stables.* Master's thesis, Clemson University, 2016.

Whitelaw, Robert N. S. and Alice Levkoff *Charleston: Come Hell or High Water.* Columbia: R. L. Bryan and Co., 1975.

Wigge, Mary. "Mapping a Spanish Donkey's Long Journey." *Washington Papers.* 29 January 2015. https://washingtonpapers.org/ (accessed 1 November 2020).

William M. Bird and Co. "Celebrating 150 Years." https://wmbird.com/ (Accessed 4 May 2002).

Williams, Roy. *Rice to Ruin: The Jonathan Lucas Family in South Carolina, 1783–1929.* Columbia: University of South Carolina Press, 2018.

Youatt, William. *The Horse; with a Treatise on Draught.* London: Baldwin and Craddock, 1838.

Yuhl, Stephanie. *Golden Haze of Memory: The Makings of Historic Charleston.* Chapel Hill: University of North Carolina Press, 2005.

Zierden, Martha. "Big House/Back Lot: An Archaeological Study of the Nathaniel Russell House." *Archaeological Contributions* 25. Charleston: The Charleston Museum, 1996.

Zierden, Martha. "Landscape and Social Relations at Charleston Townhouse Sites (1770–1850)." *International Journal of Historical Archaeology* 14, no. 4 (December 2010): 527–46.

Zierden, Martha, and Elizabeth J. Reitz. "Animal Use and the Urban Landscape in Colonial Charleston." *International Journal of Historical Archaeology* 13, no. 3 (September 2009): 327–65.

————. *Charleston: An Archeology of Life in a Coastal Community.* Gainesville, FL: University Press of Florida, 2016.

Zierden, Martha, and Jeanne A. Calhoun. "An archaeological interpretation of elite townhouse site in Charleston, South Carolina, 1770–1850." *Southeastern Archaeology* 9, no. 2 (Winter 1990): 79–92.

————. "Urban Adaptation in Charleston, South Carolina, 1730–1820." *Historical Archaeology* 20, no. 1 (1986): 29–43.

INDEX

geldings, 6, 102, 104

Gell, John, 77

Gell's Stable, 13, 94

General Assembly, 114

Gentlemen's Driving Association, 60

gentrification, 153

George Street, 134

Georgian Revival, 154

Geraghty's City Express, 78

Germania Brewing, 89

German Fire Engine Company, 81, 103, 109

Germans, 95, 98

Gibbes, J., 107–8

Gibson, Chris, 80

Gilbert, Bradford Lee, 25

Gillmore, Quincy, 22

Given, Robert, 35

glanders, 41–42, 187n

glue factories, 42–43

Godfrey, John, 114

Godolphin (horse), 8

Goff, Theodore, 80

Goodenough Shoes, 39

Goose Creek, 47, 112

Gordon, Thomas, 52

Gothic Revival, 124, 128–30

Grace Bridge, 148

Graham, Prince, 94

Graham Robert, 76, 137

Graham Stables, 51, 76, 113, 198n

Grand Council, 114

Grand Model, 16

grain mills and suppliers, 31, 84, 133

granite paving, 23, 25

grazing, 31–34

Greene, Anne, 2

Greensword, Francis, 77

Greenville, 72

Griffith, Thomas, 52

Griggs, Henry, 69

grocery delivery, 89, 91–92, 98, 152

grooms, xiv, 37, 54, 57–58, 67–68, 80, 93. *See also* equine workers

grooming, 10–11, 30, 106, 116

Guard house, 103, 115, 194n

Guignard Street, 118–19, 159

Gus (horse), 110–11

hackmen, 82–83, 153; extortion, 82

hackneys, 56, 70–71, 81–83, 87, 134, 146, 192n

Haesloop, Henry, 133

haint blue, 154

Haiti, 94

Haley Stables, 133

Halifax, Shawn, 162

Halsey Lumber, 106

Hamburg, 72, 84

Hamilton, Walter, 29

Hampstead, 75. *See also* East Side

Hampton Park, 56, 101, 114, 117, 194n

Hampton, Wade, 9, 56

Hands. *See* equines, size

handcarts, 66

Harleston, 18, 34–35, 82, 130, 139, 151–52, 165

harnesses and harnessing, 3–5, 30, 47, 62–64, 86, 104, 111, 113, 148

harness makers, 35–36, 80, 98, 10, 147

Harness Maker's Illustrated Manual, 35

Harper Brothers Stable, 13, 136–37

Hasbrouck, Charles Dudley, 106–7, 112

Hasell Street, 73, 87, 123, 132, 134

Hatfield, John, 13

Hayne Street, 78, 147, 153

Hawes, Benjamin, 64

Hawes, Jeremiah, 36

Hawkins and Petrie, 64

hay and haylofts, 31, 76, 115, 120, 128–29, 133, 136, 139, 154, 169

Hayne Street, 83

Hearse. *See* funeral carriages

heat, 16, 50–51, 112, 117, 167–68, 170–71; mitigation, 37, 170. *See also* climate

heavy horse. *See* draft horse

Heinsohn Grocery, 98

Hercules (enslaved coachman), 57, 68–69

heritage tourism, 159–72

Heriot Street, 29, 42

Herman, Bernard, 126

Hewet, George, 64

Heyward, Daniel, 66

Heyward, Dubose, 57, 122, 151

Heyward, Nathaniel, 62

Heyward Washington House, 122–24

Hiatt, Ben, 69

Hibben, Andrew, 71

Hibernian Hall, 156

Hickson, H.J., 137

Hinson, Glenn, 10

hire out system, 93–95

Historic Charleston Foundation, 129

historic district, xvi, 151, 160, 164–66

historic preservation, xvi, 149–55, 160, 200n

history, as tourist draw, 156–60

Hockaday, William, 133

Hoffman Livery Stable, 78

Hogan, Leo James, 107

Hogan, Michael, 106, 194n

Holbrook, Harriot, 25

Holloway family, 78–79

Holmes and Watson (horses), 118–19

Holmes, C. R., Jr., 80

Holmes family, 99

Holsteiners, 6

Hontze, A. W., 49

Horlbeck Brothers, 120

Horlbeck Street, 137

Horres, Belvin, 141

Horres Stable, 137

Horry, Daniel, 77

Horry, Elias, 94